The BUSINESS of Art

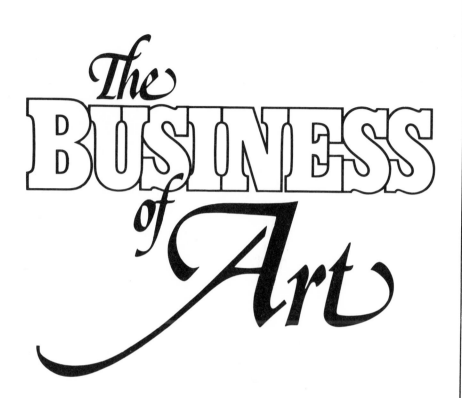

The BUSINESS of Art

Edited and with an introduction by
LEE EVAN CAPLIN

Published in cooperation with the National Endowment for the Arts

Prentice-Hall, Inc.   Englewood Cliffs, N.J.

Prentice-Hall International, Inc., *London*
Prentice-Hall of Australia, Pty. Ltd., *Sydney*
Prentice-Hall of Canada, Ltd., *Toronto*
Prentice-Hall of India Private Ltd., *New Delhi*
Prentice-Hall of Japan, Inc., *Tokyo*
Prentice-Hall of Southeast Asia Pte. Ltd., *Singapore*
Whitehall Books, Ltd., *Wellington, New Zealand*

©1982 by
Prentice-Hall, Inc.
Englewood Cliffs, N.J.

Library of Congress Cataloging in Publication Data
Main entry under title:

The Business of art.

Includes index.
1. Art–Economic aspects. 2. Art–Marketing.
I. Caplin, Lee Evan.
N8600.B875 1982   706'   81-21041
                               AACR2
ISBN 0-13-106518-1
ISBN 0-13-106500-9 {pbk}
Printed in the United States of America

Foreword

by
Livingston Biddle
Chairman, National Endowment for the Arts,
1978-1981

One of the ironies of history is the position which artists have occupied in society. While revered and respected for the works they produce, many artists—if not most—are unable to support themselves wholly from the creations they provide for our enrichment. This is especially the case in times of fiscal restraint. Artists need to develop maximum avenues for support. Methods developed by the business community can be very helpful to artists in making their creations known and better appreciated by increasing numbers of people.

This book grew out of the continuing efforts of two federal agencies, the National Endowment for the Arts and the U.S. Small Business Administration, to offer technical business assistance to individual artists.

In order to test how to present information in this complex area, four pilot conferences were held in different cities across the country. Since then, more than 50 have followed, and the opportunity now exists for artists in all states and territories of the United States to have access to this type of valuable information.

Many of the perceptions of the conference panelists—artists, dealers, lawyers and business experts—are included here. Their opinions are diverse and reflect the unique experience of the world of the visual artist. One idea that emerges is that there is no one path for artists to follow in approaching the arena where art works are bought and sold. At the conferences, several artists emphasized the statement: "All the clichés are true, and the rules are made to be broken."

Nevertheless, many concepts are vital to understand and useful to apply. This book is an attempt to state the concepts clearly and concisely so that more artists will have the opportunity for self-sufficiency and will be able to organize the business side of their lives in such a way as to allow more time for the creation of their art.

I am privileged to express gratitude for the special initiatives taken by Joan Mondale and by Vernon Weaver, former Administrator of the Small Business Administration, in beginning these significant collaborative efforts; and I express particular appreciation to James Sanders, the present SBA Administrator, for carrying them forward toward expanded goals.

A Close Look
at the Business of Art
and the Artist

by

Lee Evan Caplin

◆ ◆ ◆ ◆

LEE EVAN CAPLIN is a television producer, an attorney, and a practicing artist. Formerly the Assistant to the Chairman of the National Endowment for the Arts, and Director of the federal program "The Business of Art and the Artist" from 1978 to 1981, Mr. Caplin has published numerous articles on the relation of art to business. Mr. Caplin currently lives in New York City and is married to concert pianist Gita Karasik.

◆ ◆ ◆

Between September 1979 and May 1980 over 4,000 artists gathered together in Los Angeles, Chicago, and New York City, where, for perhaps the first time, two federal agencies combined forces in four major events to assist art in America. Blue jeans and paint-stained windbreakers merged with three-piece suits, and an air of lively curiosity and expectation filled the auditoriums at L.A.'s and Chicago's Museum of Science and Industry, and New York's American Museum of Natural History. After 18 intense hours at each location, artists were still talking, listening, taking notes, exchanging names.

The events were conferences, cosponsored by the United States Small Business Administration (SBA) and the National Endowment for the Arts, to give artists basic business and marketing information.

This apparent unlikely pairing has a rational basis embedded in the purpose and philosophy of the two agencies involved.

The National Endowment for the Arts (NEA) is the federal agency that is charged with giving support to all aspects of the arts in America. It not only supports the arts through grants but also supports artists and arts groups through technical assistance— helping them to be better organized, and to get on their feet financially. NEA also has been involved in advocacy efforts to try to get members of the private sector to become involved with supporting the arts. One segment of the private sector has been the business community.

The business community at large has primarily been active in supporting the arts as a patron—purchasing art for office buildings, giving support to symphony orchestras, dance companies, museums and theaters. However, the business community also possesses the practical knowledge of how business affairs are run— knowledge potentially very valuable to artists or arts groups in managing their own affairs—and in making the most of opportunities to earn income.

Each year as the Endowment's budget is reviewed by Congress the questions inevitably come up: "Are artists hooked on the federal dollar? How much do they really help themselves?" The NEA/SBA joint project seemed like an ideal opportunity to start answering those questions in the most positive of ways.

The Small Business Administration offers a variety of assistance projects for the small business person. It makes loans and loan guarantees, and gives technical assistance to individual entrepreneurs or businesses. However, there is one major distinction between the purposes of the Arts Endowment and of the SBA: SBA gives direct support only to groups or individuals who are trying to make money, while NEA gives grants only to individuals, or to art groups which are tax exempt and therefore primarily not engaged in making a profit. However, indirect or technical assistance to individuals is ground common to both agencies.

SBA brings to this new partnership a widespread "delivery mechanism" for technical assistance. It has field offices in all fifty states and territories that give business training sessions to all aspects of the small business community. While SBA does not have programs that deal specifically with artists, artists occasionally have found their way to SBA training conferences on accounting or establishing business operations. Nevertheless, SBA has previously given no specific attention to the arts. And most of the arts community is unaware that SBA gives technical assistance applicable to the arts.

The National Endowment for the Arts realized that it could help SBA develop a mechanism to train artists in business and marketing affairs that would respond to some real needs in the arts community. So with SBA to purvey technical information, and NEA to help develop that information, the two agencies began their task of putting together a training program for artists.

The development of this partnership received interest and support from the wife of the Vice President of the United States, Mrs. Joan Mondale. As hononary head of the Federal Council on the Arts and the Humanities, Mrs. Mondale saw the NEA/SBA alliance as embodying the goal of the Federal Council—that the Council should act as a catalyst in involving other Federal agencies besides the Endowment in assisting the arts. With Mrs. Mondale's strong endorsement, the project was off to a fine start.

NEA's Visual Arts Program—dealing with individual painters, sculptors, printmakers, photographers and varied craftspersons—was chosen as the most practical area on which to focus this first program. Since the area of visual arts is so broad, subject areas dealing with art marketing and specific problems of artists are best addressed both by practicing artists who have "made it" in the financial sense and who understand the business aspects of their activities; and by accountants and lawyers who, in the course of their practice, handle artists' affairs.

In its training activities, SBA traditionally uses lecturers picked from its "service corps of retired executives" (SCORE) and an "active corps of executives" (ACE). These experts are business executives who donate time to SBA to assist in training and advising small business people. While such resource people often do not have familiarity with the arts community, the Arts Endowment found them especially receptive to tailoring their remarks to fit the artists in the audience. With an array of experts from both the arts and business communities, NEA and SBA felt that the subjects would be fully addressed.

Three pilot conferences, in Los Angeles, Chicago and New York, were planned. These cities were picked because of the size of their arts communities, and because of the quality of SBA's District Offices. The key to the success of these conferences was identifying and engaging local conference cosponsors. Such cosponsors would take part in the planning and execution of the conferences, and would continue to be available on the local level for future artist training efforts by SBA. The Los Angeles cosponsor was the California Confederation of the Arts. In Chicago and New York, cosponsors were both the state and the city arts agencies. An additional cosponsor in New York was the Foundation for the Community of Artists. These organizations gave unselfishly of their time and resources to supply the essential support so critical to a successful program.

The response was amazing. Whereas SBA's past experience in training led it to believe that no more than 200 applicants would attend each conference, about 1,000 artists attended in each city. In Los Angeles, there was such an overflow crowd that there had to be last-minute closed circuit TV coverage in an adjoining auditorium. In New York an entire second conference was scheduled to accommodate nearly 1,000 additional artists who were unable to fit into the auditorium during the first New York conference.

During the course of the four two-day conferences, over eighty panelists appeared. On the first day artists talked about planning; an artist's accountant talked about arts accounting problems; and experts explained the intricacies of insurance, retirement plans, money-lending sources, banks, credit, tax and the law in relation to the arts. Monona Rossol, of New York's Center for Occupational Hazards, described health hazards facing artists and art buyers from the materials used in making art. The second day was all about marketing. Successful artists from various corners of the arts community, experienced in traditional or alternative marketing possibilities, spoke on such subjects as galleries, museums, alternative spaces, and commissions. Dealers who were involved as brokers, middlemen, or direct sellers of art, spoke about marketing art in those settings. According to the evaluation forms and other responses the Endowment has received, artists found the program format ideal. Certain areas, such as law and accounting, are so complex that they deserve specific attention if they are to be explained fully. However, NEA and SBA simplified their presentations within a larger context, sensitizing artists to the need for legal and accounting advice, and devoting more time to some of the specifics of *where* and *how* artists go to sell their work.

Surprisingly, some artists who were approached to serve on panels were at first skeptical about the program. They feared such a conference might emphasize elements antithetical to art. But ultimately all agreed that artists could generally benefit from exposure to business and marketing basics.

Despite the practical purpose of the conferences, it was far from a simple "How To" program. The basic philosophy of those who make their lives in the arts was explored thoroughly by the artists on the panels. As these artists later unfolded their stories it was evident that they wanted to make certain that people in the audience, who call themselves artists, were not putting the cart before the horse; art is not so much a business as it is a calling and it is not so much the manufacture of products for sale as it is a matter of producing something because one is obsessed with producing it, and only then wondering, once the art is produced, what should be done with it. On the one hand, artists who had developed formulas for success did not want to reveal their formulas to the audiences. In many ways such formulas were unique to those artists. On the other hand, some of the speakers did not care to admit that there are any business-oriented steps that artists could or should take. Painter Ed Moses suggested, "There's art, there's stuff that looks like art, and there's stuff that just looks good. If you're into the last two, you're into business." The point being that "if the art is good, it will speak for itself." In the words of sculptor Bruce Beasley, however, "If you hide your light under a bushel, nobody will see it, but first you must be sure there's a light."

Several of the artists' presentations were discouraging, in their hesitancy to validate a business element in "getting one's art out." Painter Philip Pearlstein urged that each artist ask the question, "Do I have talent?" He said that the dropout rate of artists over 30 suggests that many *are* asking themselves that question. "There are very few artists over 50," Pearlstein said.

Other panelist-artists, who are adept at promotion and marketing, made the assumption that everyone in the audience had work that he or she was proud of, and therefore it was valid to probe the extent to which business techniques were adaptable to the professional structure surrounding the making of art. They were able to identify means by which artists could go further in promoting and selling their own work.

A significant point was made that in all instances there is a quotient of "luck," and a quotient of "quality" involved in any success by any artist. Painter Joan Snyder called hers a "Cinderella story." Larry Bell was unable to explain what he had done to promote himself other than by doing his work, observing those he admires, and "emulating their style" in handling their own affairs. Most subscribed to doing only what is comfortable in terms of self-promotion. What may be easy for one artist, such as shaking hands at gallery gatherings, or setting a market value on a price of art, may be anathema to another. Sculptor Sylvia Stone admitted that she tended to undervalue her work and preferred to let her dealer establish the prices. Conceptual artist Newton Harrison even advised his fellow practitioners, with some humor, to cultivate the "appearance of incompetence" for the purpose of conducting business affairs, since any attempt on their part to compete on an equal footing with other business practitioners would only lead to greater exposure and susceptibility to the various government rules and regulations.

Artist June Wayne suggested that government agencies lack sophistication about the unique business problems of the arts. To those who draft tax legislation, an artist's overhead looks suspiciously large compared to the slim profits or repetitive losses the artist's tax return may reveal. Because Congress assumes that the only credible reason for pursuing any business or profession is to make taxable profits, the persistence with which artists pursue their unprofitable activities greatly puzzles and vexes both our lawmakers and our enforcers. As a result, for an artist to fit into the tax laws is, according to Wayne, "for an eagle to fly while wearing an ox-yoke."

The traditional rules of business do not always apply in the business side of the arts. Gallery owner Ivan Karp stated that he chooses the artists he represents on the basis of how he responds to their work—not on the work's marketability.

One theme of conflict recurred and was never fully resolved: some artists felt that planning was essential in having a professional career as an artist. Other equally successful artists felt that any plan is out of place—that it stifles one's creative instincts. Painter Jim Rosenquist gave his view by quoting President Eisenhower: "A plan is nothing, planning is everything." On balance, however, everyone seemed to profit by some aspect of the conferences. Few expected to be given a list of "ten easy do's and don'ts" for becoming a successful painter or sculptor. But despite their individualism, most artists share many of the same problems and needs. As they listened and asked questions, artists were able to arrive at a balanced view of the various options available to them in marketing and promoting their work.

Certainly the gatherings themselves were significant events apart from the valuable information conveyed. Many of the artists in the audience had never seen or heard dealers such as those on stage. Many had never been in the company of artists of major reputation, such as appeared in the three cities. There was great value in the audience's listening to sculptor Fred Eversley on the one hand, showing clear knowledge of how to market art work, or Bob Graham on the other hand, suggesting that there is little an artist can do in marketing art work; that his work somehow seemed to sell almost by itself. On a human level, it was reassuring to encounter colleagues of one's own discipline or geographic surrounding, who attended the conferences to get the same information, and to be able to communicate with these people afterwards at the receptions that were held.

The Endowment, for its part, certainly does not advocate treating art as a business or art works as commodities for sale. Rather, its main role in participating in the project is to make available as much technical business and marketing information as possible, so as to offer the broadest range of choices to artists pursuing their callings as professionals.

As a result of the pilot program "The Business of Art and the

Artist," the Endowment and SBA produced a documentary video tape and a conference organizer's manual to be used in presenting workshops throughout the country.

This volume can supplement these workshops, and is a useful introduction to the business side of art for all those who have not yet received such technical assistance. The material presented here is not meant to be inclusive, nor is it supposed to supplant courses in business and marketing. Rather, it is a first step towards understanding many aspects of "survival" for artists in a commerce-oriented society. The artists, dealers, and business professionals who have contributed their thoughts in producing this book hope it will help you discover the types of questions you ought to be asking either yourself or those whom you enlist to help you. They hope that their views on the professional side of art will illuminate and demystify many seemingly technical and complicated details that might seem burdensome to those who just want to make art. Their ideas apply to all forms of visual arts and crafts. Whether the topic is sculpture or the Los Angeles art scene, the information can be generally useful. Artists as a group are less eager to share "techniques" that have worked for them. Dealers, too, sometimes are reluctant to be candid about their colleagues and the practices they use. But for the first time, gathered in one place, a composite of the art scene is depicted by what is said—and what is left unsaid—by the authors of this book.

Larry Bell once stressed that each of us is responsible for the best and the worst of what happens in our careers. What you won't get by reading this book are any "Ten Commandments" for becoming a successful artist. What we hope you will get is a better sense of what you really want from your art and how far you are willing to go to achieve your goals. If you can place all the elements of your art and the business of art in perspective, you will have achieved a lot, especially in terms of being responsible to yourself as an artist and as a professional. For some there may be a period of time when fame and fortune are a reality. For others, there may be a perpetual obscurity. In between are many variations on the theme, as well as behavior patterns ranging from the promiscuous to the recalcitrant. Sylvia Stone made a keen observation when she said that "making art is one of the true areas where we have a kind of independence and serve our own sense of morality. It is one of the free activities still left to some of us. And I say: 'Use it. Use it and enjoy it.'"

Table of Contents

Part Two: PROTECTING

Part Three: MARKETING

Part Four: DEALING

Part Five: FINDING ALTERNATIVES

The editor would like to gratefully acknowledge the assistance of Elsie Walker, National Endowment for the Arts Fellow, 1981, in the preparation of this manuscript.

Planning

1

Artists and Planning

by

James Rosenquist

◆ ◆ ◆ ◆

JAMES ROSENQUIST is an artist and a member of the National Council on the Arts.

◆ ◆ ◆ ◆

The question I ask myself when art and business are discussed together is, "Has art grown into a desk job?" I started drawing in 1949—or even before that—but I arrived in New York in 1955. The Third Avenue El was just being torn down, the Colosseum wasn't built yet, and the Whitney Museum was still on 54th Street. At that time the art world was very small. The number of galleries was few, and I would say the number of people who collected avant-garde art—which meant that it had come from young living Americans—was perhaps less than a dozen.

While art, historically, has always been related to communication, in 1955 in New York many famous underground artists lived within a few blocks from each other but did not know each other, had never met each other. In the '50s, Jim Harvey—the man who designed the Brillo box—who used to travel to the Middle East, brought back slides of his travels and invited the whole art world to come and see the slides down at Coentie's Slip. So everybody and his brother showed up, and I was surprised to find that people did not know each other. I met Ad Rinehardt—one of America's most famous artists—for the first time. Major artists were not in close contact. In the late '50s, American artists such as Baziotes, de Kooning, Gottlieb, Guston, Kline, Motherwell, Newman, Pollock, Still, Rothko and others had tremendous underground reputations. They had worked for years—some of them, like Franz Kline, in the WPA programs—yet they hadn't had one-man shows and they were already in their late forties or older. Some of them would get up at the Friday Night Club and broadcast their art. They'd talk about it, be assertive about it, defend it; and they were, I would say, very self-conscious about their work. They talked among themselves. They would try to establish the work; in other words, they were not cool about it. They were *hot* about it compared to the next generation, called Pop Artists, of which I was a part.

22

When I arrived on the art scene, the art audience had already begun to increase. In 1958 de Kooning had a show, and one of his paintings sold for the highest price for a living American artist—$14,500. Just after that, Jasper Johns appeared on the scene. He seemed to be a reactionary to a style in painting sometimes described as drips and splashes. Actually it was called "abstract expressionism." His style resulted in critics trying to group artists in a "movement," but they were not all alike.

At that time in New York, Ivan Karp, Henry Geldzahler and Dick Bellamy would prowl the streets, going to artists' studios to discover new talent. They actually went from door to door to find out who lived in each loft. I think this was the first time artists were solicited. Young unknown artists felt they didn't have a chance to show their work when they saw someone like de Kooning walk down 57th Street in an old Levi jacket and bedroom slippers, looking very poor. If *he* wasn't doing well, how could a lesser-known artist expect to do well?

One day in 1960 I ran into Bob Indiana. He said, "Guess what I saw, Jim. I saw a dirty new collage of Bob Rauschenberg's behind a big glass table on Park Avenue! Let's go out and have a drink and celebrate!" So we celebrated Bob Rauschenberg's breakthrough. At that time artists supported themselves any way they could. Some did commercial art jobs, some worked on construction jobs, and some sold coffee in Madison Square Park from the coffee stands. I painted billboards and created window displays for Bonwit Teller and Tiffany. Rauschenberg also did window displays for Bonwit Teller. We all had to make a buck.

When Henry, Ivan, and Dick started looking for people, Henry was a curator at the Metropolitan Museum, Ivan was at the Castelli Gallery, and Dick was about to open his new Green Gallery. Dick asked me to be in his gallery. I knew I could make a living at that point, so I quit my commercial artist's job just to paint. I was very happy. I lived frugally, and was able to live on very little. I could eat breakfast for twenty-five cents at the Seamen's Institute! I found it a tremendous luxury to be able to live in a cosmopolitan city and not have to deal with it except to dream. The dealers urged me to hurry up and have a show as fast as I could, but I was happy just to live with my pictures and simply let things happen. My paintings were like my companions, and I wasn't consciously trying to sell them. But then Dick sold some of them to Bob Scull, the Tremains, Dick

Baker, Jan Streed, Morton Newman and others, for prices ranging from $350 to $1,100.

In the 1950's you could walk into the Whitney Museum annual exhibit and buy almost anybody's painting for a thousand bucks. Then things started to heat up. People became interested in art—I don't know why. Leon Menuchin bought practically a whole show for Brandeis University. People followed his lead. Harry Abrams, who had been buying French Impressionism and Old Masters' works before that, saw what Leon had done and began buying young artists' work. John Powers saw what Harry and Leon bought, and he bought what they bought. So collectors of young unknown American artists began to proliferate.

ART AS A BUSINESS

I've been asked, "How does an artist relate to business?" and "Can I plan a career as an artist?" As for planning, Eisenhower once said, "A plan is nothing. Planning is everything." Being an artist, whatever that is, involves constant questioning of everything. It is very difficult to set out a plan in a businesslike manner because a happy accident could happen and someone might like your worst work.

Artists work in unknown territory. If it were known, they probably wouldn't be artists. This is difficult for an artist to realize, but it's also more difficult for an audience to understand. However, when an artist is through with a work, then strange things can happen, like people wanting to be near it, people talking about it, and people wanting to own it. When this happens, artists usually don't know what to do.

My first experience in relating to business was like building a better mousetrap. I never had to ask my friends or potential buyers to visit me. One day Barbara Durkee visited me. She told her husband Steve about my work, and he told his dealer Alan Stone. Alan told Ileana Sonnabend, and she told Bellamy and Karp, and they told Leo Castelli. Jasper Johns even asked to come to my studio. He said, "Where did you learn to paint like that?" People beat down the door to my studio. Artists, then, were usually indifferent to galleries; they didn't expect much money, only the possibility of having their work on view in a neutral space. Before I had any reputation, I never had to schlep my paintings anywhere. That's how it happened with me. Other people's introductions to a gallery and to business happen differently. Frank Stella just walked into the Castelli Gallery, and Leo asked him, "What do you paint?" Frank said, "I paint. I just paint, man." The artists of the '60s and the '70s were a little luckier because they didn't have to solicit their art. In the '80s there is an entirely different situation. There are many more artists living in New York City, and there are many more galleries. I like it that way; there is more to look at, more to investigate.

All through the '60s my daily routine was waking up with a hangover about ten o'clock, painting all day, at five o'clock renting a tuxedo from Silver's Tuxedos, going up to 57th Street to an opening, going up to the Jewish Museum to Rauschenberg's opening, or somebody else's opening, or my own opening, then going out, staying out till one or two in the morning, waking up with a hangover, working the next day, renting another tuxedo at Silver's (or keeping the same one), going out again—every night of the week! Sometimes I was invited to three dinners at a time. Life was fast and fun.

But getting back to that planning thing: planning is like looking for your wallet under a street lamp when you didn't lose it there in the first place. When I started planning, I wanted to be a mural painter. I tried to go to school where they would teach me mural painting. All these men teaching had read books about it, but they had never done it. I looked around and I saw billboard painters painting, and I thought, "Gee, those guys can handle any kind of space. They must know how to handle paint and brushes." So I went right into billboard painting as a master billboard painter—no apprenticeship, no nothing. I learned a great deal from my helpers: David Mishnick, a sculptor who had come from Russia in 1927 and had shown his work with Arshile Gorky; Solly Schnee, Harold Bernstein, who had a lot of knowledge about paint. These old-timers were like teachers to me. They told me what *not* to do. It was like going to school—but it was a tough commercial business.

Successful artists as well as businessmen use creative thinking to get from point A to point B. The attempt to repeat an approach or a style that has been successful in the past in order to achieve new success can lead to a dull result. Creative, successful artists and businessmen rarely approach the same thing in the same way twice. Art isn't really done for any reason other than a means of the artist's self-expression. Business, on the other hand, is traditionally done to make money.

Now art may not be done to make money, but that doesn't rule out its value. The problem for any artist has always been either having money and no time, or a lot of time and no money. The ideal life for an artist would be to live in a cosmopolitan city and be free from the burden of having to make a living. And, however one accomplishes it, that freedom from "making a living" could be essential to being an artist. I think a problem comes when an artist does start to sell something, for then he becomes connected with business and his life is no longer free from that involvement.

For myself, I don't have the slightest idea of how to allocate time between art and making money except on a case-by-case basis. I really have no plan at all. The reason I work, the reason I make things, is to physically illuminate some feelings I've had. Then they exist outside of myself in some kind of form, so when I am old and grey I'll be able to look at them and realize that I was alive at a certain period. I really regard it almost like a philatelic thing. When I'm dead, that's outside the human condition and I don't care any more about the works.

There's a whole new crop of young artists who grew up surrounded by materialism, as I did, but who try to plan their art careers like the climb up a corporate ladder. I can't imagine an artist's life being as steady as that. People who don't know what an artist does ask me, "Are you doing pictures for magazines now? What are you doing this for?" My answer is that I'm not doing art for anyone but myself. The reason *why* is that if I did art for somebody other than myself, I wouldn't know what to do. I don't have to paint something this color or that color because of someone else's reason. I can do anything I please. And that's the lovely, scary thing. It's challenging to go into a room with a canvas and know that you can do anything you want to do. This is probably a Far Eastern attitude about learning. You confront yourself totally, whether you're able to work or not.

So, getting back to the idea of planning, to an artist's mind there are no holds barred, no barriers. The only thing that stops you is the old Catch 22 thing, the financial problem that you just don't want to deal with. Yet you have to face it.

When I began painting, James Michener came to my studio and said, "I want to buy that painting." I said, "I'm sorry; it's already been sold. Richard Bellamy sold it." He said, "I'd like one just like it, or something like it." I felt that the look of my art wasn't like anything else being done at that time, so I was very reactionary and

I said, "No, I can't possibly do that." Now if he hadn't said what he did, I might have made four more paintings similar to that one, or studied it further. But I viewed his request as an interference. I was very sensitive then!

Just a few years ago it wasn't fashionable to want one's son or daughter to be an artist. Now sons and daughters are encouraged to study art because it could be possible to make a handsome income from it. I can't think of art as a desk job. Avant-garde artists still face hardships in spite of a current government attitude that art is alive and well in the United States. Artists have a hard time getting credit, getting hospital care. Their work is sold, and resold quickly for high prices in a short time, and the artist gets only the first piddling commission from a dealer—or may not get paid for years. Artists can't contribute their work to museums for a tax deduction as art collectors can, because the government says the only value coming from an artist's work is the cost of the materials! Back in the 1960's, when it was lawful, the art dealers' association carefully scrutinized donations, so there were very few overvalued works. The person possibly most responsible for stopping contributions was former President Nixon, who donated his writings for an unrealistic deduction.

Artists' heirs are often stuck with a huge inheritance tax on unsold works, and have to sell them off cheaply to be able to pay the taxes. There are a great number of artist problems pertaining to business and taxes. If the speed of thinking of the IRS and the government could accelerate at the same rate as the speed of artists' and inventors' thinking—that is, linked with communication—I think we could get away from a guns or unemployment society and get into space without bringing war with us.

During the time I've taken to write this, the current acceleration of the change of events regarding government support for the arts, business support for the arts, and the fate of the National Endowment for the Arts under the new administration has changed drastically. The new government senses a need for extreme budget cuts in every area except military spending. In the *New York Times*, during the height of the Vietnam conflict, the annual government military contracts to major corporations were published. If one added up the cost of all the arts activities in the United States for the same year, including dance, music, museums, theater, and even large Hollywood films, it wouldn't be a drop in the bucket compared to the enormous military expenditures for Vietnam.

On a television program on Sunday, April 28, 1981, the panelists seemed to agree that art should become a business in order to be able to make it on its own. Mr. Herb Schmerz, of Mobil Oil, stated that art groups should be able to function and survive as a business. Mr. Schmerz was happy to announce that art finance should be left to the private sector and will happily be taken over by big business. One panelist said that art in America is alive and healthy, and always was, despite government support. Another panelist suggested that viewers should send their ideas to their congressmen.

I remember a time not long ago when art barely existed in New York. And the future of art in America doesn't look good now. In this great country of ours, let's encourage the arts and humanities, and new forays into visual art. Let's build one or two fewer missiles and provide the National Endowment for the Arts—with its history of a hands-off attitude—with a healthy, growing budget. Let's not let large corporate control lead us into "1984."

2

A Perspective on Planning

by

Bruce Beasely

◆ ◆ ◆ ◆

BRUCE BEASELY is a sculptor with works in the permanent collection of the Museum of Modern Art, the Guggenheim, and the Musée d'Art in Paris, among others. His large sculptures can be seen in public places such as the Federal Courthouse in San Diego and the San Francisco International Airport.

◆ ◆ ◆ ◆

I have been asked to address the rather vague area of planning in regard to a career in art. I am not sure what this encompasses, but I know for certain that I did not plan to be an artist. It just happened just as falling in love happens.

Although I myself cannot imagine being anything but an artist, I do not believe in soliciting others to follow me in this field. Art is a joy too precious—and painful—to proselytize. Therefore, I extend my sympathies and, of course, my warmest feelings for anyone who has the art monkey on his or her back.

I am asked what can be expected when you have been bitten by the art bug. You can expect challenge, the joy of expression, exploration; and sometimes exploration that leads to exhilarating accomplishment. You can expect frustration, self-doubt, and loneliness. You can also expect damn little practical support.

THE ESSENTIAL DILEMMA

There is much known history about artists and money problems, and a lot of it is true: Michelangelo fighting with the Pope over payments, Van Gogh writing his brother for more money. The stories are endless, and they point to a terrible historical dilemma: an artist must have money to live and to make art. But the motives for making art are not financial. This puts artists' needs in direct conflict with their motivation. In fact, artists are economic victims of their own aesthetic, which of course is not news to anyone who is an artist.

The purpose of this chapter is to shed some light on this dilemma. Perhaps the reason I was asked to address this question is that some years ago I made a decision to throw myself on the world of galleries and sales of my art for my sole livelihood. I am therefore supposed to know something about it.

I am not sure this is true, nor am I sure that I know any more about it now than I did when I made the decision. However, in looking back on that decision (which at the time was made more in passion than in logic), and also in observing and sharing the lives and careers of friends who made both similar and dissimilar choices, I have thought of some things I have learned which I would like to share. Maybe they will sound simplistic and obvious, but they have been lessons to me.

MAKING CLEAR CHOICES

Basically, I would say that the artists I have known who have had rewarding and successful careers are those who have been able to make very clear choices about their priorities and expectations. Once these priorities were selected, they wasted no emotion on the other things they gave up.

I want to make it clear that when I refer to a successful artist I do not necessarily mean financially successful. To me a successful artist is one who continues to make art, and is not more than fifty percent bitter about the rest of life.

If you teach for a living, the pay per hour is good, but for some it is aesthetically draining; if you drive a cab you have to put in more hours, but it's less complicated. If you work in California you don't have the New York scene; if you live in New York you can't work outside as you can in California.

To cast in bronze is expensive. If you work in plaster, people won't pay as much for it. If you work monumentally you can do only a few pieces per year. If you work small, you can't be in the shows of monumental work.

These tradeoffs are endless, and in addressing the specific and terrifying question of how one can make art and also make a living, there are a myriad of answers, and all of them have a good part and a bad part.

My most sincere advice is to take a hard look at your desires, your abilities and your temperament, and then pick the solution that is the least repugnant.

I purposefully put the phrase as "the solution that is the least repugnant," not as the best, because that is how I see it. The best part is the art you are going to make. The negative part is that somehow you have to get some money in order to do it. And believe me, there are no perfect solutions.

BE AWARE OF DRAWBACKS

If you are rich to start with, you and others will wonder if you could have made it on your own. There are the same and even greater doubts about marrying for money. If you teach, there are time constraints, and for some there are aesthetic drains and the general diversion of your time and energy that university involvement demands. For many, selling their art has its drawbacks also. It requires the drive to sustain a regular output even at difficult times. Some have difficulty in letting the work go once it is finished. It requires that your prices be set by what the work will really sell for rather than by what you think it should be worth; this often requires facing painful realities. Some artists find the whole business aspect of galleries and sales to be unpleasant.

My decision to try to live off my work and cut the bridges to teaching in the early days involved my acquiring a mechanical skill to fall back on when nothing sold, and also being willing to live very cheaply for many years. I do not mean to go into a long lament on the suffering and starving artist, but there is more than an element of truth in the cliché. If you are going to depend on the sales of your work as your means of livelihood, you must expect to go through a period of very real deprivation. This may mean forgoing a family, living in genuinely inadequate conditions, and, in every material sense, living a lousy life. On the other hand, this will also be a period of great excitement and reward as you hit a stride with your work that was previously prevented by the demands of school or regular work.

There is, of course, no guarantee that your learning the elements of business will produce any financial success in your art. After all, we are not talking about earning merit badges or getting into heaven.

Hopefully you will have found out your work capacity, discovered the depth of your ideas, and produced a good body of work.

For myself it has been a good choice and one that I would make again. It is not, however, as good as it often looks from the other side of the fence. I am under constant pressure to produce and exhibit. I must actively seek out and enter into competitions for sculpture commissions that are often time-consuming and unrewarding. Aside from the actual making of the art, it is a rather practical life—full of details of crating, shipping, photographs, installations, etc. And there is, of course, no certainty that because things sold this year they will sell next year. But I am not complaining. I made my choice, and when the payoff isn't worth the pain, I will make another choice.

But it would be a critical mistake to eat myself up with bitterness about the bad part that came automatically with the choice I made. If I am going to live off my work I must pay more attention to the business part than if I had another source of income. It is just like sweeping up the studio or changing the oil in the air compressor; it isn't interesting or aesthetic but it is a reality that has to be dealt with.

KNOW YOURSELF

So, basically what I am saying is this: pick where you want to be and go there without looking over your shoulder, without looking back. If you are gregarious and good at self-promotion, do it. If you are not, do as much as you can stand; realize that you are making a choice not to do more; and don't be bitter about your not being better at it.

If you love working in the mountains, great. But don't bad-mouth the New York "conspiracy." If showing in public is painful, don't show. If you can't manage a variable income, get a secure job.

These are a lot of don'ts, but I also have some do's: do make art; do make good art; and do make it all through your life, because, really, that is the only reward you can expect.

Selling your art is nice; public acclaim is nice; but it's like the warmth of a sunburn. It's superficial and shortlived.

Be practical but only about practical matters. Expect damn little, but expect a lot from yourself—because finally your relationship with the art you make will be the major source of joy and sorrow in your life.

3

Modes of Doing Business

by

Harvey Horowitz

◆ ◆ ◆ ◆

HARVEY HOROWITZ, Chairman of the Board of the Volunteer Lawyers for the Arts, is a partner in the law firm of Squadron, Ellenoff, Plesent & Lehrer, of New York City. Mr. Horowitz is a member of the arts and entertainment committees of the City Bar Association of the City of New York, and is Adjunct Professor for Performing Arts and the Law at the City University of the City of New York's Graduate School.

◆ ◆ ◆ ◆

SELECTING A BUSINESS ENTITY

When an artist or a group of artists sets out to conduct a business venture, several types of business entities can be utilized. However, to determine which form of entity best suits a particular need, various factors should be considered. Among them are tax considerations, record-keeping obligations, formalities necessary to establish a particular venture, whether federal tax exemption will be sought, what legal liability the venture and its individuals might be exposed to and, in general, the impact on conducting business that the structure would have.

Depending on particular needs, one or more of these factors may have greater significance than the others. It is almost impossible to generalize what should be foremost in the minds of artists beginning a business in terms of selecting a structure. Even if circumstances would not warrant a highly structured business entity, it still is useful to have a working knowledge of these various formats since interaction with them is almost a certainty if one begins conducting a business.

STARTING OUT AS A SOLE PROPRIETOR

The simplest and most direct manner of starting out is to conduct a business individually under one's own name. Under such circumstances, the business itself has no separate identity legally or otherwise from the person conducting the business. The individual is liable for commitments made and is personally liable to pay taxes on any income the venture produces. No separate tax returns have to be prepared for federal income tax purposes. Items of income and expense are reported on Schedule C to the individual's Form 1040 federal income tax return. There are no formalities necessary when starting a business under an individual's own name. Very often, if the type of business does not warrant any further formalities, an individual should not seek to overly structure the activity. Therefore, doing business under one's own name should be seriously considered as an initial step.

CONDUCTING BUSINESS UNDER A TRADE NAME OR AN ASSUMED NAME

A slight variation from conducting business under one's own name is individually conducting business under an assumed or trade name. The tax and legal ramifications of conducting business under a trade name are substantially identical to those attaching to conducting business under one's own name. The business is not a separate legal entity for liability or tax purposes, and, again, the individual conducting business is personally responsible for debts and taxes on income earned. Similarly, no separate federal income tax return is required to be filed. The added formality necessary to conduct business under a trade or assumed name is that in most states the individual would have to file a form of certificate disclosing the true identity of the person conducting business, and the trade name being assumed. Most states also require that a copy of the certificate be displayed at the place of business, and most banking institutions require a copy of the certificate for the purpose of opening a bank account in the trade name. Although conducting business under a trade name does not differ from conducting business under an individual's own name, some persons believe the assumption of a trade name adds a certain cachet to the business venture. There are opposing opinions on this point, but both have validity. In some instances, it is possible that the use of a trade name might make the business venture appear more substantial. In some fields, however, it might be important to establish the reputation of the individual involved, in which case it would be preferable to conduct business under an individual's name. As was noted above, the formalities of conducting business under a trade or assumed name are rather minimal, and the costs, including filing fees and photocopies, of a business certificate should run under $50.

FORMING A PARTNERSHIP

When two or more individuals set out to conduct business, usually some structure is required. The most common form when two or more people come together is a general partnership. Just as with a person doing business under an assumed name, the general partnership does not have a legal or tax identity separate and apart from the individual partners. Accordingly, partners are liable for debts incurred by the partnership and taxes must be paid by the individuals on the income earned by the partnership. Even though taxes on partnership profits are payable by the partners, the partnership is required to file a separate partnership tax return reflecting the financial activity of the partnership and the identity of the partners. State and local partnership returns may also be required. A partnership is a consentual arrangement between two or more individuals to conduct business together. It should be noted that the agreement to conduct business as partners can be a tacit as well as an express agreement. In most states, the agreement need not be written and an oral partnership agreement might suffice to constitute individuals as partners. While it is recommended that individuals desiring to form the partnership do so under a written agreement, it is important to note that an oral or tacit understanding can give rise to the partnership status. This is significant because of the legal rule that each partner can legally bind the partnership and each partner is legally responsible individually for all of the partnership's debts and obligations. Accordingly, if two people set out to conduct business, and one of the individuals orders supplies or enters into a lease, the other individual could be held liable for these obligations if it is later determined that the partnership status was created by tacit agreement between the parties. In forming a partnership, it is generally useful to have a writing setting forth the rights and obligations of the parties to each other. For instance, one party who may be contributing more time or funds to the partnership might desire a greater participation in profits. Also, if there are several individuals involved, the parties might wish to delegate responsibilities for certain matters among various partners. However, it is important to note that no matter what the agreement is among the partners, as far as other individuals and entities are concerned, each partner is fully liable for partnership obligations. Consider, as examples, two persons entering into a partnership arrangement and (1) deciding that one individual would have a ninety percent partnership interest, while the other has a ten percent interest; or (2) agreeing that each shall have an equal interest in the partnership. Notwithstanding the fact that either of these agreements would be binding and valid as between the partners, if one of the individuals in either partnership example signed a partnership lease, then the other partner would be fully liable for the lease obligations.

THE PARTNERSHIP AGREEMENT

The formalities for setting up a partnership usually include a partnership agreement, which can take the form of a rather simple letter of understanding signed by the partners, and the subsequent filing of a certificate of partnership with a state or county office. Again, the requirements for filing vary from state to state. But, in general, a certificate of partnership is filed and copies are needed for the purpose of opening a bank account. Also, most states require that a copy of the partnership certificate be displayed so that the public knows the identity of the individuals involved in the partnership venture. The cost for setting up a partnership, including filing fees and photocopies, is usually under $50.

SETTING UP A CORPORATION

The most structured form of doing business is the corporate form. All states have adopted some form of corporation law which contains the requirement for establishing a corporation. Again, as was the case with a doing business certificate and a partnership certificate, the requirements vary from state to state. Generally speaking, however, the corporation is formed by the preparation and filing of a charter or certificate of incorporation. Unlike the situations with persons conducting business under an assumed name or as partners, a corporation has a separate legal identity from that of its stockholders, officers, and directors. Accordingly, a corporation is responsible for its own debts and obligations and is liable for taxes on income earned by the corporation. Most states permit at least two forms of corporations, the first being the business corporation or stock corporation and the second, the nonprofit or not-for-profit corporation.

ESTABLISHING A NON-PROFIT CORPORATION

Usually the requirements to establish a nonprofit corporation are greater than those required to establish a business or stock corporation. For the most part, the nonprofit corporation mode is adopted where the goal is ultimately to obtain some form of tax exemption that is needed for the purpose of soliciting contributions or receiving grants from federal or state agencies. To be able to quality for nonprofit status in most states, the organization must be established to serve a public, charitable, or educational purpose rather than pursue a purely business or commercial goal. As an example, nonprofit corporations have been established to run art schools, to award fellowships, or to conduct training or educational programs. Since most artists are pursuing their profession with a view toward financial gain, it is unlikely that they would select the form of doing business as a nonprofit corporation as their primary business mode. Accordingly, there is intentionally excluded a fuller discussion on the requirements for establishing a nonprofit corporation and the requirements for securing tax exemption. In all events, it is advisable to consult an attorney if you are considering such a move.

STRUCTURE OF A CORPORATION

In most states, a business corporation may be established by one or more individuals to pursue any lawful commercial or business goal. Most states allow one person to incorporate, although some states may require a greater number of individuals to be incorporators. A business corporation consists of the individuals who own the corporation and who are denominated as stockholders. Stockholders usually elect a board of directors to manage the affairs of the corporation. The board of directors in turn elects officers to carry on the day-to-day business management of the corporation. Directors of a corporation need not be stockholders, and officers are not required to be directors or stockholders. A corporation's charter or certificate of incorporation usually does not contain a lot of detail regarding the operation of the organization. Accordingly, it is customary for a corporation to adopt bylaws at an early stage of its existence to set forth the procedures for operation. The bylaws usually contain procedures for stockholder voting, convening of meetings, and election of directors. Bylaws also include similar provisions for conducting meetings by directors.

While the procedure for establishing a sole proprietorship and partnership is quite simple, the procedure for establishing a corporation is more complicated. Accordingly, while it is possible in most states to form a corporation without using a lawyer, some consideration should be given to whether legal advice should be sought. The filing fees for establishing a corporation are approximately $100, and legal fees can range from $250 to $500. Additionally, most states require the payment of an annual franchise tax or corporate fee tax, even if the corporation has had little or no activity.

TWO OTHER BUSINESS STRUCTURES: LIMITED PARTNERSHIPS AND TRUSTS

Thus far, we have briefly reviewed three forms of business structure: (1) the sole proprietorship (whether under an individual's own name or an assumed name); (2) a general partnership; and (3) a corporation. These three categories are the ones most likely to be considered when one or more persons sets out to conduct business. However, to complete this presentation, mention should also be made of two other forms of legal entities—a limited partnership and a trust.

Limited partnerships

A limited partnership is a hybrid form of entity having some characteristics of a general partnership and other characteristics of a corporation. A limited partnership is generally utilized where investments to the business venture are being sought and certain tax benefits and profit distributions are contemplated. In the cultural and arts community, this vehicle is most frequently used in the theatrical field when money is being raised from investors to produce a play. A limited partnership consists of one or more individuals or corporations who are called "general partners" and one or more individuals or corporations who serve as "limited partners." (In this regard, it should be noted that certain state laws may prohibit a corporation from being a general or limited partner or limit its power to become such. As is the case with other forms of doing business, the rules applying to the formation and operation of a limited partnership are governed by state law. Accordingly, these laws may differ from state to state.) The general partners of a limited partnership, like the partners in a general partnership, have full liability for partnership debts. Limited partners, however, have only limited liability for partnership debts. This limitation is usually an amount equal to the money invested in the limited partnership. To this extent, the limitation of liability for limited partners is somewhat analogous to the limited liability of corporate stockholders. As in a general partnership, taxes on the income earned by a limited partnership are the responsibility of the partners. The allocation of profits and losses for the purpose of computing taxes is governed by an agreement of limited partnership. Establishing a limited partnership requires more formal steps than is the case with the general partnership. Usually a certificate of limited partnership has to be filed in a state or local office and notice of the formation of a limited partnership published. Since it is a somewhat complex form of business venture, it is suggested that professional advice be sought before establishing a limited partnership.

Trusts

The other form of entity is a trust. Trusts are usually established by a deed or instrument of trust or by a last will and testament. Trusts are not frequently utilized as a vehicle to conduct business, and it is unlikely that anyone pursuing a business career in the arts would opt for this mode of doing business. A trust is a separate legal entity and consists of one or more trustees who manage the trust and one or more beneficiaries who are entitled to receive the benefit of income generated by the trust. Because it is highly unlikely that the trust mode of business would be used, no further discussion on this legal entity is included.

CHOOSING THE RIGHT BUSINESS STRUCTURE

As stated above, the three modes of doing business most frequently utilized are sole proprietorship, general partnership, and corporation. The decision as to whether to conduct business as a sole proprietorship or as a partnership is more a result of necessity than of choice. Clearly, if more than one individual is involved in a venture, but those individuals do not want to incorporate, the partnership mode of business results directly from the decision to associate with others and conduct business. Accordingly, the primary issue to be considered when starting a business venture, in terms of opting for a mode of doing business, is the question of whether or not to incorporate, since (1) in most states an individual can incorporate; (2) a corporation is permitted to have only one shareholder, director, and officer, and (3) self-evidently, more than one individual can form and operate a corporation. In this regard, the individuals should assess the financial, practical, and tax considerations adherent to incorporating.

From a management point of view, operating a corporation imposes an additional burden in terms of record-keeping and reporting. At the early stages of operation, a certificate of incorporation or charter has to be drawn, bylaws prepared, and officers and directors elected. Since a corporation is a separate legal entity, it is required to file tax returns annually and the entity will pay taxes on corporate profits.

An exception to this rule is the "Sub-Chapter S" corporation. Provided that conditions and requirements contained in the Internal Revenue Code are met, stockholders of a corporation can file what is known as a Sub-Chapter S election with the Internal Revenue Service. In such a case, from a tax point of view, the profits and losses of a corporation are picked up by the stockholders on their personal tax returns. In such a case, the individual stockholders would pay taxes on the profits of the corporation rather than the corporation paying taxes directly on such profits. Since the tax rules for Sub-Chapter S elections are specialized, it would be advisable for individuals considering such an election to seek professional tax assistance.

SELECTING A CORPORATE NAME

Additionally, when setting out as a corporation, it is necessary to select and clear a corporate name. The purpose of clearing a name is to determine whether the corporate name selected is substantially similar, or the same as, the name of an existing corporation. If the name is similar to an existing corporate name, most states will not allow it to be used for fear of causing confusion in the minds of the public. Most states have a rather simple procedure for checking or clearing corporate names. The fees are usually modest for this service. Another practical consideration relates to banking arrangements. Since a corporation is a separate legal entity, banks often require corporate financial statements for a corporation if a loan is being requested. Very often, a bank might also request the personal guarantees of stockholders before making a loan to corporations. In addition, banks require the filing of certain corporate resolutions which designate the names of individuals authorized to sign checks on behalf of the corporation. Additionally, corporate meetings of stockholders or directors may be required in connection with substantial business transactions such as leasing space or equipment. The reason for such corporate action is that landlords or suppliers of equipment usually require written evidence that the stockholders or directors have authorized the corporation to enter into the contemplated agreement. Most organizations that request corporate resolutions, be they lending institutions, landlords, or equipment suppliers, usually have their own form of corporate resolutions which they will supply to a prospective lessee or bank customer.

DIVIDENDS AND COMPENSATION TO STOCKHOLDERS

Another practical consideration relates to the way in which funds can be distributed to stockholders. These procedures primarily concern the tax effect on withdrawal of such funds. The only manner in which corporations can distribute funds to individuals is by way of compensation or salary for services rendered, or as dividends. Most states require that dividends can be paid only out of corporate profits. Accordingly, when a dividend to stockholders is declared, the corporation is required to pay a tax on the profits that generate the funds for the dividend. In addition, the individual stockholders receiving the dividend must pay income tax on the amount received. The corporation is not entitled to take a deduction for the amount of dividends paid to stockholders. Compensation or salary for services rendered can be paid by the corporation out of any funds and constitute a corporate business deduction for tax purposes. The amount of compensation paid to a stockholder can be reviewed by the Internal Revenue Service which has the authority to question the amount paid if the IRS feels the amount is excessive for the services performed. If the IRS determines that the amount of compensation paid to a stockholder for services performed is unreasonable, it can disallow the deduction the corporation has taken for the payment of compensation and treat the amount as a dividend. In such a case, the corporation would be required to pay tax on the amount distributed. Generally speaking, the test for determining whether an amount paid as salary to a stockholder is reasonable or unreasonable is based on the particular factors and circumstances involved. What the IRS generally does is examine to see what the prevailing salary for similar services would be in the particular field of operation. It is only when the amount in question is considerably in excess of that prevailing rate or where in actuality very few, if any, services have been performed that the IRS will find the salary is unreasonable.

ADVANTAGES OF THE CORPORATION

While it is apparent that some problem areas exist in terms of doing business in the corporate mode, there can, on the other hand, be substantial benefits. The most significant of these benefits is that the stockholder is protected from liability for corporate debts and obligations. Accordingly, if the corporation borrows money from a bank and is unable to repay it, the bank has no recourse against the stockholder. Additionally, if the corporation owes taxes, the individual would not be responsible for these taxes. (At this point it should be noted, however, that certain officers may be personally responsible for the failure of a corporation to pay withholding or FICA taxes or, under some circumstances, local sales taxes.)

The second benefit is that the corporate existence can continue in most states for an indefinite period of time. Accordingly, if one shareholder should die or decide to leave the corporation, the corporation could still continue in existence. In the case of a partnership, the retirement or death of a partner usually leads to the termination or dissolution of a partnership.

The third benefit is the ability to spread tax liability over fiscal years different from the reporting years for the stockholders. Additionally, there might be a tax benefit in having the corporation pay taxes on profits, because in these situations, the taxable rate on these profits might be lower than the taxable rate payable if an individual had earned profits in a like amount.

The final consideration also may be a financial one. When individuals start in business, they may need most of their financial resources to carry on that business. Accordingly, the payment of corporate filing fees and perhaps legal fees might create an additional financial burden on the venture. In addition, the costs of operating through a corporate vehicle are somewhat higher since annual franchise tax fees are payable even if the corporation has little or no profit.

The ultimate decision as to which mode of doing business is most suitable can be made only after all of the above factors have been weighed. The information presented here is intended as a summary of the factors to be taken into account and should be assessed in terms of the business goals and operational requirements of the business venture.

4

Planning Your Financial Picture

by

Robert T. Higashi

◆ ◆ ◆

ROBERT T. HIGASHI is a Certified Public Accountant with the firm of Weil, Higashi, Hallal and Ettinger in Santa Monica, California. Many of Mr. Higashi's clients are artists.

◆ ◆ ◆ ◆

Struggling to survive can be disastrous to your work. I believe that economic freedom, the ability to work and live where you want to and not where you have to, is dependent upon economic success.

Once achieved, however, economic success creates other problems. Tax rates rise as high as 50 percent in our society. The state may add 11 percent to this startling figure. On another level too much success, or "too many toys" as the saying goes, can cause a maelstrom of budget problems, and that is an equal distraction. To the person faced with these facts, financial planning becomes imperative. Generally it encompasses tax and investment planning. It may also lead to retirement and estate planning.

But don't be turned off by these words up front. It's not just bookkeeping, taxes, and being prudent we're discussing here. More than that, it's an understanding of certain basic concepts which enable you to create and become more productive as an artist.

UNDERSTANDING "ACCOUNTING"

First, let's demystify the term "accounting." The techniques of business are not as complicated and sophisticated as you might think. Once understood they are easy to apply, not only by multinational corporations but also by individuals struggling to survive.

Everybody has a different idea about what accounting is: it is a set of books, financial statements, invoices and receipts. Accounting encompasses much more than any one of those things, but it's simple to understand. Accounting is nothing but the recording, classifying, and summarizing of economic data, a science of economic transactions. This data is usually rendered in terms of dollars and cents, but it can also be used in terms of "units," i.e., a number of paintings or sculptures.

I find many times that artists are not aware of the real help and assistance this business tool can bring to them. I can't express strongly enough to you my feeling that accounting is of value to the artist who has passionate dreams of creating, of making something new and unprecedented. Artists are always asking, "Why does the businessman have all the money?" The answer is that the artist often does not recognize and adopt the tools used by shrewd, wise, calculating businessmen. That may be a large part of why even some successful artists are behind in this area of economic achievement.

Yet the need to feel self-sufficient and create a proper environment seems paramount among artists. So I think it does us no harm to regard art as a profit-making venture, a way to make money and to sustain yourself and your work.

CASH PLANNING

One of the most fundamental principles of accounting is budgeting, or "cash planning." This is a very helpful tool because it enables you to predetermine your cash needs. At the same time it helps monitor your economic performance. Basically, cash planning is the system of comparing your estimated cash flow with your actual cash flow, both in and out. To write a budget you simply design a calendar that shows perhaps a six- or twelve-month period. Then you take into consideration all the financial ingredients of your life, the cash you require and your fixed obligations—studio facilities, equipment, helpers, supplies and research, automobile expenses and insurance, good food, drink and laughs—whatever makes up your life. When you total the cost of all these things you determine your financial needs.

Next, you determine your cash flow from the sale of art, lecture fees, grants and loans, perhaps teaching salaries or royalties. You determine when you can expect this money to arrive and you mark it on your calendar. Now you have a comparison of the cash required and the cash expected, and from that you can make sound financial decisions.

As things happen and conditions change you simply reorganize the figures. You update your plan for the next month, week, or year. When you revise your plan as the need arrives you become better at it, falling closer each time to that "bull's-eye" which is your desired financial situation. That opens up all kinds of interesting possibilities.

Suppose in the beginning you wanted only a kiln and a glazer. In time, you decide to make your studio more useful. It needs more ventilation for ovens, more electrical power, a skylight to provide natural light, shelving, a wall taken out. These things cost money, and if your budget projections suggest that such studio additions could really happen you will undergo changes in the way you approach your work. Thus, budgeting becomes a tool for personal and professional growth.

There are other benefits to consider. A budget compels you to coordinate various aspects of your life. A budget determines just exactly when you will be short of cash, whch gives you ample time to arrange financing from a bank, dealer, agent, relative, or friend. Perhaps most important, a budget places you in positive control of your financial future. After all, if you're experiencing a shortage of money, you are hardly a rarity. And yet you don't have to be a victim of circumstances if you use this tool of foresight.

That's a simple description of how a budget can work for you. Now let's view a more complicated use of it.

BUDGETING IN ACTION

I was once assisting a sculptor who experiments with color and light. His needs include expensive materials and a $100,000 piece of equipment which produces the desired effect of light and color.

The sculpture he wanted to produce was a large piece. Labor and overhead were added to the budget. However, without sophisticated accounting techniques we couldn't devise a reasonable, accurate projection of the cost.

The way of most artists is to wait for a commission before they begin a large work. "I will create a work, present the work, and I will get my money." While this is a safe approach to budgeting for doing a large work, it certainly was not productive in the mind of my client, who couldn't wait for that to begin. He had the inspiration then, and the probable cost to him was phenomenal, including a projected payroll of $6,000 per month for the four months he estimated were necessary to create the work. That was a lot of money to pay toward something which he might or not be able to sell. He had no guarantee someone would purchase the sculpture for the high price he planned to ask.

The large financial risk involved was, to him, worth taking. It was even exciting, because to him, belief in himself made it important that he take a risk. If an artist is really good it would seem natural that people would help him fulfill his creative power and passion. Often this is exactly what happens.

The first step in the artist's conception of the plan should be the budget. How much will it cost? Where can the money come from? A sound budget is a conceptually complete blueprint for action.

In the case of my client, the work was eventually sold to an important art collector for a substantial amount of money. And I will return later to the creative financing which helped this project. First, however, let's discuss another basic, important accounting tool.

KEEPING RECORDS

Record-keeping, or bookkeeping, is essential to your operation. It tells you whether you operate at a profit or loss, and how much of a profit or loss.

You have two basic reasons for keeping records: (1) for your own edification as you keep track of your affairs, and (2) for your obligation to statutory authorities—the federal, state and city governments.

The Internal Revenue Service is the most imperative reason for keeping records. The IRS requires that you keep "adequate books and records," to substantiate the income and expenses declared on your income tax return; the responsibility of satisfying them with the legitimacy of your claims rests entirely upon you.

No one has ever really formalized a definition of adequate books and records. As far as the IRS is concerned, if it can follow your records, then your records are adequate. The IRS presumes that every person in business opens a bank account, so generally, the basic foundation of books and records consists of bank statements and canceled checks.

The bank keeps records of your monthly statements, cash receipts, and canceled checks. At the end of the year some banks, for a fee, can also give you a computer printout of all your checks. All of these are individual documents of the funds you've spent. The bank records them for you, and all you need do is compile and classify the various documents. Now you have a whole financial picture, a record of how you spent money. You could sit down with that and summarize a year's activity in a few hours.

In addition you should keep any invoices, bills of sale, receipts of various kinds, and any business documents. The sum total of all these documents will constitute adequate books and records. A clear picture of your financial history will greatly assist your projections for the future.

Bookkeeping systems vary from keeping receipts and invoices in a shoe box and tabulating them once a year, to your own mini-computer which produces monthly financial statements and other financial reports. In between these extremes are manual, pegboard, and computer service bureau systems. Depending on your particular circumstances and needs, any one of these systems may be appropriate. The wide range of systems may seem confusing to you. I recommend that you hire a Certified Public Accountant to help you choose and install the right system.

ACCOUNTING SYSTEMS

Cash basis method

The most simple type of accounting system is called the cash basis method of accounting. This system records income when it is received in cash, and expenses when they are paid in cash. It is the most commonly used method of accounting because of its simplicity.

However, the cash basis method merely tracks the cash through your business. It doesn't tell you how much people owe you, how much you owe others, or what you have in inventory.

Accrual method

To obtain this information for your records you should adopt the accrual method of accounting. This is a more complete method of reporting economic transactions because it recognizes income when you earn it and expenses when you incur them.

Suppose you owe your welders $20,000. You haven't paid them yet. But at the end of the year you can record an expense of $20,000 based on the accrual system, thereby allowing yourself a deduction for the sum of money you owe. Conversely, if you shipped an art piece to a customer and billed him $40,000, but you haven't been paid yet, then this transaction must be recorded as income under the accrual accounting method. But you also can report and deduct the expenses incurred.

The accrual method proposes to tell you what really happened in an economic transaction. That's a closer picture of the truth than the cash basis method of accounting.

Records are just as important for your own personal reasons. You should keep an accurate, detailed record of all the artwork you produce and the location of each work, whether it's in your studio, a gallery, a museum, or a private collection.

INVENTORY YOUR WORK

You should take periodic inventories to determine whether your artwork is all physically accounted for and located. This documentation of your total output is of great importance to you. There are cases of art either lost or misplaced by galleries and museums. Such institutions handle the work of many artists. Through the passage of time and a lot of activity, a work may become mishandled or misplaced, damaged, or lost. An agreement must be reached that the galleries and dealers will inform the artist when a work has been sold and to whom. This way you will know when your share of the sale is due.

Suppose you consign 15 paintings to a gallery and six months later that gallery sends you a statement which says they have only 13 of your paintings. Where did the other two go? Maybe those two paintings represent $15,000 each in total sales, and to you maybe they represent, net after commission, $21,000. Could you possibly be out $21,000? If your records are not meticulous and accurate you could run into big problems. You have no effective means of representing yourself, and that leaves you at the mercy of someone else, which is where you don't want to be.

Before you send your work on consignment, you should obtain a written agreement with the gallery as to who is responsible for insuring the goods. Many times a work is damaged in transit, or while being unpackaged and handled by a gallery. If there's no prior agreement you may be subject to loss, and at best there may be an argument as to who is responsible and who gets the tax write-off.

Suppose you have an exhibit. Besides this *certificate of insurance* you should obtain a *written agreement of responsibilities*. This should be a clear-cut agreement as to what exactly this artist must provide and what the gallery must provide in terms of the kinds of space, the kinds of help, and the kinds of expense reimbursements. If these matters are not resolved in advance, they may later become the subject of disputes, not only with both parties, but with the IRS too if it reviews your early income and expense record to verify the correctness of your income tax return.

These matters are the general conduct of business, a system which says that before you have an exhibit, and before you transact any major business, you should prepare a list of things which must be resolved. Contrary to being a lot of added work, this attention to organization and good record-keeping pays off in many ways. It contributes to your creative output and productivity by furnishing you with timely information about the cost and expenses of your work. It relieves the anxiety of "not knowing." It eliminates the lack of effectiveness which always accompanies disorganized business.

PLANNING YOUR TAXES WISELY

The subject of "taxes" is very broad and stimulates a great deal of thought and a lot of questions. A complex network of taxes raises money for the government. Tax laws are complicated, dynamic, and everchanging. By giving special concessions to various segments of society, Congress uses tax legislation to effect desired social results. In effect, what government does do is give certain groups more money through tax incentives, thereby avoiding the need to have a special Congressional appropriation of money for the same purpose.

Tax is a euphemism for money. A tax break is less open to criticism. It is more disguised. So when we talk about taxes, we're not talking just about a painful obligation, but also about a way to obtain more money or preserve the money you have. The situation is not hopeless, as some people think. You are not entirely a victim of circumstances. Our system of taxation is a system by self-confession in that you are left to confess your income and expenses. That leaves you in control of the situation. You must remember that you can minimize your taxes by arranging your affairs in the most tax-advantageous manner with the aid of a skillful, creative tax planner.

FEDERAL TAX

"The Government" represents federal, state, county, and city governments. Federal and state income taxes are the most important because they're by far the highest—up to 61 percent. To a lot of people, including writers, musicians and artists, tax consultation is vital to their livelihood. Artists, I feel, are among those most needing assistance. They often don't make as much money or do as well economically as other professionals. The artist is a true small businessman, albeit somewhat oblivious to making money.

Most states have income taxes. Each state has its own individual rates and laws. The various state rates reach as high as 11 percent. In rare instances some cities such as New York have income taxes.

The stakes are high with the federal rates going up to 50 percent.

STATE AND LOCAL TAXES

The next major tax to consider is a state, county or city sales tax. Each state governs its own rates and laws. Most states assess a tax ranging from 2 to 7 percent based on the sales price of goods and sometimes services. This tax may be passed on to the purchaser in some states or assessed against the artist. In either case, accurate records must be kept of the sales and sales taxes collected and paid. The artist must check with his own state or municipal authorities to learn what he must do to comply with the law.

Say you're an artist living in California. You sell a painting for a thousand dollars to a collector who walks into your studio, and you neglect to add the 6 percent sales tax. You sell another painting for a thousand dollars to a friend. Because you want to give this person the best price possible, you again leave off the sales tax. Now you owe to the State of California a bill of $120, which comes out of your sales price.

In my experience many artists have unknowingly failed to charge sales tax on art sold directly out of their studio. The sales tax people, as a result of subsequent audits, have assessed these artists the uncharged 2 to 7 percent plus penalties and interest. This assessment comes long after the money has been spent, and results in a real hardship. What you must do then is file for a resale license, qualifying yourself as someone who is in business and incurs sales taxes, and charge the appropriate sales tax as any other merchant would.

OTHER TAXES

There are other taxes to consider. Each city usually charges a business license tax, generally based on gross receipts. You should always keep adequate records to compute these taxes. Moreover, there are penalties that are levied when these taxes are neglected.

There are federal and state payroll taxes, with each state having its own individual laws. When an artist hires employees, he is required to withhold federal social security and income tax deductions from their pay and remit to the government as required. Most states also have a state payroll-withholding requirement. Quarterly and annual payroll tax returns and year-end W-2 forms must also be filed. The combined rates are usually no more than 10 percent of the gross payment. However, here again the reporting of payroll requirements is very precise, and violations result in substantial penalties.

Many states have personal property taxes. Those are assessed by the municipalities. Unlike all the other taxes previously mentioned, personal property taxes are not computed and reported by you. The state or county sends you a tax bill for payment.

The tax laws are numerous and complicated. They require a Certified Public Accountant to help you interpret them, and to understand what is required of you by law.

I once represented an artist who, when he came to me, hadn't paid any taxes for years. Furthermore, he had no notion of how much money he had made each year. With this client, I sat down and wrote a story—the story of his life based on the last few years. In this way, we tried to piece together his sources of income.

When asked what his activities had been in a given year, he said, "Oh, that year I had an exhibit. The rest of the year I didn't work. I just went to Africa." Later, however he presented me with a tattered bundle of notes. It turned out to be statements of bank deposits totaling $40,000, which he had "kept for some reason." I asked him, "Where did all that money come from?" to which he replied, "I don't know, Bob, it came from all over."

The reason he hadn't kept track of his income was either that he didn't know it was his responsibility or he didn't accept it as his responsibility. Explaining where the money went to was not so difficult. We had canceled checks. Some of them qualified as deductions. But the sources of the bank deposits were a problem. The consequences were that the government said that unless he could prove otherwise, that $40,000 was income.

DEDUCTING BUSINESS EXPENSES

Expenses are a basic concept in taxation. All business expenses are deductible against business income. Business expenses are defined as those that are ordinary and necessary to the conduct of your work. The definition is broad and yet it specifically excludes all expenses of a personal nature, such as food, shelter, clothing, and entertainment. It includes the cost of your work: your supplies, facilities or studio, employees, utilities, rent, telephone bills, auto expenses, travel and promotion, and anything further that relates to your work—including your accounting and legal fees.

Travel and expenses to out-of-town exhibits and dealers are often incurred. Also, the meals and lodging during that time are deductible. Since many of these expenses are paid by cash, the IRS requires that a "concurrent" diary or daybook be kept to substantiate the cash expenses. You can use this diary for all other cash expenses during the year. If the diary is properly documented, actual receipts are needed only for those expenditures over $25.

If your studio is in your home, you must allocate a portion of your home as your work area. A part of your utilities, maintenance costs, and all other work-related concerns are deductible.

TAX LAWS THAT APPLY TO ARTISTS

Certain tax laws apply more to artists than others. Artists often receive prizes and awards, or fellowships and endowments. Some of these are nontaxable, such as those awarded by the government. Most awards are structured to be nontaxable because the burden to the artist is understood. Those that are taxable are the ones that include a stipulation for some *quid pro quo*, such as a commitment to teach or produce. The IRS regards this commitment as payment for services rendered, or "taxable income."

But some tax laws do not work to the benefit of artists as much as others. There's the concept of donating art to a charitable organization. If a collector donates art to a museum, he can deduct the full market value of that work. But if an artist donates his own work of equal value to a museum, he can deduct only the actual cost to him of its production, i.e., the cost of "paint and canvas." This often seems negligible to the artist.

The concept of "taxable income other than cash" is another tax matter that relates particularly to artists. Take the example of one artist selling his painting to another artist, who in turn gives his own painting to the first artist. In other words, they exchange artworks. Under the IRS Code you can deduct as a business expense only the cost of your painting—the price of the "paint and canvas." If that cost was $50 and the painting is worth $1,000, then your reportable taxable income on that transaction is $950. Another example of "income other than cash" is the case of the artist who receives services as payment for his work. Suppose a dentist pays you for an art piece with $1,800 worth of dental work. The law requires that you report the value of this service as income.

These are some of the tax laws that particularly relate to artists. There are other more intricate laws to consider, which are more complicated and require more than a simple explanation. But the three that I have mentioned—fellowships, awards and prizes; donating art to charity; and taxable income other than cash—are basic to your understanding of the tax obligations.

There are also certain electives, or "loopholes," which benefit the artist. There is a 10% investment tax credit on the cost of equipment used in your work. There's a 10% to 15% tax credit on business equipment connected with energy conservation. There's a 15% to 20% rehabilitation tax credit on the cost of improving commercial structures over 30 years old, which may be applicable to some artists making improvements to their studios.

CORPORATIONS AND TAX DEDUCTIBLE RETIREMENT PLANS

A "corporation" can be utilized by artists as a means of tax saving. Under such a format, the artist does business as a corporation. The corporation is a legal taxpaying entity. The corporate form of doing business is used by many "high earning" professionals such as doctors, lawyers, CPAs, architects, etc. The major advantage of using the corporation is the ability to "shelter" otherwise taxable income in a qualified profit sharing or pension plan. Presently the maximum tax deductible contribution into a qualified "defined contribution" profit sharing and/or pension plan is $41,500.00.

A very successful artist may be able to adopt a special retirement plan called a Defined Benefit Plan that given the appropriate circumstances could require a tax deductible contribution into the plan of double the maximum deductible contribution of the defined contribution plans.

The contributions to the plans are then reinvested in stocks, bonds, savings accounts, T-bills, etc. The income from these investments of plan assets are "tax free"until such time as the beneficiary withdraws the assets.

The plan assets are available to the artist upon his retirement. There is no age requirement. He may retire when he chooses. The plan assets are held in a trust and are protected from the artist's creditors and any legal action against the artist. When the artist dies, the plan assets may be excluded from his estate if his beneficiaries elect to receive the distribution in installments instead of in a lump sum amount.

As you can see, there may be tremendous tax advantages from the use of corporations and qualified profit sharing and pension plans. Great care and planning must be taken in utilizing these tools. A CPA and an attorney who specialize in these corporations and plans must be retained to assure that all of the complicated laws and regulations are complied with.

IRA AND KEOGH PLANS

There are two types of tax deductible retirement plans available to artists who are individuals not operating as corporate entities.

The first plan is called the Keogh Plan. The maximum tax deductible contribution each year is $15,000 or 15 percent of your "earned income," whichever is less. The earnings of the plan assets are tax free but you cannot withdraw money from the plan until age 59½ without a tax penalty.

The second type of plan, called the IRA Plan, is similar to the Keogh Plan. The maximum tax deductible contribution in this plan is the lesser of $2,000 or 100 percent of your "earned income." As in the Keogh Plan, if you withdraw money prior to age 59½ you are charged a penalty tax.

As you can see, corporate retirement plans allow you to deduct and invest tax free substantially more money than do the Keogh and IRA Plans. There is also no penalty tax for early withdrawal of funds, just a normal income tax.

CREATIVE BUSINESS—OR KEEPING THE MONEY YOU MAKE

Now you have a basis for studying your obligation to the various tax laws and also some methods of preserving your income. If you progressed financially at the same rate as you read this chapter, you now have some money. Since *some* money is rarely enough for artists with large dreams, we can proceed with the more creative aspects of business.

One dream you can't afford is the illusion that someone will just walk down the street, recognize your genius, lift it out of obscurity and drop it into the audience's consciousness. Dreams should be well thought out and realistic if we expect them to come true—but that's not saying they have to be small and insignificant.

Let's recall my client artist who experimented with light and color. This individual's art involves a large need for space, high technology, and expensive materials. It's obvious the artistic process is costly. If his business had not been creatively well planned and well managed it couldn't even have begun. But it did begin, and it continues to happen for this artist, because of the ingenuity necessary to make it happen and the foresight to see that it could.

In the beginning I assisted this artist in obtaining an interim business loan based upon using a blanket lien on his own finished inventory. In other words, the bank had a legal ability to take art pieces and sell them if the loan was not repaid. Banks often won't agree to such a loan, but in this case we were able to persuade a local bank by relying on the importance of the artist and his work. Creative business evolves from an artist's need to create. The creative energy from one feeds the other.

Many creative ways of making money were born out of desperation. A thoughtful plan may be part of the process, and yet the act is still triggered by desperation. Usually, when pushed to that point, you find you must put other aspects out of your life, unfortunately including your creative work. What we are really talking about in this chapter is how to avoid distraction by this all-consuming effort to make money. What you must do, then, is construct a financial plan for the future. Let's call it an "action plan."

Obviously, before you commence with your plan of action, you need a professional consultant to assist you. You need to rely on someone, just as you need a doctor for what hurts you. This business is too complicated for you to master it all and then administer the medicine yourself.

Hire someone who is reliable and qualified. Obtain referrals from people you have confidence in, and whom you respect. Ask yourself if this individual truly understands what your needs are and can articulate them back to you. No matter how technically qualified this person is, if he can't communicate with you he won't be able to help you. What it takes from you is a personal awareness that this person truly feels and understands your needs. If your consultant has your best interests in mind, then the two of you working together can accomplish a great deal. A good business consultant can bring new skills to an artist, as well as an application of these skills. Once an artist discovers this for himself he also discovers a new arena for his creativity.

RISK VS. RETURN

Investment planning is a highly creative endeavor. How can you best posture yourself for keeping the money you make? Consider the money that you don't immediately need to live on and to conduct your business with. That is the residue you use for investments, such as your work, your studio, real estate, stocks and bonds.

Everybody wants to make money with money. In business there is one thing to keep in mind: the concept of risk and return. The more chance there is of making money, the larger the risk. Many people who profess to know a lot about business lose sight of this concept. And yet you can't expect to make a lot of money unless you are prepared to take a lot of risks. An expectancy of high returns brings high risks, and low returns should involve low risks.

ESTATE PLANNING

Estate planning is the thoughtful planning of how to preserve your estate from death taxes, both federal and state. It also provides for the orderly distribution of your assets. My first question to a client concerned with estate planning is this: "Is it necessary?" Death is something we should provide for, but estate planning should be looked at in its proper perspective. Although it is necessary, it should not have undue attention placed on it. Be concerned with living, not with planning for death.

SUMMARY

If the article provokes your thinking, clarifies some concepts that you've heard but never understood, it has accomplished something. The relationship between creative output and supportive business concepts is tied closely together. Think of this chapter's numerous concepts as being a complement to your artistic activities.

5

Estate and Gift Tax Planning

by

Ira M. Lowe

◆ ◆ ◆ ◆

IRA M. LOWE is a senior partner in the firm of Lowe, Bressler and Kaufman, specializing in art law. He is a member of the Washington, D.C., New York and Massachusetts bars.

Mr. Lowe wishes to acknowledge the invaluable assistance of attorney Betty Battle of Washington, D.C., and the expertise of Frank Williams, CPA, of Glens Falls, N.Y.

◆ ◆ ◆ ◆

The media called it "the inheritance of the century." Pablo Picasso left no will when he died at the age of 91 in 1973, leaving more than 250 million dollars in art works piled in three villas in the south of France plus $40 million in other assets. Instead he chose to leave his heirs to struggle over the estate in a fractured family version of "Guernica." It is remarkable that they were able within four years to reach agreement on the division of nearly 40,000 works of art.*

The Picasso "family" resembled one of his Cubist creations. His widow Jacqueline and his son Paulo were the legal heirs at the time of Picasso's death. The remainder of the family, all alienated from Picasso before his death, were three legitimate grandchildren, offspring of Paulo (Pablito, Marina, and Bernard), and three illegitimate children (Maya, Claude, and Paloma), offspring of mistresses Marie Thérèse Walter and Françoise Gilot.

Intestacy laws, in the absence of a will, govern designation of heirs and shares. Only after the French Government in 1972 passed a new law which gave inheritance rights to illegitimate children and applied it to this case did Maya, Claude, and Paloma become eligible as heirs. Each was allowed half the share of a comparable legitimate heir.

Before final settlement of the estate, son Paulo died of alcoholism in 1975, Pablito committed suicide in 1973, and mistress Marie Thérèse also committed suicide.

The French law (*dation en paiement*) which permits estate taxes to be paid in art works (or assets other than cash) saved the estate from having to borrow or to sell quantities of art at forced sale and

---

*1,885 paintings, 7,089 drawings, 3,222 ceramic works, 17,411 prints, 1,723 plates, 1,228 sculptures, 6,121 lithographs, 453 lithographic stones, 11 tapestries, 8 rugs.

depressed prices in order to raise cash for taxes. The cream of the collection was painstakingly selected by the French Government for payment of taxes and will be housed in the Picasso Museum as a French national monument.

Imagine if Picasso had died as a resident of the United States! There is no *dation en paiement* for payment of estate taxes in this country. Payment is due in cash nine months after death unless an extension is granted. Even if the executor were able to spread payment of taxes over the allowable number of years if it qualifies as a "closely held business," there would be immediate obligations to pay state death taxes, funeral costs, administrative costs, legal fees, and support for family members. And where would these funds come from.

What if Picasso, with an estate of over $290 million, had died as a resident of the United States without a will (intestate). It was certainly too late after death to bequeath the historic art collection to a museum and qualify for the charitable deduction. And too late to reduce the taxable estate by any other form of gifts.

The estate, in the absence of a will, would be divided according to the laws of intestacy, which vary from state to state. Generally the surviving spouse receives the first $50,000 plus one-half the balance, the other half going to surviving issue (linear descendents), or if none, then to surviving parents, or if none, the entire estate to the spouse.

WHAT CONSTITUTES AN ESTATE?

Your *gross estate*, for federal tax purposes, includes the value (at date of death, or six months thereafter, at the election of your executor) of all property owned by you at the time of death. It also includes the value of all property in which you hold an interest or benefit right or expectancy or general power of appointment at death.

It is simple to identify most property which you own, for example a car or house with title in your sole name or the portfolios of prints and the lithographic plates in your studio. It is more difficult to identify your interest in an employee pension plan or the right to income from a trust (both are benefit rights) or a legal right to inherit a savings bond held in joint title (an expectancy) or the unrestricted right to name beneficiaries of a trust fund (a general power of appointment) or the right to borrow money on a life insurance policy (an incident of ownership). All of these are values includible in the gross estate.

Property may be tangible or intangible. Tangible property includes such things as real estate, household goods, personal possessions, works of art, stocks and bonds, savings certificates, bank accounts, non-qualified pension and profit sharing plans, and survivor's annuities purchased by the decedent. Intangible assets include patents, copyrights, trademarks, leasehold interests, accounts receivable and debts owed to you.

From your gross estate are subtracted certain expenses and deductions, such as funeral and other administration expenses (including dealer's commission and fees for selling art work to raise funds for taxes and probate expenses); debts and claims against the estate; unpaid mortgages; and net losses during administration. This is the *adjusted gross estate*.

Your *taxable estate* is the adjusted gross estate less any marital deduction (unlimited in estates of decedents dying after December 31, 1981); lifetime taxable gifts and charitable contributions.

Cumulative lifetime gifts. The total amount of taxable lifetime gifts, above the annual exemptions, made after 1976 is added to the taxable estate.

Tentative tax. The unified estate and gift tax is applied to the total amount of the taxable estate and the lifetime gifts made after 1976 to arrive at the tentative tax.

Tax credits. To complete the computation, tax credits are applied to determine the total tax due based on date of death according to the following table:

Unified Estate Tax Credit		Exemption Equivalent
(A dollar-for-dollar offset against the tax computed on the taxable estate.)		(Signifies the amount of estate property which is sheltered from tax.)
1982	$62,800	$225,000
1983	79,300	275,000
1984	96,300	325,000
1985	121,800	400,000
1986	155,800	500,000
1987	192,800	600,000
and subsequent years		

The maximum tax rate is 65% for decedents dying in 1982, 60% in 1983, 55% in 1984, and 50% in 1985 and subsequent years. When fully phased in, the 50% tax rate will apply to taxable gifts and bequests in excess of $2.5 million.

The minimum rate starting at $225,000 is 32%.

When the unified estate tax credit is fully phased in, in 1987, the actual payments according to the tax rate will thereafter be between 37% and 50%.

HOW THE ESTATE TAX WORKS

Present law, as expressed in the Economic Recovery Tax Act of 1981,* continues to consolidate gift and estate taxes and effectively provides one tax rate for transfers of assets, whether by lifetime gift or by inheritance. Thus the value of lifetime taxable gifts is added on to your estate at death and is subject to tax at the unified rate.

The taxable estate does not include gifts made before 1977, although gifts made between January 1, 1977, and December 31, 1981, will be included above the $3,000 annual exclusion in effect during that period of time. Gifts above the $10,000 annual exclusion starting in 1982 will similarly be included in the taxable estate. Nor does it include assets held by you in trust for the benefit of another, but it does include assets held by another in trust for your benefit if you have power to control disposition of the assets by will. Life interests held by you are not included because the interest terminates upon your death. Excluded from the gross estate are Keogh plans, individual retirement accounts, qualified pension and profit-sharing plans (under certain conditions), social security benefits, workman's compensation awards payable to the survivors but not to the estate, wrongful death benefits, and a share of joint property which was purchased with funds of the co-owner.

Special rules apply in states where community property law prevails. In general, one-half of property acquired as co-owners by husband and wife while under the jurisdiction of community property states is included in the estate of each. State laws vary and should be consulted for particular application.

Of all "properties," the types that most frequently present problems are jointly owned property and life insurance, which will be discussed in greater detail.

*Effective in most instances as of January 1, 1982.

WITH—OR WITHOUT—AN ESTATE PLAN

Consider the case of Aida, a serious painter with talent and sensitivity. She lives with her two teenage children, 13 and 15 years old, in a rented studio loft in SoHo, and is divorced from a penniless photographer husband who is remarried and struggling to support a second wife and small child. Aida sells four or five major canvases each year and has an annual income of $25,000, which includes dividends from $50,000 of inherited IBM stock and $8,000 annually from part-time teaching activities. Her studio and storage contain most of her life work, approximately 150 paintings and 226 drawings. As a result of a recent gallery exhibition which received favorable reviews, several large paintings sold for $3,500 and a number of drawings brought $300 each. Ten years ago an uncle left her a beach cottage on Long Island, then valued at $80,000. She uses the cottage on weekends, lives there in the summer, is indifferent to the appreciation in value of the waterfront property, and wants it to be kept for the children to use in future years. Last year Aida purchased a $50,000 ordinary life insurance policy through the junior college where she teaches, naming the two children as beneficiaries and hoping that the proceeds would provide for their support and education in case she dies prematurely.

Without an estate plan

What if Aida dies unexpectedly? Her estate, which includes art works valued at $296,500 computed on 50 percent of retail sales price, real estate appraised at current value of $133,500, life insurance of $50,000, IBM stock of $50,000 and $20,000 in cash and personal property, would total $550,000.

Without an estate plan, federal estate taxes would be slightly over $100,000* and estate expenses (funeral, administrative, and legal expenses) as much as $30,000, requiring that the IBM stock, life insurance, and available cash be used immediately to pay these obligations. In addition at least $10,000 in art works must be sold within the nine-month period after death to fund the balance due. It may be unrealistic to depend on sales of that amount within such a short period. Even a one-year extension may be inadequate. The

---

*Based on the unified credit and IRS provisions effective in 1982. Results differ considerably and favorably to the taxpayer from years 1983 on, based on increased unified credits.

executor may argue successfully that there is reasonable justification to extend payment of tax over 14 years because art works were part of a closely held business.

An extension would partially solve the problem of taxpaying. But what happened to Aida's hope that the life insurance would provide for the children's education? And what about their immediate and future support needs?

With an estate plan

What steps could Aida take to protect the estate for the children?

- She could assign ownership of the existing life insurance policy to the children (giving all incidents of ownership) and remove $50,000 from her taxable estate.
- She could purchase an additional, $50,000 term life insurance policy (extending over the ten-year period of greatest need for educational and support expenses) in the name of the children, give them ownership in the policy, and make successive annual gifts to the children to cover the amount of premium payments.
  Or she could purchase an additional ordinary life insurance policy and assign it to an irrevocable trust outside the estate, making annual gifts of premium payments to the trust to benefit the children upon her death.
- She could make annual tax free gifts to her two children of art works for five years, amounting to $100,000, which would remove this amount from the value of her taxable estate and would thus provide assets which the children could liquidate from time to time for emergency use.
- She could make charitable bequests in her will of 80 paintings (appraised at 50 percent of the sales price of $3,500 each), deducting $140,000 from her taxable estate.

After removing $290,000 as suggested above from her gross estate, she would have a federal tax on the $260,000 remainder of about $11,000. Quite a difference between this and the $100,000 tax bill before adopting estate planning strategies! The liquidity of IBM stock would be sufficient to pay estate expenses and taxes; the children would have immediate access to life insurance proceeds (outside the estate) adequate for support and educational needs.

Thus a properly tailored plan could provide maximum security for both Aida and her children with minimum shrinkage of assets.

ESTATE PLANNING GOALS

There is more to planning an estate than merely writing a will. Your primary goal should be to facilitate maximum enjoyment and use of property during lifetime; your secondary goal should be to provide for the smooth transfer of the estate at death according to your wishes and with the least diminution in value and burden to beneficiaries. Tax considerations are of major concern to the planning of an estate, but they are not the only considerations. There are others involving personal needs and human relations which are paramount.

Much depends on when you begin to plan the estate and on individual personal and family needs. A photographer just ten years out of school with a wife and two small children will have different objectives than will the single mature artist whose studio houses more than a thousand works of art and whose painting sales bring income of over ten thousand dollars for a single canvas.

Goals are determined by analyzing your own special situation. Ask yourself these questions:

- What will happen in case of serious illness or incapacity? Or premature death?
- What if your spouse dies first? Or if both you and your spouse are killed simultaneously in an accident?
- Who will take care of the children? Are there funds for their support? Education?
- Should assets go directly to the children? Or to a trustee for their benefit?
- Is there a change in marital status in the offing? Is your spouse likely to remarry? To have another family?
- Is your spouse competent to manage the inherited assets and likely to pass them on to your children? What if the surviving spouse remarries and chooses to pass the assets to another family instead?
- Does your spouse have separate property which when your inheritance is added will cause unnecessarily high taxes and shrinkage in the second estate? Will the surviving spouse

receive more income than necessary for a lifetime? Will the excess be taxed again in the second estate?

- Is the core collection of art of sufficient value and interest to warrant establishing a foundation or trust to preserve and place the art in appropriate institutions?
- Will your beneficiaries maintain and preserve the art works in accordance with your wishes? Will they maintain the integrity of the art works, preserve the physical condition, exercise care in offering the art for sale or placing it in museums to protect the historical value of the body of work?
- Should the core collection of your work be donated to a museum? Now? Or on death?
- Should gifts be made now to family members, friends, or museums?
- Have circumstances changed since you drafted your will or created a trust? Should changes be made?
- How will the assets be valued and distributed at death?
- How will the estate pay taxes and estate costs without an unfavorable forced sale of works of art?
- Who will be executor of your estate?

ESTATE PLANNING ADVISORS

If you were selecting a doctor, you would seek a specialist who has experience with your particular ailment. You should seek estate planning advisors with the same care, inquiring as to their professional expertise, sensitivity, and knowledge of your special problems.

An attorney is essential to many aspects of handling estate matters. Only an attorney familiar with estate planning should draft a will or a trust or advise on writing certain contracts. He should be selected with the same care exercised in choosing an executor of your estate. A certified public accountant should be brought in to prepare financial statements and income tax returns, and to assist with accounting matters. An appraiser may be needed to value assets. And a life insurance underwriter will be needed to advise on and arrange for purchase of a policy suited to your needs. The optimum result will be obtained if these efforts are coordinated; the attorney is in the best position to undertake responsibility for the overall estate plan and to call in the other advisors as you direct him.

ESTATE PLANNING STRATEGY

Thomas Hart Benton at the age of 80 pondered the problem of estate taxes on the large number of his unsold works for which no buyers had been found.

> ... It actually has become so bad that I seem to penalize my heirs by painting a picture....The Feds have got it now so that just by comparing me with market values they make me a multimillionaire on paper and I have got to pay taxes for which I have no money ... the best solution would be to destroy all unsold works before I die....

Of course there are other ways of creating a zero estate for tax purposes without destroying your legacy. Such a drastic step should not be a necessary part of an estate plan.

Should you have an absolute aversion to estate and gift taxes, there are ways to achieve a zero-base estate for tax purposes. If your taxable estate is valued at less than the Exemption Equivalent, there is no estate tax to pay because the unified credit exempts entirely this base amount from tax. Also, if married, you may pass unlimited amounts to your surviving spouse tax free by using the marital deduction.

One way to escape tax altogether on estates over the exemptions is to bequeath the remainder to a qualified charitable institution. This may or may not be the happiest solution for your heirs.

Estate planning strategy should be tailored to your personal lifetime goals and particular testamentary wishes. At first glance it may appear ironic that one's goal in life may be to labor hard in order to build an estate of growing value so as to provide security for dependents, but to best accommodate testamentary wishes it may be wise to reduce the value of the taxable estate. The ideas are not at cross-purposes if proper estate planning concepts are applied.

The important planning concepts highlighted below are basic to estate planning and apply to any artist's estate regardless of size.

- Maintain an accurate *inventory* record of art works to assist in identifying, locating and valuing your assets. Include the cost of materials and fabrication with each item.
- Include in your inventory an estimated valuation which you deem to be reasonable for estate tax purposes.
- Consider structuring your artistic activities to qualify as a closely held business.

- Under many circumstances, avoid formation of *joint title* to property except for your marital residence and small joint bank accounts held for convenience. Consider severing existing joint titles and reforming ownership as tenants in common.
- Reduce art inventories by selling works and using the profits to fund the purchase of *life insurance* to provide liquidity for tax obligations and family needs in the post-death period.
- Avoid inclusion of life insurance proceeds in your estate by assigning all ownership rights in the policy to a beneficiary. It is better still if the beneficiary takes ownership in the policy in the first place.
- Fund life insurance premium payments made by the beneficiary with annual gifts, taking advantage of the *$10,000 annual exclusion*.
- Consider the "present value" of money and defer tax payments wherever possible.
- Reduce the size of the estate before death by annual tax-free gifts of up to $10,000 in art works to each family member and other beneficiaries, taking maximum advantage of the *$10,000 annual gift exclusion*.
- Take advantage of "gift-splitting" which allows a spouse to join in passing an additional $10,000 tax free each year to each donee.
- Take advantage of the *marital gift tax deductions*.
  But consider the impact of *marital gifts* on estate taxes and costs in the second estate when the surviving spouse dies. Avoid "overqualifying" the second estate.
- Take optimum advantage of the *marital estate tax deduction*. But avoid overloading the second estate.
- Consider the advisability of establishing a marital or special purpose *trust* to manage assets and distribute income to your beneficiaries. Consider tax advantages of a bypass trust, a generation-skipping trust.
- Choose beneficiaries carefully. Consider direct bequests to children above what your spouse will need or want. Consider appointment of a guardian for children who may be left without a parent.
- Reserve a selection of art works from each type and period of production, building an *historic collection* which will represent your life work. Hold this collection for appreciation,

selling from it, as necessary, for income, and exhibiting from it in selected museums and institutions.

- Consider the advantages of a charitable bequest of art works and make arrangements during lifetime for transfer at death of a part or all of the historic collection to a museum or charitable institution. A *charitable donation* of the historic collection excludes it from taxation in the estate, and assures its preservation.
- Do not overlook the advantages of medical insurance, social security, employee disability and retirement plans and death benefits, and the possibiltiy of setting up your own self-employed (Keogh or IRA) retirement plan.

THE FIRST STEP—AN INVENTORY OF ASSETS

Value the estate

It is understandably difficult to place a dollar sign on your work. It is, however, a practical necessity in dealing with potential estate assets. Until you have an accurate idea of the value of your estate, with awareness of what constitutes the estate, you cannot intelligently make plans for its disposition. Too often artists fail to project the potential value of art in the studio or storage place or fail to realize the appreciating value of forgotten or rejected or even unfinished works. In many notable case histories only a small part of an artist's inventory has been sold prior to death, followed by startling appreciation in value thereafter.

Maintain an accurate inventory and document file

By developing careful habits of clearly identifying, signing, and dating each work and by keeping an inventory with accurate descriptions as to size, media, date, exhibitions, insurance value, sales price, current location, awards and any facts relating to provenance, you can assist in reducing the administrative burden of handling the estate. Photographs of art works facilitate identification and are a valuable part of the inventory record.

All legal documents are of prime importance to settlement of the estate. These include income tax returns for at least the five preceding years, bank statements, records of bank deposits and safe deposit boxes, certificates of investments, stock and bond certificates, life insurance policies, birth certificates, marriage certificates, documents of title, deeds of trust, trust documents, mortgage and loan documents, business records and contracts (including sales contracts, dealer contracts, loan exhibition contracts), and current will.

Review assest for liquidity, change of title, or form of investment

Once the approximate present-day value of the entire estate is determined you should consider which items provide liquidity to meet cash requirements in case of emergency, disability, or estate obligations. Stocks, bonds, savings certificates, life insurance, and death benefits are ready sources of cash, but art objects are not readily saleable and produce no revenue until sold. Consider, as well, the form of title in which the asset is held to determine whether it can be assigned (a life insurance policy, an annuity), whether a joint tenancy (real estate) should be severed, whether certain assets should be sold and converted to cash or other form of investment.

JOINTLY OWNED PROPERTY

When Morris Louis died in the early 1960s, his wife claimed ownership as the surviving joint tenant of the 577 canvases mostly found rolled up in the basement of his Washington, D.C., house.

Few paintings had sold during Louis' lifetime. The artist relied almost entirely on his wife's income from teaching activities as a source for funds for materials and studio, and she therefore provided "consideration" sufficient to substantiate joint ownership with the artist in his works. By law joint tenancy assets pass directly to the survivor outside of probate or the laws of intestacy but are subject to taxation.

Consideration test

It may surprise you to learn that jointly owned property is included entirely in the taxable estate of the first tenant to die unless the survivor can show individual contribution to its cost from separate funds. Failure to provide evidence to the Internal Revenue Service of the survivor's contribution may cause the entire value to be included in the decedent's estate.

However, this does not apply in the case of joint tenancy (by the entirety) between husband and wife. One half of the value of jointly held property is taxable in the estate of the first spouse to die and the value of the property held at the surviving spouse's death will be includible in his or her estate.

Advantages and disadvantages

The creation of a joint tenancy limits the donor's ability to transfer the property and requires the consent of the co-tenant to sever title in order to sell it, to make a gift to a third party or trust, or to pass it to another heir. It can be conveniently used in small estates to assure continuity in ownership of a family residence, a family car, and similar property, and has the advantages of avoiding probate and the accompanying costs. Thought should be given, however, to other forms of title for assets in larger estates.

Tenants in common

The treatment of joint property does not apply to an interest in property held as tenants in common in which each holds an undivided interest and can freely sever his identifiable share and transfer it to a third party or to heirs. An interest in a tenancy in common is included in the estate of the deceased only up to the value of his declared share. This permits a wife to will her share as a tenant in common to a child upon death and allows the surviving husband to retain his share as before.

Life insurance

You may be shocked to learn that if you purchase an ordinary or term life insurance policy on your life and if the policy permits you to change beneficiaries or to borrow money on the cash value of the policy, or if it is payable to your executor or estate, the entire proceeds of the insurance will be included in your taxable estate at death. Also includible in your estate is any policy owned by another which is required to be paid to your estate or to the executor or designated to be used for payment of your estate taxes. A life insurance policy in which the decedent holds any "incidents of ownership" is taxable in his estate. "Incidents of ownership" refers to the holder's right to affect or enjoy any economic benefits of the policy, for example the power to alter beneficiaries, to revoke assignment or transfer of title of the policy, or to borrow money on the policy.

Ownership in an existing policy can be assigned and given to a spouse or other beneficiary and thus remove from your estate the appreciation in value over the cash value at the time of the assignment. Like any other gift, the assignment of a life insurance policy is taxable on the value at the date of gift, approximately the cash value at that time. To determine if your existing policy is assignable it is necessary to read the fine print: to succeed in removing it from your taxable estate it is necessary to transfer all "incidents of ownership."

An insurance policy can be given to a lifetime trust which is funded with the proceeds upon your death, with benefits flowing according to your instructions to a surviving spouse or children or other beneficiaries. Many banks or trust institutions will act as trustee for such a trust, holding the life insurance policy for a nominal fee until your death, receiving annual gifts from you to cover the cost of premiums and using the $10,000 annual exclusion.

If a new policy is being purchased, consider the advisability of having someone other than yourself as the owner, for example your spouse, who can be a beneficiary, or you can designate the children as beneficiaries.

VALUATION

Your art works are your life if you are a serious artist. And when you die, they may be the main part of your estate. The problem of how to value works of art has plagued artists, dealers, appraisers, insurance agents, lawyers, judges, and tax collectors for years. Each may claim a different value, depending on the special purpose of the valuation.

The lawyer for an artist's estate may claim in the estate tax return a low value; the IRS may claim a high value; and the Tax Court judge may decide upon a value in between. One appraisal may be high for purposes of a charitable contribution and deductibility of taxes, while the IRS may challenge that amount and insist on a lower figure.

The living artist can deduct only the cost of materials when giving a work of his own creation to a tax-deductible institution, but once he dies the value of his art is placed at fair market value on the date of death or six months thereafter. Fair market value is defined by estate tax regulations as "the price at which the property would change hands between a willing buyer and a willing seller, neither being under any compulsion to buy or sell and both having reasonable knowledge of relevant facts."

The deductibility of selling costs, including dealer's commissions of 25 to 50 percent, transportation, insurance, and other charges, is permitted "if the sale is in order to pay the decedent's debts, expenses of administration, or taxes, to preserve the estate, or to effect distribution."

Internal Revenue Service regulations require that an appraisal of an expert or experts, under oath, of works of art with a value of over $3,000 shall be filed with the estate tax return. This must be accompanied by an affidavit of the executor as to the completeness of the list of property and as to the disinterested character and the qualifications of the appraiser(s). The expert must be qualified to appraise the particular type of art object; the IRS is free to challenge the qualifications and to employ its own appraiser. To assist in this difficult area the Internal Revenue Service has an Art Advisory Panel of 18 members, which includes representatives of museums, universities and dealers, who meet three times annually to review and evaluate appraisals.

The estate executor bears the burden of supporting the estate's valuation; he may be assisted by records of valuation kept by the artist prior to death. In fact the Internal Revenue Service in some instances will accept the artist's own evaluations. By distinguishing between "finished" and "unfinished" works an artist can shed light on the value of his art.

Determination of fair market value encompasses many factors: recent comparable sales; the costs of selling; costs of preparation for exhibition; framing; shipping and transportation; dealer commissions or fees; the cost of replacement; terms of the sale; the time and place of sale, and any unusual circumstances which affect price. Sudden increase or decrease in value requires justification.

Selection of an appropriate appraiser is crucial to an acceptable appraisal. The appraisal of an expert whose reputation is recognized as trustworthy and who is established as a specialist in the particular field will be given more weight by the IRS than the appraisal of one who is less well known. It is important to inform the expert that the appraisal is for submission to the IRS for estate tax purposes (or for a gift or charitable contribution). And it is equally important that the chosen appraiser not be in a position to reap personal gain from his own appraisals.

While the IRS may claim the full and highest market value, the David Smith case provides striking proof that it can be successfully argued that if an estate was forced to sell valuable art works in bulk in order to pay estate taxes and related costs, the market value would be reduced considerably.

Sculptor David Smith sold fewer than 80 pieces of sculpture during his lifetime, and at his death in 1965 the main body of work which comprised his estate consisted of 425 pieces of welded sculpture. The executors computed a value of $714,000 for the art and paid taxes totalling $244,495. In 1969, one week before the three-year statute of limitations would have precluded any further claims by the IRS, the IRS revalued the estate at $5,256,918 and claimed additional taxes of $2,444,629. The executors challenged the claim, and in its decision the United States Tax Court conceded that the impact of simultaneous offering for sale of a large number of such art works would reduce significantly the return on the hypothetical retail value. In addition the court considered the fact that Smith's stature had not been fully recognized before his death, that the bulk of Smith's work was located inaccessibly at his studio at Bolton Landing, New York, and that the size of the sculptures (many over ten feet in height) was a factor influencing marketability and value.

As finally determined by the Tax Court, the Smith estate was valued at $2,700,000, which equaled an amount midway between the executors' and the IRS evaluations of the sculptures and was based on the estimated amount which could be obtained in a bulk sale. Additional deductions were allowed for (a) costs incident to the sale of those sculptures required to be sold in order to pay the decedent's debts, (b) taxes, (c) administrative expenses, and (d) expenses necessary to preserve the estate and to effect distribution of the estate, which constituted most of the expenses. Deductions were not allowed for selling costs attributed to sales not considered necessary to pay the foregoing debts, taxes or expenses.

As finally assessed, the estate had to pay only an additional $69,944,* resulting in a total estate tax of $314,439 rather than the $2,689,124 sought by the IRS.**

---

*Tax rates determined by Internal Revenue code then existent.

**Furthermore, the increased fair market valuation at date of death to $2,700,000 raised the basis of computation of estate income taxes from post-death sales of sculptures, entitling the estate to an income tax refund of approximately $400,000 with a net gain, resulting from the Tax court suit, of about $330,000 for the heirs. The executor's original evaluation of approximately 3,000 Smith drawings and paintings at $15 each was left standing.

The court in the David Smith case did not establish specific criteria that would apply to every artist's estate, but wisely chose an ad hoc approach which permits the flexibility necessary to a fair decision in the unique circumstances of each artist's estate.

THE $10,000 ANNUAL GIFT TAX EXCLUSION

Now we look more closely at one of the most effective and important estate planning tools, the $10,000 annual gift exclusion. You are permitted to give to any number of donees up to $10,000 in value each year exempt from gift tax and free from the requirement to file a gift tax return. This tax-free gift may be in a variety of forms including cash, a work of art, forgiveness of a debt, or even payment of someone else's tax obligation. It can be made to a spouse, a child, or any other party.

By making regular annual gifts to family members a donor can pass a significant portion of a modest estate. For example, a gift of $10,000 each year to each of two children for ten years permits a tax-free transfer of $200,000.

If you have a spouse, this benefit is doubled if he, or she, joins in gift-splitting. An additional $10,000 can be passed to each donee annually, or $400,000 altogether could be passed tax free over ten years. Additional gifts to grandchildren, other family members or friends can increase the tax saving.

The major limitation on the $10,000 exclusion is that it must not be the gift of a future interest, an interest whose possession or enjoyment begins at a future date.

If the gift exceeds $10,000 in value, a gift tax return must be filed and gift tax paid effective on the donor's date of death on the amount in excess of the unified credit.

LIFETIME GIFTS

Aside from the personal satisfactions of gift giving, there are important estate planning aspects involved in making lifetime gifts. Appreciation in value is passed on to the donee, a gift of income producing property passes income from a high-bracket donor to a low-bracket donee with tax savings, the taxable estate is reduced, and the unified credit of, for example, $62,800 in 1982, postpones or negates actual payment of gift taxes on amounts up to $225,000.

The gift carries with it the donor's basis or actual cost. The artist's basis in works of his own creation is limited to the cost of materials, exclusive of his own labor. In the hands of the artist, his work is "inventory" and subject to ordinary income tax on any profits from sale. When an artist gives a work of his own creation to a charity he can deduct only his low cost basis; when he gives his art to another, the recipient assumes the same low basis and is subject to ordinary income tax when it is sold.

Contrast this with the collector who purchases an art work, whose basis is the purchase price (his cost), and who holds a capital asset taxable at the lower capital rate and deductible at the full fair market value if given to a charity.

A startling change in basis occurs when an art work is inherited from the artist-creator. All assets in the estate, including art works, receive a stepped-up basis equal to the fair market value at the date of death and take on the character of a capital asset.

Clearly the recipient of art from the creator fares better when he goes to sell an inherited work than when he sells a lifetime gift. But the estate must bear the burden of appreciation and tax. Especially for smaller estates there are decided advantages to holding art assets until death and passing to the heirs the full benefit of the stepped-up basis. There may be additional advantages in retaining the art as part of the core collection for testamentary bequest to a charitable institution.

The decision in each case involves weighing and balancing goals and advantages. Consider whether you need to pass the benefit of appreciation on to dependents during your lifetime or whether they will benefit most from a bequest which carries the stepped-up basis.

There are important ways to make lifetime gifts without unfavorable tax consequences. Take advantage of the $10,000 annual gift tax exclusion to make annual gifts to each beneficiary without tax or the requirement to file a gift tax return. Married couples may protect from tax $20,000 in annual gifts to each donee by gift splitting.

Remember that taxable gifts above the annual gift tax exclusions will be added back into the total estate when estate taxes are computed. It behooves you to keep accurate records and evidence of all gifts to avoid later disputes with the IRS.

Charitable gifts

It should be ascertained whether the charity is qualified and whether it is a public or private charity, or a private operating or distributing foundation.

Depending on the type of charity there are percentage limitations based on the adjusted gross income. Gifts unrelated to the charitable purpose of the institution receive a reduced deduction; only one-half of the appreciation above the cost basis is deductible if it is a capital asset.

Charitable deductions against income tax can be taken only in the year in which the gift property is actually transferred to the institution or the artist relinquishes control. Should you wish to have the best of both worlds you might consider lending art works to a chosen museum during your life on an indefinite loan basis. By including in your will a testamentary bequest of the art to the museum, you insure that your estate will receive full benefit of a charitable deduction of the fair market value at the time of death.

MARITAL DEDUCTION

Effective beginning 1982 the existing limits on the marital deduction are removed for both gift and estate tax purposes. Gifts and bequests between spouses are therefore no longer subject to any gift or estate taxation.

TRUSTS

Everyone knows that "you can't take it with you!" but you *can* make arrangements that put a string around your worldly assets and control their distribution for as long as the lifetime of the living beneficiary plus 21 years. You can set up a trust to accomplish your special purpose, whether it is to manage assets for minor children or an improvident wife or to sprinkle income to low-bracket taxpayers and realize income tax savings or to bypass estate taxes on the death of the first beneficiary.

The trust vehicle is a simple arrangement whereby one person (or trustee) holds title to assets for the benefit of another. Trusts can be created which accomplish the dual purposes of providing professional administration of financial assets or property and permitting maximum savings of income and estate taxes and probate costs.

A living (intervivos) trust is one which comes into existence during the lifetime of its creator. It can be changed during lifetime (revocable) or it can be permanently established once and for all (irrevocable). While a revocable trust escapes probate and accompanying costs, and may provide income tax savings only if you have no right to control or receive income or benefits from the trust, your gross estate will include the entire revocable trust assets for estate tax purposes. The second estate of the life beneficiary, however, escapes estate taxes on the trust. The reason is that the revocable trust becomes irrevocable upon your death.

An irrevocable trust which comes into existence during your lifetime and in which assets are placed completely beyond your control, will not be included in your gross estate. While gift tax may be assessed on assets given at the time of creation of the trust, both probate costs and estate taxes will be avoided. There is, however, genuine reluctance to part with assets so completely during lifetime.

Careful consideration should be given to assure the validity of the trust under your state law. Otherwise the trust may fail and those assets which are in the estate may be distributed by an executor according to the will, or by the laws of intestacy. Only an attorney skilled in drafting trust documents should be entrusted with this task.

There are numerous types of trusts to accomplish a myriad of purposes. The types most commonly used for estate planning purposes can only be highlighted here:

- The *marital trust* receives the marital deduction share of the estate, provides professional financial management of assets, and gives the surviving spouse income benefits wihtout losing control of the assets. It should consist of non-terminable income-producing assets which will be largely consumed during the spouse's life. It receives the advantage of the estate tax marital deduction but is fully taxable upon the death of the surviving spouse.

- The *bypass trust* may be established for the balance or share of the decedent's estate. Though taxable at your death, it escapes tax on the death of the surviving spouse and is a tax-saving device for protecting and passing appreciating assets to the next beneficiary.

- The *pour-over trust* may receive assets such as death benefits and life insurance proceeds which come from sources outside the estate. The validity of the trust depends on state law; complications may be avoided if the trust is in existence prior to ratification of the will and the trust document is properly incorporated by reference in the will.

- A *short-term or Clifford trust* may provide income tax savings by placing income producing assets in the hands of a trustee to pass income on to lower-bracket beneficiaries. At the end of the term the assets revert to the grantor. Because of the reversion the entire trust is includible in the grantor's estate.

- The *generation-skipping trust* may be used to pass assets from a grandparent through a child and on to a grandchild without incurring tax when the child dies, on the first $250,000. Above this amount a generation-skipping tax is applied, roughly equivalent to the estate tax. The $250,000 exclusion from tax in the second estate is available for each child of a grandparent, and could be used to pass $1 million free of tax through four children to unlimited numbers of grandchildren.
- A *trust for minors* may be desirable where there is no surviving parent who can competently manage assets for the minor's support and education or where it is desired to achieve income tax and estate tax savings on the surviving spouse's death by sprinkling income and by passing assets directly to children.

A trust is not for everyone. Unless there are income-producing assets of at least $200,000, many trust institutions and banks are reluctant to act as trustee. Trust management fees can consume as much as 4 percent of the annual income. Institutional management is traditionally conservative in placing investments and usually prefers low-yielding securities and certificates to more glamorous and higher income investments.

Trustees should be sensitive to your personal wishes, to the trust purposes, and to the needs of the beneficiaries. Choose a trustee as carefully as you choose your executor. In some cases it may be the same individual.

BEQUESTS TO CHARITABLE INSTITUTIONS

Prior to his death Mark Rothko engaged in estate planning. The results filled the press and art journals and dragged on for three years after his death and through seven court cases. There are lessons to be learned in studying what Rothko intended for his estate and what went wrong with the plan which he apparently approved before his death. Rothko sought to reduce estate taxes by willing almost his entire estate, valued at $43 million, to a charitable organization.

The Mark Rothko Foundation was established as a charitable organization under New York law with the purpose of giving financial assistance to mature artists. In his will Rothko bequeathed $250,000 and the family residence and its contents to his wife and the entire residue of the estate to the Mark Rothko Foundation. No provision was included for his two children if his wife survived him. Rothko's widow died only six months after his death, and his two children contested the will. Under New York law a disposition to a charitable organization is valid only up to one-half of the estate if challenged by a spouse or a child with a claim to the estate. The challenge was upheld by the courts and the children were awarded their share of the estate. The legal conflict encompassed other main issues, most notably the conflict of interest of some fiduciaries. The manner in which the Rothko will and estate were handled has resulted in criminal judgments and sizable fines of $9,252,000 against the offending parties.

The effort of Rothko to pass art works or the proceeds thereof to a charity was clear, and accomplished tax savings to the extent that the charitable contribution was acceptable after close scrutiny by the Internal Revenue Service and the courts. Rothko's problem was that he chose individuals as executors, dealers, and trustees who had serious conflicts of interest and who violated their fiduciary duty and the ethical standards of their position for personal gain.

Charitable contributions have long been recognized as an estate planning device for the rich, but there may be considerable advantages for the not-so-rich in donating property to a tax-exempt institution. For the artist, charitable testamentary bequests in his will are fundamental to estate planning. Aside from the marital deduction, which is available only to married persons, and the use of trusts, which must be funded with a certain amount of liquid or income-producing assets, no other concept provides such substantial impact on minimizing estate taxes. Charitable bequests reduce the taxable estate and at the same time provide assurance to the artist of maintenance and preservation of a selection of his work.

The artist is advised to select the charity with care. There should be prior consultation with an appropriate staff member in advance of drafting the will to determine whether the bequest will be accepted and whether conditions or restrictions concerning exhibition, labeling, loan or deacquisitioning may be stipulated. A separate agreement with the institution should provide the necessary assurances. Alternate charitable donees should be specified in the event circumstances change and the chosen charity is unable to receive the bequest.

Consideration might be given to donation to a non-profit corporation or foundation set up for your special purposes. Your lawyer and accountant can advise you as to whether the value and nature of your assets justifies creation of a new foundation and whether it can be structured to qualify as a charitable institution under existing laws.

DRAFTING THE WILL

Having completed an inventory and tentative valuation of assets, having decided on beneficiaries and executor(s), having reviewed joint property and life insurance, having considered setting up a trust or charitable foundation, and having negotiated with a charitable institution to receive charitable bequests upon death, you are now ready to draft or redraft your will.

Should you die without a valid will the state steps in to distribute your estate, most likely in a way you had not intended. Each state law governing intestacy is different, but in general the surviving spouse will receive up to one-half the estate with the remainder distributed to all surviving children. If there is no spouse your surviving children will be the heirs, and if there are none, then it passes to their lineal descendents or to next of kin. A spouse, including an estranged one, has inheritance rights and, if dissatisfied with a will, may step in to claim a statutory marital share (or dower or courtesy rights) to one-third or one-half the estate, depending on state law. Children born out of wedlock may, in some states, be ineligible for any share.

No matter how small the estate, it is preferable to direct the disposition of your assets by will. The proper drafting of a will requires expert advice of an attorney because there are important inclusions or omissions which can affect such things as the flow of income to the family members immediately after death and before settlement of the estate, the appointment of a guardian for minor children, the disposition of personal property, the division of assets among survivors, and designation of the executor, as well as other provisions which may result in unnecessary burdens or expenses to the estate.

Prior to passage of the Economic Recovery Tax Act of 1981 the law permitted a gift tax marital deduction for the first $100,000 of gifts to a spouse and for 50 percent of gifts to a spouse in excess of $200,000. An estate tax marital deduction was allowed for transfer to a surviving spouse up to the greater of $250,000 or one-half the adjusted gross estate. Transfers of terminable interests generally did not qualify for the gift or estate tax marital deduction.

The newly enacted law removed the quantitative limits on both the gift and estate tax marital deductions and provides that certain terminable interests also qualify for those deductions.

Therefore, if you have a will that provides your spouse with an amount equal to the maximum marital deduction it should be reviewed immediately to determine whether the entire estate is intended to pass to the spouse.

This chapter is not the appropriate vehicle for a detailed discussion of will drafting. There are, however, several points to be considered by the artist beyond the rules generally applicable to will drafting:

- Unless there are special reasons for making a bequest of a specific item in the estate, one particular work of art for example, it is preferable to give your trusted executor discretion to make an equitable division of such items among clearly identified beneficiaries. If a specific bequest of an art work is indicated and it has been sold or destroyed prior to death, the gift will fail unless an available alternative is specified in the will.
- It is advisable to consult the charitable organization in advance to be certain of their willingness and ability to accept a bequest. Alternate beneficiaries should be named in the event an individual may predecease or an organization may no longer exist.
- You could direct the executor to reserve major art works for specific museums or charitable donations, or such decisions could be left to the discretion of the executor.
- Include provision for administrative expenses in connection with maintenance, storage, shipping, and insurance of art works in the hands of the estate. The residuary estate will be charged with these costs unless you direct that recipients deduct the costs from their inheritance.
- In certain cases, the will should provide that administrative costs of handling and disposing of art works for which the estate is charged shall be deducted from the gross estate before computation of tax.

- Provision should be included in the will to authorize the executor to sell works of art as needed for payment of tax obligations, administrative costs, legal fees, and family expenses, and to allow deduction from the gross estate of the costs of selling art works, including fees and sales commissions.
- Include a clause in the will which specifies disposition of copyrights to all bequests of art works or other copyrightable assets. Copyrights extend 50 years beyond the creator's death and are transferred separately from the art object itself. If no provision is included in the will for transfer of a copyright, it will pass to the residuary estate.
- In instructions to the executor, clearly specify that directions as to disposition of the estate not be changed or may be changed only after consultation with a panel of experts.

COPYRIGHTS AND THE WILL

Pictorial, graphic, and sculptural works are eligible for copyright protection from the moment of creation under the Copyright Revision Act of 1976. The duration of a copyright is for the life of the creator plus 50 years. Beginning in 1978 there is a distinction between ownership of the material object (a work of art) which is copyrightable and ownership of the copyright itself or of one of the exclusive rights under copyright: the right to reproduce, the right to prepare derivative works, the right to distribute copies, or the right to exhibit publicly. Sale of an art work does not include the sale or transfer of the copyright or exclusive rights. Only by written agreement or a transfer in writing can the copyright or an exclusive right be transferred.

A will may provide for a bequest of a specific painting to a named beneficiary, but if nothing more is said, the copyright will be retained by the estate and passes to the residue of the estate. It is therefore important to include in the will specific provision for transfer of copyrights to the beneficiaries of your choice or a direction that the copyrights shall pass along with the works of art.

It is equally important not to overlook the question of transfer of copyrights when making lifetime gifts of art works. While the gift may be completed by merely handing it over, the copyright is still yours and will remain in your estate unless it is transferred in writing.

Copyrights are not treated as capital assets and are taxed as ordinary income assets.

DEALER CONTRACT

Franz Kline provided in his will a bequest to his friend Charles Egan of two paintings to be selected by the beneficiary "prior to the disposition of my works by my executrix." After Kline's death it was discovered that the two paintings selected by the beneficiary had been sold, one to the Art Institute of Chicago, the other to the dealer himself, Sidney Janis. The court found that neither sale had been finally consummated prior to Kline's death and that the dealer, whose consignment contract had terminated, no longer had authority to sell the paintings. The beneficiary was given the paintings according to the wishes of Kline.

Unless the dealer's contract specifically extends a dealer's "agency" status beyond the lifetime of an artist (as in the case of the David Smith estate), the dealer's contract terminates immediately on the date of death of either party. The dealer cannot negotiate sales or continue to represent the artist's estate without specific authorization in writing, either by the original contract or by subsequent agreement with the executor.

A provision in the dealer's contract which may greatly facilitate estate matters and the need for immediate liquidity would be agreement by the dealer to advance an amount of cash to the estate while continuing to hold certain art works for sale. Where the artist has a long-standing dealer relationship and profitable sales record, it may be possible to conclude a buy-out agreement in case of death. In exchange for a favorable bulk price as specified by the artist the dealer would agree to purchase within a limited period of time a certain number of works consigned to the gallery. The cash received by the estate would be available for administrative costs, taxes, and immediate family needs. This has the advantage of liquidation of a part of the estate without necessarily forcing public sale of art works under unfavorable conditions, and also establishes the value for those pieces sold.

The dealer may be advised to purchase life insurance on the artist payable to him, in order to provide liquidity for purchase of a specified number of art works on death. As in the case of buy-sell agreements in the corporate world, a dealer buy-out could be funded by a life insurance policy on the artist's life, owned and paid for by the dealer himself. This could be a term policy, renewable and maintained as long as the artist and dealer continue their relationship. The policy should be structured so that it is not taxable in the artist's estate at death.

PAYMENT OF TAX

If the gross estate does not exceed the applicable exemption (including taxable lifetime gifts), there is no requirement to file an estate tax return. Unless an extension is granted the estate tax return and the total tax are due and payable nine months after death. An interest charge at the current rate announced by the IRS is due on any amount overdue, and if there is not reasonable cause for delay, a further penalty may be charged. The executor may request an extension for filing on or before the due date. The extension for filing is limited to six months, and obtaining an extension for filing does not operate to extend the time for payment of the tax.

However, an extension to pay the tax may be granted if the assets are part of a "closely held business" of which the artist was a sole proprietor and which constitutes at least 35 percent of his adjusted gross estate. In such cases the executor may elect to pay estate taxes in not more than 14 years with 4 percent interest due annually on the unpaid balance.

It would be helpful if the artist added a little window dressing to show evidence of business formalities. Such things as printed stationery, business cards, and use of a business name on the annual income tax forms are useful bits of evidence of business activity. If the artist sold some art works directly from the studio or put a sign on the door, the executor may be able to show that it was a proprietorship or a business entitled to tax deferment privileges. Proof of an effort to sell his works assists in establishing a profit motive and provides justification for deduction of art-related expenses from annual income tax, fortifying a claim that it is a "business." A record should be kept of selling efforts, participation in competitions and juried shows, and awards or prizes received.

Such an extension may be of great assistance for an estate consisting mainly of works of art and other non-liquid assets.

STRATEGY FOR THE ARTIST WITH A SMALL
ESTATE

Even the small estate can benefit from estate planning. An estate valued below the Exemption Equivalent has no tax problem because of the Unified Credit, nor does it require filing of an estate tax return. A marital estate using the marital deduction may pass free of tax. And lifetime marital gifts made to the surviving spouse can help to escape taxes.

In small net estates assets can safely be left in joint tenancy and passed outside of probate with savings of administrative expenses. And gifts or charitable donations provide estate tax saving. Ownership of life insurance that will tip the total above the magic tax-free amounts is better assigned to another. A marital gift or bequest, however, should not add unnecessarily to the surviving spouse's estate or pass more than can be consumed in a lifetime, because the marital deduction is not available to reduce taxes on the second estate. Above all, do not make a lifetime marital gift which is willed back to you unless it will pass free of estate tax. The better disposition of the gift is to the children.

Marital and by-pass trusts

Assets that qualify for the marital deduction may be passed outright to your spouse or placed in a marital trust or a trust which gives the spouse income for life and the right, without restriction, to designate by will the beneficiaries. These assets are not taxed in the first estate by virtue of the marital deduction, and should be assets which will be largely consumed during lifetime (if the trust permits lifetime invasion) because the remainder will be fully taxed upon the spouse's death.

The balance of the estate, above the marital deduction share, may be placed in a by-pass trust, giving the spouse income for life and the remainder to the children or other named beneficiaries at the spouse's death. By-pass trust assets will not be taxed in the spouse's estate because they are held in trust. In addition to saving taxes, the second estate will save probate and administrative costs.

These trusts are most effective for moderate or large estates, but can be employed in the small estate for special situations where the testator wants to provide management of the assets and assure that the corpus will be preserved and passed on to the children or specified beneficiaries. There are minor expenses in setting up a trust and annual management fees. It is generally uneconomic to establish a trust for assets under $200,000; the trust vehicle is best reserved for special situations where the tax savings appear worthwhile or where the beneficiary is a minor child or cannot be depended upon to manage the estate alone.

BENEFITS

The holder of minimal assets can gain future security by seeking outside employment which offers employment benefits such as group medical insurance, disability and retirement benefits, and qualified group life insurance. Inquire about the availability of these benefits before taking on an employment commitment. Qualification for social security benefits requires a number of years' employment and contributions in accordance with the requirements. Your local Social Security office will provide information explaining the qualifications and benefits, which may be the bedrock foundation of your old-age security or disability support.

Inflation and appreciation are increasing the value of your estate each year. At 10 percent inflation, a $200,000 estate will more than double in eight years and in 15 years it will be four times its original value! When your estate reaches the level above the Exemption Equivalent, it is time to employ the suggested estate planning strategies. This may be sooner than you think!

OVER A MILLION DOLLARS

You need not be endowed with Picasso's genius or prolific productivity to amass a multimillion dollar estate, but without benefit of deductions or estate planning your tax burden may be considerable. This realization should stir your creative instincts to contemplate significant charitable bequests and creative gifts which will make the estate costs more palatable.

Harry Callahan and Aaron Siskind, the photographers, have already completed arrangements for the donation of a collection of their negatives to the Center for Creative Photography, University of Arizona. The sculptor, Jacques Lipchitz, who lived in the United States since 1940 and died in Italy in 1973, directed in his will that 518 of his original terra cotta and plaster models be donated to a charitable foundation. His will provided that the plasters remain untouched and unreproduced, except for photographs. Although the value of these works has not been publicly revealed, this value, which is considerable, is removed from Lipchitz' taxable estate and the objects are preserved intact.

Ask your friends like Louise Nevelson and Georgia O'Keeffe what they have done, and begin a mini-plan of your own. More than ten years ago Robert Rauschenberg established a foundation called Change, Inc., with an illustrious Board of Directors involved in the arts. Change, Inc., assists professional artists in need of immediate small grants. Situations recognized by his Board as an emergency, such as fire, medical catastrophe and utility turn-offs, will result in financial assistance.

This is one of many possible creative estate planning ideas. Your own plan can benefit from your ingenuity, and both you and future generations will be enhanced.

Protecting

part two

6

Safeguarding the Uniqueness of Your Work: Copyright, Trade Secret, Patent and Trademark Law

by

Robert Wade and Richard L. Stroup

◆──◆──◆

ROBERT WADE has been the General Counsel for the National Endowment for the Arts since 1972. Previously, he served on the staff of the General Counsel to the Comptroller General of the United States. From 1966 to 1969 Mr. Wade was in private practice in Washington, D.C. He is also a photographer.

RICHARD L. STROUP is an associate with the firm of Finnegan, Henderson, Farabow, Garrett and Dunner in Washington, D.C., and frequently lectures to arts groups.

◆ ◆ ◆ ◆

The members of the art community are continuously creating literary, musical, choreographic, visual and audiovisual works in their respective fields. During this creative process, artists often develop new methods, materials, articles and information useful in their profession. As they market and sell their products and services, they may adopt and use certain logos and trademarks to identify their art and services and to distinguish them from the art and services of others. Each of an artist's creative developments and marketing efforts represents a substantial investment of creative energy, time and effort which deserves protection and compensation.

The copyright, trade secret, patent, and trademark laws provide artists with legal means of protection and compensation for their creations, developments, and trademarks. However, unless artists are aware of these protections and the manner of obtaining, keeping and using them, the law is of little relative value. It is, therefore, the purpose of this chapter to present a practical overview of the protection available through copyright, trade secret, patent and trademark law. The chapter will outline the application of these laws to artists and their works, the scope of protection available, the manner of securing the protection, and the use of the protective rights to compensate artists for their work and shield them from unfair practices.

COPYRIGHT

The copyright law often offers the easiest and least expensive way for an artist to protect his work. Copyright protection is available for a broad variety of artistic works, and there is no initial cost for receiving copyright protection. Under the new 1976 Copyright Act, which became effective on January 1, 1978, an artist receives a copyright at the moment an original copyrightable work is created in a fixed form. Thus, every working artist has, at least initially, some rights under the copyright law.

The apparent ease in obtaining copyright protection may be deceptive. An artist unaware of the existence and scope of available copyright protection will receive no benefit from the copyright law. It is important that an artist, or his representative, be aware of the availability of copyright protection and take the necessary steps to exercise these rights to ensure that they are not lost inadvertently.

Protections granted by copyright

The copyright law provides the copyright owner with a broad category of rights. Those rights are statutorily defined as the following exclusive rights:

(1) to reproduce the copyrighted work in copies or records or tapes;

(2) to prepare derivative works based upon the copyrighted work;

(3) to distribute copies or phonorecords of the copyrighted work to the public by sale or other transfer of ownership, or by rental, lease or lending;

(4) in the case of literary, musical, dramatic, and choreographic works, pantomimes, motion pictures and other audiovisual works, to perform the copyrighted work publicly; and

(5) in the case of literary, musical, dramatic, and choreographic works, pantomimes, and pictorial, graphic or sculptural works, including the individual images of a motion picture or other audiovisual work, to display the copyrighted work publicly.

The above rights significantly protect an artist and his artistic creations. Through copyright, a songwriter, poet or playright has the right to control, license or present (1) the reproduction of his work in books or magazines, (2) the preparation of adaptations of his work into other forms, (3) the distribution of the work, its reproductions and adaptations, (4) the performance of his work by others, and (5) the display of his work in public. Painters, sculptors, potters, printmakers and photographers have all of the exclusive rights, except the right to perform, since their creations are generally not capable of being performed.

The exclusivity of an author's rights has limits. A copyright only prohibits another from actually *copying* the identical or a substantially similar work. For example, if one artist in New York creates one painting and a second artist in Los Angeles, without seeing or being aware of the New York artist's work, creates an identical painting, the first has no rights against the second. Even if the second painter had access to the work of the first, there is infringement only if the second painting was copied and is "substantially similar" to the first. Finally, there is a certain amount of use, designated "fair use," which is permissible without the authorization of the artist. Examples of fair use might include copying a work for the purposes of criticism, comment, news reporting, teaching, scholarship, or research.

An artist's copyright in his work grants him numerous opportunities to obtain compensation for his creation. For example, a painter can receive royalties for the reproduction and sale of his work by a museum, as well as the reproduction of the work on post cards, greeting cards, and china. A sculptor of a work can license the reproduction and sale of scale models of his work and receive a commission on each sale. The potential is almost limitless. The owner of a copyright can keep all rights to himself, sell the entire copyright, or license only selected rights under special terms.

For work created after 1978, the 1976 Copyright Act affords the artist and his heirs the right to terminate transfers and licenses of copyright made by means other than by will. When this termination right is available, the artist can revoke the earlier transfer and has the option of keeping future rights for himself, renegotiating the terms of the transfer, or transferring the rights to other interested parties. This right is extremely beneficial to artists who originally received little if any compensation for the original transfer and who later became established and highly recognized. The termination may be effected at any time during a five-year period beginning at the end of 35 years from the date of execution of the grant; or, if the grant covers the right of publication of the work, the period begins at the end of 35 years from the date of publication of the work under the grant or at the end of 40 years from the date of execution of the grant, whichever term ends earlier. The termination is effected by serving an advance notice in writing, signed by the owners or their agents, upon the grantee or the grantee's successor in title.

Finally, the copyright grants a copyright owner a number of remedies which can be asserted against a person who without authorization copies a copyrighted work. The remedies available against an infringer include temporary or final injunctions against future infringement; impounding and destruction of all copies or phonorecords and of all plates, molds, masters, tapes, films, negatives and other articles by means of which such copies or records may be reproduced; and damages and profits. It is also possible to receive attorneys' fees.

Copyrightable works of art

A broad range of artistic works can be protected by copyright. Copyrightable works of authorship include the following broad statutory categories:

(1) literary works;
(2) musical works, including any accompanying works;
(3) dramatic works, including any accompanying music;
(4) pantomimes and choreographic works;
(5) pictorial, graphic and sculptural works;
(6) motion pictures and other audiovisual works; and
(7) sound recordings.

These broad categories apply to works of fine art, such as oil paintings and sculptures, and works of applied art, such as manufactured vases and greeting cards.

Copyright protection is available for the original works of artists who fix their works in any tangible medium of expression. Copyright can provide protection for artistic works expressed in or on physical articles such as books, periodicals, manuscripts, notes, cards, sketchbooks, records, films, tapes, magnetic disks, canvas, clay, paper, and almost all physical objects on which an artist's expression can be fixed. In addition, copyright law applies to both two-dimensional and three-dimensional works of fine, graphic, and applied art. For example, photographs, prints, paintings, drawings, photoengravings, etchings, lithographs, sculptures, art reproductions, maps, globes, charts, technical drawings, diagrams and models are all protectable by copyright. Similarly, motion pictures, musical scores and lyrics, pantomimes, and sound recordings are protectable.

An artist can protect his works of applied art through copyright. Copyright protection is available for artistic works included in or on utilitarian objects such as clocks, lamps, textiles, jewelry, china, dolls, jewelry boxes, candlesticks, chandeliers, and a host of other items. The design in a work of applied art, however, is protected by copyright only if the design incorporates a pictorial, graphic, or sculptural feature which can be identified separately from and is capable of existing independently of the utilitarian aspects of the article. Thus, a hand-painted design on a vase would be protectable, whereas a Bauhaus-inspired chair in which form and function are blended would not. If the pictorial, graphic or sculptural work contained in or on a useful article is copyrighted, the copyright will afford the copyright owner protection against unauthorized reproduction of his work in useful as well as non-useful articles.

Copyright protection is available not only for original works but also for compilations and derivative works which feature some degree of creativity and originality. A derivative work is a work based upon one or more pre-existing works and can be a translation, musical arrangement, dramatization, fictionalization, motion picture version, sound recording, art reproduction, abridgement, condensation, or any other adaptation or transformation of an earlier work. A compilation is a work formed by the collection and assembly of pre-existing materials or of data that are selected, coordinated, or arranged so that the whole constitutes an original work of authorship. In the field of art, a derivative work might be a reproduction of a work of art in the same or a different medium of expression. Works falling within the "reproduction" category would include lithographs, photo engravings, and copies of previously existing paintings, sculptures and similar works. An art book including illustrations of several art works is an example of a compilation.

While derivative works and compilations that contain some original work are copyrightable, the copyright protection for a derivative work or compilation of pre-existing material extends only to the material contributed by the author of the derivative work or compilation. The author does not receive any protection for the pre-existing material. Thus, the infamous bearded and mustachioed Mona Lisa ("L.H.O.O.Q.") by the artist Marcel Duchamp would have been copyrightable, but Duchamp would not have been able later to stop Salvador Dali from making his own copy of the original Mona Lisa painting. It should be noted that if the pre-existing work is protected by a valid copyright, the artist creating the derivative work or compilation should obtain permission to copy the pre-existing work. If the artist fails to secure the permission, he or she may infringe the copyright in the original work and may be sued.

In order for a work of art to receive protection under copyright law, it must contain some degree of creativity and originality and be fixed in a tangible medium of expression. Creativity refers to the nature of the work itself, while originality refers to the nature of the artist's contribution to the work. Fixture means that the art is fixed in a material object so that it can be perceived, reproduced, or communicated for a period of more than momentary duration.

The issue of creativity is highly subjective and the courts have traditionally been very hesitant to make such judgments. As a result, a work need only display a minimal amount of creative authorship to satisfy this requirement. Similarly, the requirement of originality (not to be confused with novelty) is easily satisfied if the work is original to the artist, i.e., it is not exactly copied from the work of another. Often, any distinguishable variation created by the artist in an otherwise unoriginal work of art will constitute sufficient originality to support a copyright. For example, the courts have found sufficient originality in reproductions of oil paintings on scarves, engravings made from original paintings of old masters, and an accurate reproduction of Rodin's "Hand of God" sculpture. The general rule of thumb for the artist is "when in doubt, copyright the work." Leave it to the copyright office (or perhaps eventually the courts) to make the rare decision to deny a copyright application on the ground that the work lacks creativity or originality.

Certain subject matter is not protectable under copyright. Copyright generally protects the author's particular expression, not his ideas embodied in the expression. The copyright statute specifically provides that copyright protection for an original work of authorship in no case extends to any idea, procedure, process, system, method of operation, concept, principle, or discovery, regardless of the form in which it is described, explained, illustrated or embodied in such work. Also, works that are not fixed in a tangible form of expression are not protectable. For example, an author cannot obtain a copyright for a choreographic work that has not been notated or recorded, or a speech or performance that has not been written or recorded. Titles, names, short phrases, and slogans; familiar symbols or designs; mere variations of typographic ornamentation, lettering or coloring; and mere listing of ingredients or contents are not protectable. Similarly, works consisting entirely of information that is common property and containing no original authorship are not protectable. For example, standard calendars, height and weight charts, tape measures, schedules of sporting events, and lists or tables taken from public documents or other common sources are not considered to be copyrightable.

While a copyright may be obtained for artistic designs used with objects of applied art, a copyright does not protect the mechanical or utilitarian aspects of the applied art. Therefore, a copyright for a design on a useful article, such as a plate, would provide its owner with the right to stop others from copying his design and placing the copied design on plates, canvas, or any other tangible item. The copyright would not, however, afford its owner any greater or lesser rights with respect to the making, distribution, or display of plates in general. Furthermore, a copyright does not include any right to prevent the making, distribution, or display of photographs used to advertise a useful article with a copyrighted design or to stop commentaries or news reports relating to the distribution or display of the article.

The works of art protected by copyright are usually not protected by the law of patents and trade secrets. In general, a copyright covers an artist's expression, while trade secret and patent law more closely protect information, processes, devices, materials, and applied inventive concepts. In certain instances, however, a person may be able to receive both a copyright and a design patent for a particular work of applied art. Thus, the design on a watch or a lamp base may be protectable under both a copyright and a design patent.

Ownership and transfer of copyrights

Copyright protection is easy to obtain and, if an artist properly protects his work, the protection lasts throughout an artist's life and beyond. As soon as an artist creates a copyrightable work in a tangible form of expression, he immediately receives copyrighted protection for that work. A work is created when it is first fixed in a copy in which the work can be read or visually perceived directly or with the aid of a machine or device. Whenever an artist fixes a copyrightable creation in a tangible form, the work is copyrighted. Thus, as soon as an artist commits to paper a book, play, poem, novel, lyric, or musical composition; or records or places a work on tape, record, film or video tape; or sketches, paints or sculpts a work of visual art, the work is copyrighted.

Who owns the copyright to a work of art? Generally, the artist, as creator of the copyrightable artwork, is the initial owner of the copyright in the work. When a work is prepared by two or more artists with the intention of merging their contribution into a single work, it is deemed a "joint work." The artists of a joint work are co-owners of the copyright in the work, and each has the independent right to authorize the use of the work. However, each co-owner must share the profits received from such use with the other(s).

When a work brings together several independent contributions into a collective whole (e.g., magazines, anthologies, etc.), it is deemed a "collective work" and may be copyrighted as a whole. The owner of the copyright in the collective work as a whole is not necessarily the owner of the copyright in each contribution. Under the new law, absent a written agreement to the contrary, the presumption is that the visual artist, whose work is reproduced in the collective work, retains the copyright. The publisher is only presumed to acquire the privilege of reproducing and distributing the contribution as part of that collective work.

An artist who creates a copyrighted work initially has rights in the material object itself and in the copyright for his work. These rights can be transferred together or separately. For example, the artist can sell the material article and keep the majority of the copyright rights to himself. On the other hand, he can transfer in writing all or some rights to the work.

Under the old copyright law, if a copyright owner unconditionally sold a painting or other work of art, the copyright privileges normally were transferred to the buyer. The law presumed that all rights were intended to be transferred in connection with the sale. Under the 1976 Act, that result is different. The transfer of ownership of any material object, including the copy or record in which the work is first fixed, does not of itself convey any rights to the copyrighted work embodied in the object. The purchaser or owner of a particular copy or record may lawfully sell or otherwise dispose of the work and display the copy publicly to viewers present at the place where the copy is located. Barring a written agreement, however, the copyright owner continues to have the other copyright rights, including the right to reproduce the work, to distribute the work, and to control the public display of additional material objects including the work. Unfortunately, the law does not give an artist the automatic right of access to his work, and without access the artist cannot really make reproductions and thereby exercise his right of reproduction. Therefore when an artist sells the only copy of a work, he should consider obtaining, by contract, the right to gain access to his work periodically to make reproductions.

There are some circumstances in which the creator is not the owner of the copyright. When a work is prepared by an employed artist who under the scope of his or her employment creates the work, the copyright belongs to the employer for whom the work was prepared. Thus, if an artist employed by an advertising agency creates a sketch for an advertisement, the copyright belongs to the agency. On the other hand, if the same artist at his home and on his own time creates a painting which is not made for his employer, the artist owns the copyright. In certain limited circumstances, works for commission may be owned by the person commissioning the work, not the artist. Under the 1976 Copyright Act, however, the artist will retain the copyright for a commissioned work unless the artist specifically transfers the copyright in a written instrument signed by both the author and the person commissioning the work.

The copyright rights in a work can be transferred, in whole or in part, by gift, sale, assignment, exclusive or non-exclusive license, or upon death, by will or intestacy. The majority of these transfers must be in writing, and all such transfers should preferably be placed in writing and then recorded in the records of the Copyright Office. Except for transfers by gift or will, an artist can and usually should receive compensation for these transfers.

Publication and its consequences

As long as the artist does not publish his work, it is protected under the federal copyright law and none of his exclusive rights will be lost. Once an artist does publish the work, however, he can lose some or all of his rights unless he places a copyright notice with the work. Thus, if an artist keeps his works to himself, he has little need to worry about formal requirements such as copyright notice or registration. Normally, however, an artist will desire to sell, distribute or reproduce his work in order to receive compensation for his artistic creation. The publication of a work is therefore a significant occurrence.

When is a work published? The word "publication" has a special meaning in the copyright law. Under the 1976 Copyright Act, publication is defined as follows:

> Publication is the distribution of copies or phonorecords of a work to the public by sale or other transfer of ownership, or by rental, lease or lending. The offering to distribute copies or phonorecords to a group of persons for purposes of further

distribution, public performance, or public display, constitutes publication. A public performance or display of a work does not of itself constitute publication.

Thus, the sale or distribution of copies of a book which includes an artist's story, poem, play, song, or script would constitute a publication. Similarly, the sale or distribution of records, cards, lamps, tapes, posters and other items containing a copyrighted work would constitute publication. The distribution of a few copies of an artist's work for review by others probably would not constitute a publication. Nonetheless, whenever an artist distributes copies of his work, it would be prudent for him to assume that publication occurs and therefore place a copyright notice on the work.

The definition of "publication" provided by the 1976 Copyright Act is significantly beneficial to artists, when compared to the old law. Before 1978, the single publication of a work without notice resulted in a complete loss in copyright. The law was strictly applied to the point that an artist by merely exhibiting his work without a copyright notice could and often did lose all of his copyright protection. Under the 1976 Act, the mere public display of work may not, in itself, constitute publication. Similarly, the public performance of a work is normally not a publication, regardless of how many people are exposed to the work. However, if the displayed copies or phonorecords are offered to a group of consumers, whole-salers, broadcasters, or motion picture theaters, for the purpose of further distribution, public performance, or public display of the work, the work is published.

The display or exhibition of a work for purposes of sale could be viewed as an "offering to distribute copies," and as such would constitute publication. Artists seeking to distribute works for public display run the risk of losing some or all of their rights by exhibiting the work without proper copyright notice. Prudence would seem to dictate that artists include a copyright notice on their works whenever exhibition is intended for purposes other than mere display. Therefore, a painting or photograph exhibited in a museum or gallery should include a copyright notice.

COPYRIGHT NOTICE, REGISTRATION, AND DURATION

Whenever a work protected under a copyright is published in the United States or elsewhere by the authority of the copyright owner, the notice of Copyright should be placed on all publicly distributed copies. The 1976 Copyright Act provides that the notice appearing on copies shall consist of the following three elements:

> (1) the symbol © (the letter C in a circle), or the word "Copyright," or the abbreviation "Copr."; and
>
> (2) the year of first publication of the work; in the case of compilations or derivative works incorporating previously published material, the year date of first publication of the compilation or derivative work is sufficient. The year date may be omitted where a pictorial, graphic, or sculptural work, with accompanying text material, if any, is reproduced in or on greeting cards, post cards, stationery, jewelry, dolls, toys, or any useful articles; and
>
> (3) the name of the owner of copyright in the work, or an abbreviation by which the name can be recognized, or a generally known alternative designation of the owner.

The law requires that the notice be affixed to copies in such a manner and location as to give reasonable notice of the claim of copyright.

The 1976 Copyright Act requires only that the copyright notice be positioned to give reasonable notice of the claim of copyright. If the notice is on the title or first page of a book, article, play, script, music sheet, or in a viewable portion of a work of visual art, the notice would be proper. For pictorial works, a notice may be placed on the face or margin of the work or on the reverse side of the work, as long as it may be seen upon examination. Placement of a notice on the reverse side of a painting would be permissible, as long as the notice is visible upon inspection. Arguably, the placement of a notice next to the work on display would be sufficient, but if an artist decides to follow such a procedure, he would have to make certain that the notice was always placed next to the work. For framed artwork, the placement of the notice on a frame permanently affixed to the work would seem to fulfill the notice requirement. However, if a frame is readily removable, a notice on the frame may not fulfill the requirement. For sculpture, the notice can and probably should be placed on the base or pedestal which is permanently affixed to the sculpture. In general, an artist should make a good-faith effort to place the appropriate notice on or with his work in a manner which reasonably notifies the public and does not unduly detract from the artist's creation.

The notice provisions of the 1976 Copyright Act permit the copyright owner to choose from a number of alternative notices. In general, the proper notice for copyrighted works (other than records or tapes) first published in 1981 would be this:

© Artist 1981.

Since many fine artists sign and date their works, the only additional action necessary to secure an artist's copyright is the inclusion of the symbol ©. The above notice is proper for use with all artistic works and also complies with the notice requirement for significant international protection. If an artist has a recognized abbreviation or other designation, he can substitute the abbreviation or designation for his name. The abbreviation or designation must, however, be recognized. Therefore, if there is any question concerning the degree of recognition, the copyright owner should use his name, not a designation.

For a few special categories, an artist does not have to include the year of publication in the notice. The copyright notice for designs and other copyrighted work placed on useful articles, such as post cards, lamps, and textiles, can be this:

© Artist.

That notice, however, will not meet the notice requirements for international copyright protection and, more importantly, will not meet U.S. requirements for most artistic works. Therefore, an artist should use this special notice only when he is sure that it is appropriate.

The omission of a copyright notice can ultimately lead to the complete loss of an artist's rights in his work. Under the previous copyright law, the failure to include a notice automatically placed the work in the public domain, and all copyright rights were lost. Under the new law, that result has been made less harsh. Omission of a copyright notice from publicly distributed copies does not invalidate the copyright if—

> (1) the notice has been omitted from no more than a relatively small number of copies or phonorecords distributed to the public; or
> (2) registration for the work has been made before or is made within five years after the publication without notice, and a reasonable effort is made to add notice to all copies or

phonorecords that are distributed to the public in the United States after the omission has been discovered; or

(3) the notice has been omitted in violation of an express requirement in writing that, as a condition of the copyright owner's authorization of the public distribution of copies or phonorecords, they bear the prescribed notice.

Thus, by taking reasonable efforts to correct an omission of a notice on a work, an artist can save most, if not all, of his copyright.

If a person innocently infringes the copyright in reliance upon an authorized copy or phonorecord from which the copyright notice has been omitted, he would incur no liability before receiving actual notice that the work was protected by copyright. However, the copyright owner would in the future probably be able to enforce his copyright against that person and others. In contrast, a prolonged failure to include copyright notice will place the work in the public domain and all copyright rights will be lost.

Within three months after the date of first publication of a work with a copyright notice, the owner of the copyright is obligated to deposit in the Library of Congress two complete copies of the best edition. Certain exemptions may be made by the Register of Copyrights, but at present an artist is generally obligated to deposit copies of his work in the Library of Congress. For a work of fine art like a single painting, photographs can be submitted. The Library of Congress can in its discretion levy a fine if a deposit is not made after a written demand from the Register of Copyrights.

Although registration in the Copyright Office is not required, registration does provide the author with some additional rights. The law provides for the registration of both unpublished and published works. In most circumstances, the most opportune time to file a registration is when the work is published. Registration establishes a public record of the copyright claim. Furthermore, a copyright owner cannot sue another for infringement until the owner either obtains a registration or applies for registration. In addition, if the registration is made within five years of the first publication date, registration will establish *prima facie* evidence of the validity of the copyright and the facts stated in the certificate. A registration also may entitle the copyright owner to an award of statutory damages and attorneys' fees. Without a registration, those remedies are not available. Finally, registration makes the recordation of assignments and other documents easier.

The registration of a copyright is a relatively simple process. Generally, the procedure consists of filling in a proper copyright form, including with the completed form one copy of an unpublished work or two copies of the best edition of the published work, and submitting the form and copies with a statutory filing fee of $10. The forms can be obtained free of charge from the United States Copyright Office. That office also has an excellent information office which will by telephone answer questions regarding copyright protection.

The requirements for the submission of copies vary, depending on the work. If multiple copies of the work, such as a book, are available, copies of the book should be submitted. In the case of many artworks, the Copyright Office often will accept visual substitutes to fulfill the copy requirement. For example, to register an oil painting, the artist could submit a photograph or 35mm transparency of the work, rather than the original. In similar circumstances, the submitted identifying material could include photographic prints, transparencies, photostats, drawings, or similar two-dimensional reproductions or renderings of a work, in a form visually perceivable without the aid of a machine or device. The copies should identify the actual size of the work and the position of the notice.

A copyright, whether registered or not, provides an artist with a significant term of protection. Ordinarily the term of a copyright is the author's life plus an additional 50 years after the author's death. In the case of a joint work prepared by two or more authors, the term lasts for 50 years after the last surviving author's death. The duration of the copyright for a work of unknown authorship or a work for hire normally will be 75 years from publication or 100 years from creation, whichever is shorter. All the above terms apply for copyrightable works first created after January 1, 1978. For works created before 1978, the rules are different. Under the old law, unpublished works were protected under state law for as long as the work was not published. Works which were unpublished before 1978 are now protected under the 1976 Copyright Act, and generally the duration of the copyright in these works is computed by either (1) the life plus 50 year rule or (2) the 75 years from creation, 100 years from publication rule, whichever rule provides the shorter protection. However, all works unpublished before 1978 are guaranteed at least 25 years of protection beyond 1978. For works that before 1978 were either published with proper notice or registered, the 1909 Copyright Act afforded protection for a period of 28 years from the date of publication or registration. Under the 1909 Act an additional 28-year renewal period could be added by filing at the Copyright Office a timely claim for renewal. Under the new Act, the renewal term has been extended from 28 years to 47 years, giving those works a potential life of 75 years. However, a timely renewal must be filed in the United States Copyright Office before the original 28-year term ends. If a renewal is not filed, the copyright expires at the end of 28 years. For works created after 1978, no renewals are required.

TRADE SECRETS

Many artistic innovations can be protected under trade secret law. For example, an artist who discovers a new secret process, such as a new method of painting, etching or sculpting, may be able to protect it by keeping it secret. Customer lists also can be protected as trade secrets. Every state in the United States has some type of trade secret law. That law is important to artists because it is often the easiest and least expensive way to protect many of their discoveries. This type of protection, however, has limits.

Under the law of trade secrets, certain information can be protected from unauthorized use. To be protectable, the information must be (1) secret, (2) substantial in nature, and (3) valuable. Information that may be protectable includes customer lists, methods of doing business, methods and techniques of making or protecting artwork, material lists, material formulas, artistic techniques, and other information of particular value that is gathered and unknown to others.

Because of the secrecy requirement, many discoveries will simply not be protectable under this law. Artistic techniques that are visually perceptible, like pottery shapes and color combinations, could easily be copied by others. This copying technique is known as "reverse engineering," and the law fully permits this, unless the product is patented.

In short, an artist can protect his developments under trade secret law only if he can somehow keep it secret. For example, if an artist invents a particular process to fire pottery and keeps that process secret, a competitor could not simply look at the finished pottery to determine how it was fired. The della Robbia family of

Renaissance Italy produced ceramics by a unique glazing and firing process which competitors never discovered.

The requirement of secrecy and confidentiality may initially offend an artist's sensibilities. Shared thoughts, techniques, and developments strengthen the artistic community and lead to increased creation in all fields of art. Artists aware of the benefits of trade secret law surely will not suddenly try to keep every little development to themselves. Such a procedure would only injure the artistic community without benefiting the individual artist. However, someone may on occasion discover or create something truly innovative, valuable, and worthy of protection. When he does, he should be aware of trade secret protection and consider its use.

Why should an artist try to keep a significant development secret? Simply, in order to keep others from misusing his idea and competing unfairly. As long as information is kept secret and confidential, the artist can stop use of the information by people who learned of it improperly. For example, the owner could stop someone who stole a secret and attempted to use it. Similarly, if an owner disclosed his trade secret to someone who promised to keep it confidential, the owner could legally stop that person from disclosing his secret. Furthermore, if the information remains secret, he can then contract to sell the information for profit.

Trade secret protection can last for minutes or for decades. The law will protect an artist's discovery as long as it is kept secret and is not known or legally discovered by others. If an artist voluntarily discloses his finding to his friends, his fellow artists may profit from the sharing, but the trade secret rights are lost; everyone may then use his process freely. On the other hand, if an artist keeps his discovery confidential, his rights may last for years. Sometimes, however, even if he does keep the information confidential, his rights may be lost. If another person through his own efforts and without knowledge of the original artist's work develops the same information, the first artist's trade secret protection ends. Suppose, for example, someone discovers that a particular chemical in a photographic bath gives his photographs a special quality. He then keeps his discovery a secret. If another photographer, without knowledge of the first discovery, himself learns that the same chemical gives him the same result, the first cannot stop the second from using the chemical or from disclosing his discovery. If the second photographer does tell others, the entire trade secret of the first is lost. Everyone will be free to use the photographic bath.

If you develop a significant trade secret, what must you do to keep that information protectable? How much will it cost? The simple answer to the first question is that you must take all reasonable steps to keep your valuable information secret. The answer to the second is that protecting trade secrets does not cost much more than your time and efforts. In that regard, the law of trade secrets is particularly beneficial because it is relatively inexpensive to qualify for protection.

There are a number of procedures to follow. First, any documents that disclose or contain the significant trade secret information should be kept in a safe place, and preferably should be under lock and key. It would be best to place a notice or stamp on any confidential documents. The notice might say:

> Confidential Information of (Artist's Name), Not to Be Copied, Disclosed, or Used for Any Purpose Without the Express Written Permission of (Artist's Name).

Confidential documents should also be placed in an envelope marked with the same notice or stamp. If you use the trade secret information in your studio, you should take all reasonable steps to control access to the studio so that others cannot steal or otherwise wrongfully learn of the information.

Other steps can be taken to better ensure that trade secret rights are not unnecessarily lost. Commercial industries often place confidential notices or signs in any work areas where trade secret information is used. Similarly, industries often require that their employees agree to keep all trade secret information confidential and not disclose it to others. Along the same lines, industries often require that even guests agree in writing not to disclose any confidential information they may learn during a visit.

If you do decide to protect certain significant trade secrets, there probably will be times when you will want to disclose your secrets to other people, such as friends or a potential buyer, perhaps. Whenever you do so, you should ask that person to sign a written agreement of confidentiality. That agreement should be signed before, not after, the disclosure. It might read as follows:

> The undersigned (name of person or corporation) in consideration for the disclosure, review and observation of the trade secrets and confidential know-how of (artist's name) promises to hold in confidence and not to reproduce, divulge, or use any and all trade secrets and unpublished know-

how observed by or given to him by (artist's name), or his agents or representatives, concerning (general discussion of your trade secret) without the written consent of (artist's name).

Name:_____

Title: _____

_____
signature

Date:_____

It is important that you take as many of these steps as are reasonable. If you do not, the courts simply will not be able to protect you.

If you design or develop something particularly useful to others, you may soon get offers for the disclosure of your secret. Under those circumstances, you can enter into a written contract which specifies the particular payment and use of your trade secret information. Often, parties are willing either to pay a percentage of the proceeds of sales of products they make using another's trade secret information or pay an initial down payment and continuing royalties. A person might even pay a lump sum for all rights.

A variety of contract terms are possible. If you enter into a contract with another person, it should be in writing. It is also important not to disclose the secret information until the agreement is signed. It would be wise to have a lawyer help in negotiating and drafting such agreements.

PATENTS

New designs, processes, tools, products, machines, or substances may be able to be patented. A patent holder has the exclusive right to make, use and sell his invention throughout the United States for the life of the patent. He can also sell his patent or license others.

There are two different types of patents: design patents and utility patents. A *design patent* is available for any new, original, and unobvious ornamental design for an article of manufacture. Design patents might be appropriate to protect ornamental designs for clothing, jewelry, furniture, hollowware, glassware, china and other articles of manufacture. *Utility patents* are available for any new, useful and unobvious process, machine, manufacture, or composition of matter or any new, useful, and unobvious improvement in those areas. Utility patents might be appropriate to protect new tools and machines used in creating works of art, new art materials such as acrylic resins, paints or glazes, and new methods or techniques for creating or manufacturing artwork.

Design patents protect only the appearance of an article, not its structure or function. In some circumstances, both a design patent and a utility patent can be obtained for a particular patentable product which includes a patentable ornamental design.

Patents can be extremely valuable to an artist. Patent law, unlike trade secret law, gives the patentee the exclusive right to make, use, and sell his invention, regardless of whether the invention can be kept secret. Patent law can also often give broader protection than trade secret law. For example, if an artist obtains a patent on a particular airbrush, he can use his patent to prevent anyone from copying the invention. Depending upon the novelty of his invention, he might be able to stop people from making, using or selling airbrushes that are similar, but not identical, to his. He can also license selected persons to make, use, or sell his invention and require them to pay him for those rights.

Patents offer a definite period of protection. A design patent can have a life of 3.5 years, 7 years, or 14 years, depending upon the application fees initially paid to the Patent and Trademark Office. Utility patents have a life of 17 years. Neither design nor utility patents can be renewed. When the patent expires, any person has the right to make, use, or sell the previously patented invention.

The degree of patent protection is defined by the claims of the patent. If an invention represents a major technical advance, the scope of protection can be extremely broad. A claim in the patent for the very first paintbrush might recite:

> A paintbrush comprising a handle and flexible, absorbent material at the end of the handle for holding paint and transferring it to a surface to be painted.

Such a broad claim would give the inventor the exclusive right to make, use and sell almost every paintbrush. On the other hand, if an artist today invented an improved paintbrush having a particular form and made from a special material, he might be able to obtain a patent for the improved brush, but the claims would have to be more specific or narrow.

Before an artist can obtain a patent, he must invent a new design or invention. However, not every new design or invention is patentable. For a new design or invention to be patentable, the law requires that it be "unobvious" over the "prior art." The terms "unobvious" and "prior art" have special meanings in the law. Generally, "prior art" refers to the knowledge and information known or available to others before the inventor made his invention. That includes all printed publications anywhere in the world and any public use or sale of similar designs or inventions in this country. Previously issued patents, magazine and newspaper articles, public speeches, and the sale and use of products in the market are all prior art.

To be patentable, an invention cannot be exactly like those already known. Even if there are one or more differences between an invention and similar previous products, a patent may still be refused if the differences are obvious. An invention must be sufficiently different in ways that would not be obvious to a person of ordinary skill in the area of invention. For example, the substitution of one known material for another, or changes in size and shape, are ordinarily not patentable.

To obtain a design or utility patent, an artist must file a formal application in the United States Patent and Trademark Office. Its address is:

> U.S. Patent and Trademark Office
> Crystal Plaza
> 2021 Jefferson Davis Highway
> Arlington, Virginia 22202

The U.S. Patent and Trademark Office has an information office to provide general information on patent protection. The Patent and Trademark Office also publishes a number of booklets and pamphlets concerning Patent and Trademark Law, which can be obtained free or for minimum fees, usually under five dollars.

To obtain a patent the artist must file an application in the Patent and Trademark Office. Once filed, the application is classified and given to an examiner who specializes in the area of the invention. The examiner determines whether the application complies with all legal requirements, and compares the invention with whatever prior art patents and publications he finds.

If you invent a new design or invention that might be patentable, it is important to act quickly. In the United States, an inventor cannot receive a utility patent for his invention unless he files an application in the United States Patent and Trademark Office within one year from the date he first publicly discloses, uses, or sells his invention. For design patents, he has only six months. In some foreign countries it is impossible to obtain patent protection unless the inventor files an application before any public use occurs in this or a foreign country.

Design and utility patent applications are complex legal documents, and it is almost impossible for a layman to prepare a patent application. Thus, you should probably consult an attorney or agent who is registered to practice before the United States Patent and Trademark Office. Attorneys and agents are usually willing briefly to discuss patent protection free of charge—but ask first. Also, a volunteer lawyer's association might be able to provide some assistance to artists interested in patent protection.

Because of the complexity of the application process, patents can be expensive. Design patents normally are less expensive than utility patents, and the prices for either design or utility patents vary depending upon the complexity of the invention and the attorneys' fees. Because of these costs, patent protection is most appropriate when an invention has commercial applications, such as large-scale manufacture or use.

The protection available from a patent can be well worth the expense. Many banks will make loans using patents as collateral. More important, if an artist has an extremely valuable invention, the exclusive right to make, use and sell it can be worth a great deal. If an invention is of use to the artistic or general manufacturing field, it probably has commercial value. Often, licensing a patent is the only way to make the largest return, particularly if the demand is great. For example, a woodcraftsman in Virginia designed and patented a process to make a wood chair. He was able to license his utility patent to a furniture manufacturer who agreed to pay him a percentage of the sales price of each chair sold. (See illustration.)

Finally, if an invention is sufficiently important, patent protection throughout most of the world can be obtained. Such patent protection, however, is extremely expensive and would make sense only if the invention were valuable in selected foreign countries.

TRADEMARKS AND SERVICE MARKS

When an artist places his artwork or services in the marketplace, it may be advisable to use trademarks, service marks, or logos to identify them to the public. These marks can help market artwork or services, and the law provides for their protection.

A trademark is any word, name, slogan, logo or device (or combination) that a person uses to identify his goods and services and distinguish them from others. A mark identifies its owner as the source of the artwork and advertises the value and uniform quality of his work and goodwill. A service mark is similar to a trademark but is used in the offering or advertisement of services.

Examples of trademarks in the art world include arbitrary and distinctive signatures or logos on paintings and sculpture, stampings of a name or logo on pottery and pewter, a printmaker's chop mark, labels used to identify an artist or gallery, marks on packaging or display information, and labeling placed on boxes.

Examples of service marks are arbitrary and distinctive words or logos used with appraisal services, galleries, artist's consulting services, interior decorating firms, and architecture firms. These

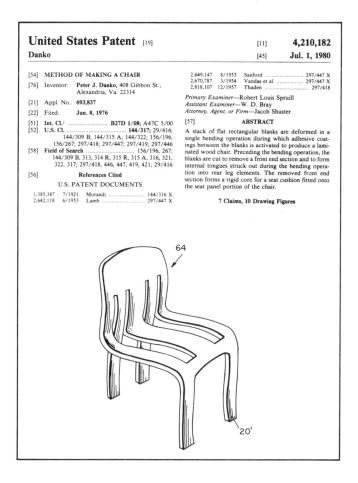

United States Patent [19]   [11]   **4,210,182**

Danko   [45]   **Jul. 1, 1980**

[54] **METHOD OF MAKING A CHAIR**

[76] Inventor: **Peter J. Danko, 408 Gibbon St.,** Alexandria, Va. 22314

[21] Appl. No.: **693,837**

[22] Filed: **Jun. 8, 1976**

[51] Int. Cl.² B27D 1/08; A47C 5/00
[52] U.S. Cl. .... 144/317; 29/416; 144/309 B; 144/315 A; 144/322; 156/196; 156/267; 297/418; 297/447; 297/419; 297/446
[58] **Field of Search** .... 156/196, 267; 144/309 B, 313, 314 R, 315 R, 315 A, 316, 321, 322, 317; 297/418, 446, 447, 419, 421; 29/416

[56] **References Cited**

U.S. PATENT DOCUMENTS

1,385,387	7/1921	Morandi	144/316 X
2,642,118	6/1953	Lamb	297/447 X
2,649,147	8/1953	Sanford	297/447 X
2,670,787	3/1954	Vandas et al.	297/447 X
2,818,107	12/1957	Thaden	297/418

Primary Examiner—Robert Louis Spruill
Assistant Examiner—W. D. Bray
Attorney, Agent, or Firm—Jacob Shuster

[57] **ABSTRACT**

A stack of flat rectangular blanks are deformed in a single bending operation during which adhesive coatings between the blanks is activated to produce a laminated wood chair. Preceding the bending operation, the blanks are cut to remove a front end section and to form internal tongues struck out during the bending operation into rear leg elements. The removed front end section forms a rigid core for a seat cushion fitted onto the seat panel portion of the chair.

7 Claims, 10 Drawing Figures

marks might be placed on stationery, envelopes, business cards, advertisements, and signs.

Trademarks and service marks are protectable under both state and federal law. In the United States a person receives protection for a mark only when he actually begins to use the mark. The geographical area of protection available under the law depends upon where the mark is actually used and whether a federal registration has been obtained.

Since an artist cannot receive protection for every mark he might wish to use, the selection of a mark is important. Some words or logos are not protectable as marks. Others may infringe upon marks already existing.

It is important to select a mark that is not confusingly similar to marks already used by others who deal in similar products or services. If one person doing business in a geographical area is using a particular mark for his gallery, a second gallery owner should not select a confusingly similar mark. If he does, the first gallery owner may sue the second to stop confusion. If he wins, the second user may have to destroy all products, signs, and labels that include the mark, and may have to pay damages.

There are procedures for discovering if a mark is already in use. Telephone directories and trade directories are a source. If the mark is to be used nationwide, or if big investments are to be made in printing and advertising, it is wise to ask a trademark attorney or specialist to conduct a thorough search.

Certain words, phrases, and logos are not protectable as trademarks. No one can obtain trademark protection for a mark that is immoral, deceptive or scandalous, or consists of a governmental flag or coat of arms. Also, the law will not protect a mark that is used in its generic or "dictionary" sense. If a person calls his art gallery "The Art Gallery," for example, he probably would not get any protection. The law considers it unfair for any one person to have exclusive rights to the generic use of a word or phrase. Similarly, it is unlikely that an artist would be allowed rights to the frequently used mark "wearable art" for clothing which is also art.

Certain marks are protectable only if the owner can establish that through prolonged and continuous use and advertisement, the mark has become distinctive and recognized by the public as representing his goods or services. Within this category are marks that are merely descriptive or deceptively misdescriptive of goods or services, marks that are primarily geographically descriptive or misdescriptive of the origin of the goods or services, or marks that are primarily surnames. Therefore, descriptive, geographical and surname marks like BEAUTIFUL, PARIS and JONES, promise little, if any, immediate protection.

The marks providing the strongest protection are those which are distinctive and arbitrary in meaning. For example, if an artist sells his paintings under a trademark like the word SOURCE, there is no generic, descriptive or geographic link between the mark and his work. Through use and acceptance the mark will strongly identify the artist's goods or services, and the law will give him broad protection. Well-known arbitrary marks in the commercial fields include the marks EXXON®, KODAK®, and IBM®. These marks are distinctive, and had little meaning when first used. Today, they are probably worth millions of dollars in sales.

One of the most common trademarks in the art field is a person's surname or signature. Under trademark law, the amount of protection given to such surnames and signatures varies depending upon the circumstances. If an artist's name is Smith and he signs his name in block letters, he will probably receive little, if any, protection. Any other artist by the name of Smith would be able to use his name and sign it in block letters. Furthermore, the Trademark Office probably would not register the mark. If an artist signs his name with a particular signature or script, he possibly could stop others from making a copy of his signature on similar artwork. Still, the protection for a surname is not great unless the name becomes well-known as a trademark through widespread use. An artist should therefore consider using both his signature and a separate word or logo as a mark.

Once an artist selects a trademark or service mark, it is important to use it properly. The law requires that a trademark or service mark be used in conjunction with his goods or services, respectively. That means that the trademark must be placed on or with the artwork or services. A trademark can be drawn or stamped on the actual artwork, used as a label, or placed on display next to the art. If an artist ships his artwork, he can use boxes having the marks on the outside. For a trademark, the use of an artist's mark merely with advertisement of his artwork will not fulfill the use requirement. For a service mark, an artist can meet the use requirement by placing the mark on his stationery, in advertisements, on signs, on envelopes, on shopping bags, or on business cards.

It is a good idea to place a warning or "notice" next to a trademark or service mark. Such notices serve to let the public know that the mark is protected under the law. If an artist has not obtained a federal registration, he can use the "TM" notice with his trademarks (VISION™) and the "SM" notice with his service mark (GRAFIX℠). If the mark is federally registered, he can use the "®" notice (COCA-COLA®). It is illegal to use the "®" notice unless the mark is actually registered in the United States Patent and Trademark Office.

Under state law, protection for trademarks or logos begins with use of the mark and initially extends over the geographical area of actual use. That protection enables the first user to prevent others from using the name or a confusingly similar mark with similar goods. Protection of the mark continues as long as it is actually used.

It is also possible to register trademarks in most states, and a mark can be federally registered in the United States Patent and Trademark Office. A separate state registration only protects the mark in the state. Federal registration grants essentially exclusive rights to a mark throughout the country, even if it is not presently used in certain parts of the United States. There are exceptions to this rule, so it would be a good idea to talk with a trademark attorney or specialist who should be able to file and obtain a registered trademark for a relatively modest fee. A federal registration has an initial life of twenty years and can be renewed as long as the mark is in use.

Once an artist adopts and uses a mark, it is important to protect the mark from confusing use by others. If there is some confusion with other marks, and the artist allows the situation to continue, his own mark loses its strength, and in time the courts will not enforce the mark against others.

The cost of obtaining legal protection for an artist's marks is small. To receive protection under state law, an artist only has to select a protectable mark and actually use and enforce it properly. For a simple federal registration, the current cost would probably be between $200 and $600 if no real problems were involved. The process for obtaining registrations for marks in most foreign countries is expensive and should be used only when foreign sales would support it.

The effort necessary to adopt, use and protect a mark justifies the cost. Marks are strong marketing tools. As an artist's artwork and services become better known to the public, his mark becomes an important asset. He may also use his mark to stop others from attempting to copy him. If necessary he can sue for damages. Finally, if a mark becomes well-known, he can license others to use his mark with products and services which he authorizes. If he is considering such licensing or franchising opportunities, he should seek an attorney's advice.

CONCLUSION

The copyright, trade secret, patent and trademark laws offer artists a wide scope of protection for their creations, creative developments and marketing efforts. Through copyright, artists can protect their literary, visual, audio and audiovisual works from unauthorized copying by others. Trade secret law enables an artist to protect his trade secrets and stop the unauthorized use of his secret information by others. Through patents, an artist can secure the exclusive right to make, use and sell his inventions throughout the United States, regardless of whether or not the inventions can be kept secret. Finally, trademark law enables an artist to market exclusively his rights and services under his selected trademarks and service marks and to stop others from using identical or confusingly similar marks. In short, the copyright, trade secret, patent and trademark laws collectively enable an artist to protect the vast majority of his works and creations from unauthorized use. Because of these legal protections, an artist can practice his art to the exclusion of others or can contractually transfer his rights and receive compensation from authorized users.

The cost to obtain the protections available under these laws is not prohibitive. When an artist creates a copyrightable work, he immediately has a copyright in that work, at no cost. By simply placing a copyright notice on the work when it is published, the artist will ensure that the majority of his rights under the copyright law will not be lost. With respect to protecting his trade secrets, an artist only has to expend the time and effort necessary to keep his developments secret. Any disclosure of the trade secrets must be made in confidence. Whenever an artist uses his trademarks or service marks with his goods and services, state trademark laws protect the artist's marks from unauthorized use, at least in the geographical area of actual use. Thus, without paying any immediate out-of-pocket expenses, an artist can receive substantial protection under the copyright, trade secret, and trademark laws.

To receive the maximum protection available under the copyright, trade secret, patent and trademark laws, an artist may need to apply for federal registrations or patents. For example, an artist can receive patent protection only after the U.S. Patent and Trademark Office issues a patent based upon a formal patent application filed by the artist or his representative. Similarly, an artist can receive additional copyright and trademark protection by registering his copyrightable works in the Copyright Office and his marks in the United States Patent and Trademark Office. Registration of a copyrightable work provides the artist with certain rights not otherwise available, and an artist cannot enforce his copyright in a court of law until he has at least filed a copyright application. The federal registration of an artist's trademark or service mark grants him essentially exclusive rights to his mark throughout the United States, rather than in the more limited geographical area of actual use. Furthermore, a federal registration of a mark provides the artist with certain rights not provided by state law. In view of the added protections provided by copyright and trademark registrations and by patents, an artist should always consider these procedures when he creates or develops a new work, invention, or mark. By being aware of the protections available by federal registration and their costs, the artist can then selectively protect his most important creations, developments and marks. Often, the additional protections are well worth the expense necessary to file applications and obtain a patent or a copyright or trademark registration.

In conclusion, there is no real excuse for not protecting an artist's creations and marks through copyright, trade secret, patent and trademark law. Many of these legal rights are available free, and an artist can secure the available additional rights on a selective basis. The protections provided by these laws can be well worth the expense. Through the use of these laws an artist can prevent the unauthorized use of his works and creations and can sue to stop others from stealing his creations and otherwise unfairly competing with him. Perhaps more importantly, the rights provided by these laws can be sold or licensed by the artist to others for direct compensation. Thus, as an artist succeeds in his creative talents and reputation, he can by law receive adequate compensation through his legal rights.

7

Insuring You and Your Product

by
Huntington T. Block

◆ ◆ ◆

HUNTINGTON T. BLOCK is the sole proprietor of Huntington Block Insurance in Washington, D.C., specializing in fine arts insurance and insurance for businesses and professionals.

◆ ◆ ◆ ◆

There is perhaps no more independent a businessperson than an artist. You may not think of yourself as a businessperson, but you are. You make something which you hope to sell. You lease or own working space, you sometimes hire assistants, you own and use the tools and raw materials of your craft, and you deal with the public. If you stop to think about it, these are the sorts of things that any business does, and in this litigious society in which we live you have the same legal responsibilities and potential liabilities as anyone else.

You also have assets to protect, but none is more important than yourself. This is supposed to be a chapter on insurance, but I hope it will be a chapter that will serve to remind you of risks you can avoid just as emphatically as it will address itself to insurance you can buy. Nothing is more devastating to an independent business person than sickness. Productivity stops, and presumably income stops as well. We all get sick at one time or another, but a lot of sickness is the result of carelessness, and to an independent artist an unnecessary illness is an inexcusable waste of time—and time is money. Take care of yourself!

GROUP INSURANCE

Hospital and medical insurance is available on an individual basis, but it's expensive. It's best to shop around for a group you can belong to. For example, if your spouse is working in a large organization, chances are you can be included as part of a "family" coverage in the organization's group policy. Perhaps you can find an artists' group which has negotiated a good program you can join.

When you enter a hospital and medical program, beware of something that sounds too cheap—chances are the benefits are cheap too. You want a hospital plan that guarantees a semi-private room in a local hospital; you want a doctor benefit that reimburses your physician in accordance with the fees he normally charges; you need to be assured of adequate expenses like drugs, operating room fees, etc.; and you want dental coverage included if it can be done so at a reasonable premium.

LOSS OF INCOME INSURANCE

Just as troubling as the expense of getting well is the loss of income while you are sick, particularly if you are faced with a long illness. Rent and taxes go on regardless of whether you're sick or well. You can usually arrange loss of income insurance at a reasonable premium if you are willing to accept a fairly long waiting period before benefits commence. For example, if you make a philosophic decision that you need loss of income insurance only for a catastrophic illness, you might be willing to accept a six-month waiting period before benefits start being paid. Such a program is relatively inexpensive, especially if it can be purchased as part of a group. Your benefit, usually payable on a monthly basis, will represent a percentage of your normal income—enough to keep the wolf away from the door, but certainly not enough to encourage you to stay on your back any longer than you must.

LIFE INSURANCE

Artists have never been great believers in life insurance, but there are some important uses for life insurance that deserve mention. If you have dependents, the need for some form of life insurance is self-evident. You may want to buy sufficient life insurance to guarantee that your mortgage will be paid off in case you die, so your family will have a place to live free and clear. You may have to buy life insurance to help guarantee a loan. These days a good deal of the life insurance that is sold is pure term life insurance, that is, just life insurance, no cash value, no loan option, nothing extra. Term is the cheapest form of life insurance available, and most money men will advise you to buy term insurance, and look to real estate or the stock market for your investment income. However, if you own an ordinary life insurance policy which has accumulated a cash value, don't overlook the possibility of borrowing against that policy at very favorable interest rates.

RETIREMENT INSURANCE

No one really likes to think about retirement, especially an artist whose productive years may never stop. Picasso certainly didn't need any retirement income. However, the IRS recognizes that many independent business people do retire, and they have established the Keogh Plan which encourages an independent to set up his or her own retirement plan, and enables annual contributions of tax free income into that plan. Any artist who has not taken advantage of the Keogh Plan is missing a great opportuntiy to save.

There are many ways to put money aside for retirement. You can buy an annuity which will guarantee a certain fixed income beginning at age 65 or 70, or however you decide to set it up. You can make a contribution to a group pension plan if you can find one to join, or you can set up your own pension plan with an annual tax free contribution under the aforementioned Keogh Plan. It's hard enough to grow old, but it's twice as hard if you have to be poor too.

INSURING YOUR STUDIO

So much for your life and health. Let's give some thought to your environment. Your studio is the center of your professional life. You may own it or lease it, but whatever you do, you have stocked it with brushes, easels, tools, and equipment of all kinds. Chances are, also, that one of the heaviest concentrations of your own work is held in your studio. Collectors and would-be dealers come to see your work. Occasionally you might share your studio with another artist or artists. The point is that even though you may embrace solitude, people tend to come and go in any artist's studio.

What can happen? Obviously a fire can be devastating, so can serious water damage from burst pipes, and so can a major theft or act of vandalism. On the liability side, someone can claim to have been injured on your premises, and sue you for negligence. All of these perils can be insured against with what is generally referred to as a commercial multi-peril policy. It is a package of insurance which, on the property side, will cover your building if you own it, all of your contents including your business-related personal property, and your liability as a building owner or as a tenant, whatever the case may be.

If you own your building, or the building that houses your studio, you should ask for a policy that provides "all risk" perils, and that guarantees replacement cost if a part or all of your building is damaged or destroyed. When arriving at a figure to use to insure your business personal property, remember all of the studio furniture and equipment, your leasehold improvements, if any, all materials and supplies, any commercial camera equipment or audio equipment you use in your work, and your art library, including catalogues, periodicals, etc. You should again insist upon "all risk" perils, and you should understand that if you don't insure to value, you could be penalized in any loss adjustment. Your inventory of your own art work, and that of other artists, can best be treated under another form of policy which will be described later on in the chapter. The commercial multi-peril policy can be extended to provide for reimbursement of extra expenses as a result of a fire or other insured peril forcing you to locate elsewhere temporarily while your own space is being repaired.

A second section of the policy deals with all of the liability exposures that arise out of the premises itself, and all of your other operations as an artist, including installations, art in public places for which you are responsible, your activities away from your studio, etc. Coverage can be extended to cover your potential liability arising out of the activities of independent contractors, your liability as a result of an alleged act of libel, slander, or invasion of privacy, and your possible liability arising out of the serving of alcohol at a business-related party or reception. If you are working in a medium that could cause eventual physical harm, such as a large steel sculpture, the policy can be extended to cover product liability. If you lease your studio space, you can even cover your liability for fire damage to the owner's walls, floors, and ceilings if it can be proved the fire was started as a result of your negligence.

Other forms of liability insurance are just as important. Automobile and truck insurance is mandatory in most states, and mandatory or not, absolutely essential to carry. Don't forget motorcycles, mopeds and tractors. If you have employees, Workers' Compensation is a statutory requirement. So is Disability Benefits in some states. In fact, if you are incorporated, you are your own employee, so you can buy Workers' Compensation Insurance for yourself. It is valuable coverage, because it reimburses an employee for medical expenses and loss of income arising out of a work-related accident or sickness.

CATASTROPHE LIABILITY INSURANCE

Finally, there is what can best be described as catastrophe liability insurance, or Umbrella Liability Insurance. Smart plaintiff's attorneys often sue for a good deal more than they expect to get, and $1,000,000 suits are fairly commonplace these days. Insurance people generally recommend substantial liability coverage, and the best way to buy it is through an Umbrella Policy which provides $1,000,000 or $2,000,000 additional liability protection on top of all of your basic liability policies.

HOMEOWNER'S INSURANCE

If you work at home, your insurance needs are tied into the Homeowner's or Tenant's Policy you buy to protect your home or apartment. However, many working artists don't realize that most such policies designed for the home specifically exclude business personal property and liabilities arising out of business pursuits. It behooves you, therefore, to ask your agent or insurance company representative to endorse your policy to recognize you are a professional artist with a studio in your home. The cost is not great, and the extra peace of mind is substantial.

INSURING YOUR INVENTORY

Finally, there is the question of your own work, your own art inventory, and that includes work in process, work in storage, work on consignment, etc. Insurance of this inventory calls for a carefully constructed fine arts policy, one that responds to a broad range of perils, and one that establishes insured value in a form easily understandable to artist and insurance adjuster alike.

Such a policy is generally referred to as a Fine Arts Policy, and heretofore underwriters have been somewhat reluctant to offer this broad insurance coverage to a working artist. Happily that attitude is changing, and the market is opening up, influenced by the persistence of various artists' organizations.

Perhaps inhibitions existed because of the stereotype of the poor, starving artist working in a four-story walk-up, classified by insurance people as a fire trap. There is nothing more devastating to an artist than the loss of months, sometimes years, of work in a major fire or burst pipe. The fact is that artists are just as concerned about so-called fire traps as are the underwriters, and while there are undoubtedly some shining exceptions, the majority of people who paint and sculpt are as careful about safety and security as is any other responsible businessperson.

Another problem has been the difficulty of establishing value, particularly for an artist whose work has as yet not attracted an active market. In fact, it is not unreasonable for insurance people to require evidence of some sort of sales record before agreeing to insure studio inventory at a particular level of value. However, if valuations can be established, according to size, medium, or whatever, it should be possible to insure not only completed works held in the studio, but also work in process at whatever percentage of completion exists at the time a loss occurs. Since the artist generally consigns his work to a dealer at a percentage of selling price, say 60 percent of selling price, the consigned value is usually the amount the artist and the insurance company agree upon for insurance purposes. The purpose of insurance is to make you whole, but no more than whole. Insurance wouldn't and shouldn't be arranged to reimburse you for more than you might expect to receive if a loss had not taken place.

CONSIGNING YOUR WORK: WHO IS RESPONSIBLE?

Artists must be careful to review the insurance responsibility when they consign their work to a dealer or a cooperative gallery. Generally the insurance responsibility lies with the dealer or the gallery, but that's not always so. If the dealer or gallery is carrying the insurance, which will be the case in most instances, the consignment agreement should be in writing, because the first document an insurance adjuster asks for after a commercial art gallery fire is the consignment agreement with the gallery's several artists.

Furthermore, when an artist submits some of his work to a juried show or to a museum show, he should determine who will be responsible for the insurance—and whether it begins when the art leaves the studio, and continues until the art returns, or if it covers only while the art is on the premises where the show is being held. Remember also that if you are sent a Loan Agreement Form by a museum or other borrower, the figure you put opposite each object you agree to lend is usually an "agreed value," and that is all you get in the event of a loss.

If a loss does occur, you will be dealing with an insurance adjuster. He is a representative of the insurance company charged with bringing your claim to a reasonable and satisfactory settlement. He isn't the enemy, and he generally tries to be fair. But he does need you to supply certain documentation to support the claim you are making. For example, if your loss involves works of art, he'll want to see the aforementioned consignment agreements so he can establish value in accordance with the terms of your policy. If the loss involves business or household personal property, he'll want to see bills of sale if they're available, and he'll want to know how long you've owned a desk, or a table, or whatever, in order to determine how much depreciation to allow. If someone has been injured on your premises, he will need to know from you all the circumstances of the injury, because he has to establish whether or not there has been any negligence on your part.

Finally, where do you go to get the best insurance buy and the best insurance service? It's usually wise to try to find a person or a firm where there is an interest in and understanding of the needs of an artist. Such people exist. All you have to do is ask around among your fellow artists, and find out which ones seem most satisfied with their insurance relationship, and who's dealing with people who seem to grasp the special insurance needs of the artist. There are even insurance people who are part-time artists!

The whole business of evaluating the risks you face is not without its rewards. You certainly don't have to buy an insurance policy in every instance. Good common sense can prevent most accidents from happening in the first place. If a studio space opens up at an attractive rental, but in a rundown building, don't be pennywise and pound foolish. Wait for a space in a well-maintained building where your neighbors have the same concerns for safety and security as do you. Remember you can be the most careful person in the world, but you can't do much about your neighbor, and the fire that his carelessness starts in his studio will most certainly spread to yours.

Think about the things that can happen to you, and think about the things you can prevent. Be particularly concerned about a catastrophe, like a major fire, a long illness, or a six-figure liability suit against you. Then begin to construct your insurance program, perhaps with the counsel of someone who knows and understands art and the artist.

8

Keeping Your Health

Health Hazards for Artists

by

Monona Rossol

◆ ◆ ◆ ◆

MONONA ROSSOL is a potter, art teacher and chemist, who in 1977 helped found the Center for Occupational Hazards. As director of the Hazards Information Center, she lectures and writes extensively on health hazards in arts and crafts.

◆ ◆ ◆ ◆

We artists like to think of ourselves as different from the general public. For example, we feel that we have little in common with industrial workers. Yet artists and industrial workers are often using and being exposed to the same hazardous chemicals, including lead, asbestos, silica, solvents, pigments and dyes.

ARTISTS AND CHEMICALS

Artists are exposed to lead in artists' paints, ceramic glazes, enamels, lead fumes from soldering, welding, and casting of lead-containing alloys such as bronze, and from working with stained glass. Artists are exposed to asbestos when sculpting asbestos-containing stones such as soapstone and serpentine, when working with asbestos-containing talcs in clays, glazes, industrial talcum powders and French chalk, asbestos-coated welding and brazing rods, old asbestos gloves and welding curtains, and many other asbestos-insulated items.

Other chemicals to which artists are exposed include many hazardous solvents such as benzene, carbontetrachloride, and n-hexane. Artists also work with dyes which are either highly toxic or cancer-causing, toxic heavy metals in pigments and ceramic colorants, silica (which can cause silicosis) in clays, glazes, stone dusts and jewelry buffing compounds, and more.

Often our exposure to toxic chemicals is greater than that of industrial workers—for four principal reasons: (1) we do not know these chemicals are in our supplies and hence take no precautions, (2) we are not careful about using our materials, (3) we may not know how toxic our materials are, and (4) we are using these materials in non-industrial settings such as school classrooms, home studios, or lofts in which ventilation and personal protective equipment are either lacking or inadequate.

Unlike many industrial workers, we usually have no union to fight for safe and healthful conditions or to promote educational programs to alert workers to workplace hazards. Instead, we often work in isolation and independently, making our own decisions about what materials to use and how to use them.

As a result we are seeing artists contracting the same types of occupational diseases that have plagued industrial workers. Artists and craftsmen are contracting work-related illnesses such as silicosis, chronic bronchitis, liver and kidney damage, crippling nervous system disorders, dermatitis, and heavy metal poisoning. Occupationally induced cancers are also showing up. A recent National Cancer Institute mortality study of artists (primarily painters) showed dramatic elevations (above the normal population) in brain, kidney, and bladder cancer and leukemia in male artists, and in breast, rectal and lung cancer in women artists.

Statistics such as these are cold and meaningless when compared to the individual stories of occupational illness and death among artists. Of the many cases of which I am aware, three particularly touch me. The first is the story of a California mural painter who contracted mercury poisoning from her acrylic paints—probably from her habit of eating while working. Her physical suffering is complicated by the mental and emotional effects of mercury poisoning. These mental symptoms have been known since the 1800's, when felt hat workers used mercury vapor to block hats. From this came the phrase "mad as a hatter," which Lewis Carroll drew on when he included the Mad Hatter character in his *Alice in Wonderland*.

The second story is that of weaver Dennis Friend, who died of inhalation anthrax (a bacterial disease which used to be called "wool sorters' disease") from working with contaminated wool. Mr. Friend left a widow and a six-week-old baby. His widow, also a weaver, has been actively alerting others to the dangers of anthrax and has personal knowledge of a number of other cases of skin anthrax among American weavers.

The third case is that of Erica Barton, a collage artist, who has been disabled by exposure to a solvent in spray adhesives. This solvent, n-hexane, is commonly present in rubber cement and its thinner, aerosol spray cans, contact adhesives, some lacquer thinners, and low-boiling naphthas. The disease it can cause is similar in many respects to multiple sclerosis.

Mrs. Barton's symptoms began as a numbness in the hands and feet and progressed to difficulty in walking, exhaustion, loss of interest, vision problems, paralysis, and other symptoms affecting the peripheral nervous system. Two years later the peripheral nervous system symptoms have mostly disappeared, but she has permanent central nervous system damage including vision problems, muscle weakness, and difficulty in controlling fine motions. Her doctor does not expect that she will ever recover completely and return to being an artist.

There are many other dramatic examples of occupational illnesses among artists, but there are even greater numbers of artists who are suffering undiagnosed, chronic illnesses which they do not know are work-related. For example, there are artists somewhere right now who are suffering from repeated respiratory infections, which are actually due to inhalation of irritating dusts or solvents. Such infections might even be manifestations of early silicosis. There are others, constantly fatigued, who are actually suffering from low-level lead intoxication, chronic carbon monoxide inhalation, or who may be in the early stages of occupationally induced blood diseases such as leukemia. These conditions are often attributed by the artists to other causes. Even well-meaning physicians who are not trained in occupational medicine commonly misdiagnose these conditions.

These artists could do a lot to protect themselves from chronic illness and aid physicians in making diagnoses if they knew what toxic chemicals were present in their art materials and what symptoms they can produce. We must educate ourselves about the effects of toxic materials and the proper precautions necessary to work safely with these chemicals.

HOW MATERIALS AFFECT US

The symptoms produced by toxic chemicals will vary with the amount of a material to which we are exposed. In general, the effects of toxic materials on the body can be divided into two categories of illness—acute and chronic.

Acute and chronic effects

An *acute* effect results from exposure to a toxic material in a single dose large enough to produce harmful effects within a relatively short period of time. It is usually not difficult to diagnose an acute illness because cause and effect are easily connected. For example, narcosis (headache, loss of coordination, nausea, and dizziness) is a common acute effect of intense exposure to solvents such as lacquer thinner or turpentine.

A *chronic* effect is harder to diagnose. Chronic effects are produced by repeated exposure to low doses of toxic materials, usually over a long period of time. Symptoms may vary from individual to individual. For example, exposure to the same lacquer thinner at lower doses over a period of months or of years on a regular basis might produce individualized chronic effects like dermatitis (if skin contact were involved), psychological problems (apathy, irritability, depression, etc.), liver damage, and nervous system damage. Another example of a chronic or long-term effect is cancer, which in some cases can take up to 40 years to develop. Examples of materials used by artists that may cause various types of cancer are benzene, asbestos, benzidine-based dyes, lead chromate used as a ceramic colorant and a pigment in some paints and inks, and uranium compounds (used in some photographic toners and glazes).

Are you at risk?

You should ask yourself a number of questions to determine the extent of your risk from exposure to toxic materials.

1. *How much do you use?* Keep track of the amounts of material you use. A pint of solvent, for example, presents a smaller hazard than a quart.

2. *Under what conditions are you exposed?* How close is your contact with the material? For example, do you get it on your hands or breathe its vapors? A pint of solvent, for instance, is less hazardous if it is used with good ventilation than if you use it in a small unvented room.

3. *How often are you exposed?* The body will tolerate exposure once a month better than daily exposure.

4. *How long are you exposed?* A few minutes' exposure to a chemical presents a smaller risk than exposure for many hours. The government standards for permissible exposure levels are based on an eight-hour day. This allows the body 16 hours to detoxify and excrete materials. If you work more than eight hours (a common occurrence among artists), you experience a substantially higher degree of hazard. The worst exposure occurs when you also work

with the same materials at home when you free lance in addition to your regular job. Lingering fumes and dusts in your home can mean that you are exposed for 24 hours a day.

5. *How toxic is each material you use?* Some materials are more toxic than others. The higher the toxicity, the less of a material it takes to cause harm. Among the most toxic compounds are those that are not easily eliminated from the body and tend to accumulate (such as lead). Learn which chemicals you use are the most dangerous.

6. *What is your "total body burden?* The total body burden of a particular substance is the amount of that substance in your body from all sources. For example, if you are an average city dweller, you already have a total body burden of lead from pollution (air, water, food, smoking) that is higher than experts would like it to be. If you add more from workplace exposure to lead-containing materials like paints, your total body burden of lead may be a source of real concern.

7. *Are you exposed to many different chemicals?* If you are exposed to several chemicals all of which can cause injury to the same organ, then the total damage to that organ is the sum of the contributions from each chemical. For example, if you are exposed to several solvents all of which damage the liver and you also consume alcohol, the total liver damage is the result of the toxic action of each of the solvents plus the alcohol. In addition, some chemicals will act together synergistically to produce an effect much greater than expected. The well-known interaction of barbiturates with alcohol is an example of synergism. Another example is smoking and inhalation of toxic dusts such as asbestos. People exposed to asbestos increase their chances of developing lung cancer by five times. If the exposed people are also smokers, they increase their chances of developing lung cancer 92 times. This is a classic example of synergism. We are only beginning to identify many more examples of this effect among various chemicals.

8. *Are you a member of a high risk group?* Government standards that specify the amounts of various substances to which workers can be exposed safely are based on the tolerances of *healthy adults*. High risk groups which may not be able to tolerate these levels include children, the elderly, those with pre-existing illnesses, those taking medication, people with allergies or sensitivities, pregnant women, smokers, and drinkers.

How toxic materials enter the body

Toxic materials must enter the body in order to cause damage. Three ways this can occur are through skin contact, through inhalation, and through the mouth and digestive system.

- *Skin contact.* The skin's barrier of dead cells and waxy layers can be penetrated by chemicals such as caustics, acids, solvents, peroxides and bleaches. Once past the skin's defenses, these chemicals can damage the skin or tissues deep beneath the skin, and some may enter the blood stream. In addition, once the skin is damaged either by chemicals or by cuts and abrasions, many other chemicals which normally would not be hazardous now are able to damage the skin or enter the blood stream. Some chemicals penetrate the skin's barrier directly and enter the blood stream without your knowing it. Among these are phenol, benzene, toluene, xylene, and methyl alcohol.
- *Inhalation.* When inhaled, some chemical vapors and fumes can damage or attack lung tissue immediately. Among these are welding fumes, resin vapors, and fumes from heating some plastics. Other chemicals such as some dusts and mists may take longer to act and can cause chronic irritation or illness. In general, the smaller the dust or mist particle, the greater the damage it can cause. Examples of chronic lung diseases are chronic bronchitis and emphysema. In addition, many substances can pass through lung tissue into the bloodstream where they can reach other organs. Examples are liver damage resulting from the inhalation of solvent vapors and nerve damage resulting from inhalation of lead-containing spray paints.
- *Ingestion.* Most ingestion of toxic materials is caused by hand-to-mouth contact with soiled hands, for example, when eating, smoking, biting nails, or licking fingers to turn pages. Inhaled dusts or mists also can be ingested when they are trapped in lung mucous, coughed up, and then swallowed.

Occupational diseases

Once in the body, each different chemical produces its own particular effects or disease. Correct diagnosis of occupational illness often requires the unique skills of doctors who specialize in occupational medicine or toxicology. Here are only a few of the many diseases that theater people might develop and a few of the chemicals that might cause them:

- *Allergies to sensitizers*: Sensitizers are chemicals that can produce allergic responses such as asthma or allergic dermatitis in significant percentages of those exposed. Known sensitizers include epoxy resins and glues, formaldehyde, polyurethane resins (diisocyanates), cold water dyes, turpentine, some wood dusts, chromium, and nickel.
- *Metal fume fever*: A temporary flu-like disease usually caused by inhalation of zinc and copper fumes from welding or soldering (not to be confused with the same early symptoms of cadmium poisoning, which can be fatal, caused by inhaling fumes from cadmium-containing metals or solders).
- *Primary dermatitis*: From acids, alkalis, solvents and all chemicals that can irritate or remove oils from the skin.
- *Allergic dermatitis*: From turpentine, epoxy, nickel, chromium, formaldehyde, and some woods.
- *Skin cancer*: From ultraviolet light, carbon black pigments, and arsenic compounds.
- *Lung fibrosis*:From silica (silicosis), asbestos (asbestosis), beryllium, and some woods.
- *Pulmonary pneumonia*: From nitrogen dioxide (from etching baths), cadmium fumes, chlorine, and ozone.
- *Lung cancer:* From asbestos, smoking, and inhalation of chromium- and nickel-containing fumes, dusts, or pigments.
- *Hepatitis*: From chlorinated hydrocarbons, toluene, and many other solvents, styrene (used in polyester resin casting), lead, cadmium, and phenol compounds.
- *Liver cancer:* From chlorinated hydrocarbons such as vinyl chloride used in old spray cans.
- *Bladder cancer*: From benzidine-type dyes.
- *Heart damage*: From carbon monoxide, methylene chloride, methyl chloroform, and barium compounds.
- *Nervous system damage*: From mercury, lead, manganese, arsenic, n-hexane, methyl butyl ketone, and all solvents to varying degrees. Both acute and chronic effects are possible, depending on the solvent.

WHAT CAN YOU DO ABOUT IT?

Use label information

Do not buy unlabeled materials. Read labels carefully, although many products (especially art materials) are incompletely labeled. For additional information, write to the manufacturer's address on the label and ask for a Material Safety Data Sheet (OSHA 20 form). Manufacturers are not required by law to give you a copy of this form, but many reputable manufacturers will. These forms include information on hazardous ingredients, fire and explosion data, health hazard data (only acute hazards—not chronic hazards such as cancer), special protective equipment and ventilation to be used with the material, and more. The quality of this information will vary greatly depending on the care with which the company prepares these forms, but they are a good addition to label information.

Use safer substitutes

1. *Use the least toxic material for each job.* Many products are more hazardous than they need to be. Compare labels on similar products to see which contains the least toxic ingredients. An example would be to substitute acetone, whenever possible, for commercial lacquer thinners, which are usually a mixture of more toxic solvents.

2. *Switch to the water-based or latex products whenever possible.* Solvents are among the most hazardous chemicals used in art. Try to replace solvent-containing products such as oil-based paints and enamels when possible. Watch for the appearance of new and improved water-based paints and inks as the marketplace responds to the restrictions placed on the sale of photoreactive (smog-causing) solvents by ecologically minded state legislatures. For example, several water-based silkscreen systems have recently been introduced to the art market.

3. *Choose products that don't create dusts and mists.* Try to buy products that are in solution rather than in powdered form, and avoid aerosol cans and spray products whenever possible to avoid inhalation of toxic chemicals.

4. *Avoid products containing carcinogens.* Contrary to popular opinion, there are relatively few carcinogens among the vast num-

ber of chemicals used in art. Keep abreast of information about cancer-causing chemicals and replace products that contain them. Remember, although there is no safe level of exposure to carcinogens, the lower the exposure the lower the risk.

Ventilate

Ventilation is the most important defense against toxic materials. Open windows and doors, air conditioners, or fans that simply circulate the air in the room are not good ventilation. In most cases, installation of proper ventilation requires professional advice. There are two basic types of ventilation: general or dilution and local exhaust.

1. *General or dilution ventilation* dilutes airborne toxic chemicals with fresh air, producing a lower, safer concentration through the combined action of exhaust fans and make-up air inlets which replace exhausted air. For example, fresh air enters a room at one end through an opening or a blower. This fresh air mixes with the contaminated air in the room, while an exhaust fan located at the other end of the room removes the mixed air to the outside.

General ventilation systems produce air currents, making them unsuitable for any dust-generating art operations, since such currents make it impossible to avoid inhaling the dust. These systems are also incapable of controlling large amounts of toxic vapors or highly toxic materials. They are suitable for operations where small amounts of materials are produced, such as in acrylic or oil painting studios.

2. *Local exhaust ventilation* captures the toxic materials at their sources before they can contaminate the general air in the room, and removes the captured material to the outside air by means of hoods, ducts, and fans. Local exhaust systems are preferred to general ventilation systems, because they do not agitate the air, they remove contaminants before they get into the general air, and they are more energy efficient. (They require smaller fans and move less air to the outside, thereby lowering heating and cooling costs.)

Examples of local exhaust systems include spray booths which use a fan to pull the spray mist away from the operator; canopy hoods over ceramic kilns to collect rising hot gases and fumes and remove them; and slot vents behind photochemical baths, acid etching baths, or at the back of air brush tables to remove airborne materials away from the operator and to the outside air.

Rules for Good Ventilation

1. Use local exhaust ventilation rather than general dilution ventilation whenever possible.
2. Have all systems designed, installed, and maintained by qualified professionals.
3. Provide adequate make-up air to replace exhausted air.
4. Arrange tables and work areas so that fresh air is drawn through the workers' breathing zones before being contaminated.
5. Enclose the source of contamination with the hood or collector so that toxic materials cannot escape.
6. Make sure that once air is exhausted it is not drawn back into the room or into some other area in which it is not welcome.

Personal protective equipment

Art processes employ a great number of toxic materials and produce dangerous byproducts such as heat, ultraviolet light (in welding, for example) and noise. The best solution is to keep on hand a variety of multipurpose protective devices.

- *Gloves*. A variety of different kinds and sizes of gloves to withstand heat, abrasion, or chemicals may be needed. To resist heat, woven fiberglass (not asbestos) gloves should be used. Chemical-resistant gloves, such as nitrile and neoprene gloves, should be chosen because of the large number of chemicals they can resist. Cotton work gloves can be used to resist abrasion.
- *Face and eye protection*. Impact-resistant goggles and face shields should be available in the shop. For welding use both face and eye protection that meet OSHA standards. (See section on OSHA.)
- *Hearing protection*. In general, hearing protection should be used if shop noise is at or above the level at which you must continually raise your voice to be heard by someone two feet away. One-size-fits-all earplugs are inexpensive in bulk and should be adequate for most shop circumstances.
- *Respiratory protection*. Ventilation, and not respiratory protection, should be the primary method employed for protection from airborne toxic substances. The Occupational Safety and Health Administration (OSHA) regulations make it clear that respiratory protection devices are to be used only when ventilation is not feasible (not likely in any art situation),

while ventilation is being installed, or for emergency situations. In addition, some people should never use respirators. Because all respirators increase breathing strain to some degree, *respirators should not be worn by most people who have heart or respiratory difficulties*. Consult your physician.

When purchasing masks, respirators, or filters, *buy only equipment that is "NIOSH-approved."*

- *Air-purifying respirators.* Respirators may be either disposable or reusable ones with replaceable filters or cartridges. Try them on before purchasing them to be sure they fit and are comfortable. Filters and cartridges provide protection only against certain types and levels of contaminants. For example, for protection from solvent vapors you would need an organic vapor cartridge, while a toxic dust filter would be needed for protection from dyes or pigment powders. Sometimes a combination of filters may be necessary. Choosing the right filters and respirators requires some thought and study.
- *Air-supplied respirators.* The two most common types of air-supplied respirators are airline and self-contained. The airline type has a hose which supplies clean air from an outside source. The self-contained type is similar to scuba-diving equipment, with air tanks usually carried on the back of the user.

Personal hygiene rules

1. Do not eat, smoke, or drink in the studio to prevent ingestion of small amounts of toxic materials. Smoking also can be a fire hazard, can increase the effects of hazardous materials on the lungs, and even can convert some materials into more hazardous forms. For example, methylene chloride used as a plastics and paint solvent can be converted into poisonous phosgene (war gas) by lit cigarettes.
2. Wear special work clothes and remove them after work. Wash them frequently and separately from other clothing. Don't wear scarves, ties, or loose clothing. Tie back long hair.
3. Wash hands carefully in soap and water after work, before eating, and during work breaks. Never use solvents to clean hands. If soap and water are insufficient, use waterless hand cleaners and follow with soap and water.
4. Wear gloves to protect hands against solvents, acids, and alkalis. Barrier creams may be used for light or occasional hand contact with irritating chemicals.

Storage and handling of materials

1. Label all containers clearly, noting both contents and hazards.
2. Use nonbreakable containers such as metal or plastic. Do not store large containers on high shelves where they are difficult to retrieve and might fall and break.
3. Do not store chemicals that may react with each other, such as peroxides with polyester accelerators.
4. To prevent escape of dust or vapors, keep all containers closed except when using them.
5. In case of accidental skin contact with toxic chemicals, wash affected areas with lots of water. In case of eye contact, rinse eyes for at least 15 minutes and seek medical help.
6. Do not sweep floors or brush dust off shelves. Use a wet mop or industrial vacuum cleaner with a filter system.
7. Dispose of waste or unwanted chemicals safely. For large amounts of regularly produced wastes, engage a waste disposal service. Do not pour solvents down the sink. Pour nonpolluting aqueous liquids down the sink *one at a time* and with lots of water to avoid reactions between chemicals. If you don't know how to dispose of a material, contact the manufacturer.
8. Clean up spills immediately so solvents won't evaporate and dust won't become airborne. Clean up flammable liquids with paper towels, place this waste in an approved, self-closing waste can, and empty the can daily.
9. Store quantities of solvents greater than one quart in approved, self-closing safety cans.
10. Do not store flammable or combustible materials near exits or entrances. Keep sources of sparks, flames, UV light and heat, as well as lighted cigarettes away from flammable or combustible solids or liquids.
11. Keep an ABC-type extinguisher handy and get training in how to use it.

Occupational Safety and Health Administration (OSHA)

The purpose of the Occupational Safety and Health Act of 1970 is to "assure safe and healthful working conditions for working men and women" by establishing and enforcing safety and health standards. All employees (not students) are protected except those in public agencies and their political subdivisions in certain states which have chosen not to come under the OSHA-approved state plans. This means that employees in state or municipal public schools in over half the states are not protected by OSHA. If you are a public employee, check to see if you come under OSHA's jurisdiction.

If you are protected by OSHA you have certain rights, one of which is to complain if you think your workplace is unsafe. In major cities, local OSHA offices are listed in the telephone book either under the Labor Department of the United States Government or under the States' Labor Departments in those states with a state plan.

The Center for Occupational Hazards*

The Center for Occupational Hazards (COH) is a national clearinghouse for research and information on health hazards in the arts, including the visual arts and crafts, theater, and museum conservation. COH has a number of programs.

1. *Art Hazards Information Center.* The Information Center, directed by Monona Rossol, researches, prepares, and collects written materials for dissemination to artists. It distributes about 50 different books, pamphlets, articles, and data sheets on art hazards. For example, there are publications to help you select the proper respirator or other personal protective equipment for your particular work, or to acquaint you with the hazards of your particular medium.

   It will also answer your letter or telephone inquiries about health-related matters directly. Enclose a self-addressed stamped envelope for a reply or a copy of their publications list.

2. *Art Hazards Newsletter.* COH publishes a four-page newsletter ten times a year. It covers such topics as new hazards, precautions, government regulations, lawsuits, a calendar of events, etc. Subscriptions cost $10 per year. Send a self-addressed stamped envelope for a sample copy.

3. *Lecture Program.* COH provides speakers on art hazards and precautions for lectures and workshops.

4. *Consultation Program.* Dr. Michael McCann, a certified industrial hygienist, conducts walkthrough surveys of art schools and art facilities and provides a written report on observed

---

*The Center for Occupational Hazards is located at 5 Beekman Street, New York, NY 10038. Telephone 212/227-6220.

hazards and recommendations for their correction. Write to inquire about fees and other particulars.

BIBLIOGRAPHY

American Conference of Governmetal Industrial Hygienists. *Respiratory Protective Devices Manual*. Cincinnati: ACGIH.

American Mutual Insurance Alliance. *Handbook of Organic Industrial Solvents, Technical Guide No. 6*, 5th ed. Chicago: Alliance of American Insurers, 1980.*

American National Standards Institute. *Safety in Welding and Cutting*. ANSI Z49.1. Miami: American Welding Society, 1973.

Barazani, Gail. *Ceramic Health Hazards*. Chicago, Ill., 1979.*

Carnow, Bertram. *Health Hazards in the Arts and Crafts*. Chicago: Hazards in the Arts, 1975.

Center for Science in the Public Interest. *Aerosol Spray Products: How Aerosols Can Affect Your Safety and Health*. Washington, D.C.

Committee on Industrial Ventilation. *Industrial Ventilation—A Manual of Recommended Practice*, 16th ed. Cincinnati: ACGTH, 1980.*

Davies, C.N. (ed.). *Health Conditions in the Ceramics Industry*. New York: Pergamon Press, 1969.

Gleason, Marion, Robert E. Gosselin, Harold C. Hodge, and Roger P. Smith. *Clinical Toxicology of Commercial Products*, 4th ed. Baltimore: Williams & Wilkins Company, 1976.

Hamilton, Alice and H. L. Hardy. *Industrial Toxicology*, 3rd ed. Acton, Mass.: Publishing Sciences Group, Inc., 1974.

Lead Industries Association. *Facts About Lead Glazes for Artists, Potters, and Hobbyists*. New York: Lead Industries Association.

McCann, Michael. *Artist Beware: The Hazards and Precautions in Working with Art and Craft Materials*. New York: Watson-Guptill Publications, 1979.*

McCann, Michael. *Health Hazards Manual for Artists*, revised ed. New York: Foundation for Community of Artists, 1978.*

*These publications are available from the Center for Occupational Hazards, 5 Beekman Street, New York, NY 10038.

McCann, Michael and Gail Barazani. *Proceedings: Health Hazards in Arts and Crafts Conference.* Washington, D.C.: SOEH, 1980.*

Moses, Cherie, James Purdham, Dwight Bowhay, and Roland Hosein. *Health and Safety in Printmaking: A Manual for Printmakers.* Edmonton, Alberta: Alberta Labour, 1978.*

Quinn, Margaret, Sharon Smith, Laura Stock, and Jeff Young (eds.). *What You Should Know About Health and Safety in the Jewelry Industry.* Rhode Island: Jewelry Workers' Health and Safety Research Group, 1980.*

Sax, N. Irving. *Dangerous Properties of Industrial Materials*, 4th ed. New York: Van Nostrand-Reinhold Company, 1975.

Siedlicki, Jerome. *The Silent Enemy*, 2nd ed. Washington, D.C.: Artists' Equity Association, 1975.

Stellman, Jeanne and Susan Daum. *Work Is Dangerous to Your Health*. New York: Vintage Paperbacks, 1973.

The Merck Chemical Index of Chemicals and Drugs, 9th ed. Rahway, N.J.: Merck and Company, 1976.

National Fire Protection Association. *Flammable and Combustible Liquids Code*, NFPA #30. Boston, 1973.

Waller, Julian and Lawrence Whitehead (eds.). *Health Hazards in the Arts: Proceedings of the 1977 Vermont Workshops.* Burlington: University of Vermont Department of Epidemiology and Environmental Health, 1977.*

---

*Ibid.

9

Understanding Financial Resources for Artists: The Visual Arts Program at the Arts Endowment

by

Jim Melchert

◆◆◆◆

JIM MELCHERT, Director of the Visual Arts Program at the National Endowment for the Arts from 1971 until 1981, is Professor of Art at the University of California, Berkeley.

◆ ◆ ◆ ◆

The Artists Fellowship category in the Visual Arts Program at the National Endowment for the Arts provides individual grants for visual artists of exceptional talent and demonstrated ability of any aesthetic persuasion. The artists to whom we award these fellowships include painters, sculptors, printmakers and artists specializing in the crafts, in photography, in drawing or artists' books, artists working in performance, video, conceptual modes and new genres.

We do not fund students pursuing their degrees or individuals who have received a major fellowship within the last two years. Primary consideration is given to artists who have never received a major fellowship from the Endowment.

The amount of a fellowship is $25,000, but a limited number of $5,000 fellowships are also given to emerging artists. During the Program's 14 years, 1,322 grants have been awarded for a total of $11,956,700. This year we received 10,162 applications, which indicates a significant and continuing increase in the number of artists who apply. In 1979, we received 7,275, in 1977, 5,865, and in 1975 we received 4,510. Statistically, it has turned out that the average age of those who apply is 35 or 36 years. Out of all the applications we receive, generally only about three percent receive funding.

We return all slides, videotapes, films and original works of art (photographs, prints, artists' books, etc.), and we make every effort to handle all the materials with care. The Endowment, however, cannot be responsible for any damage or loss, and it is always a good idea to insure your work. We do not return catalogues or reviews.

The specifics of the application process are spelled out in our guideline booklet, which is available on request from The Visual Arts Program, National Endowment for the Arts, 2401 E Street, N.W., Washington, D.C. 20506.

THE VISUAL ARTS PROGRAM

Many artists are aware of the Visual Arts Program, but often the information they have is third hand and inaccurate. Usually rumors have to do with strategies that you can use to increase your chances of getting a fellowship from the Visual Arts Program. It is sometimes tempting to think that factors other than the merit of your work are what will do the trick. For example, we hear that some artists believe it is better to use your parents' mailing address in Indiana than your own in New York, or the other way around. Actually it is not of much consequence where you are from. (If you look at statistics from previous years, you will find that about the same percentage of applications are funded from all the various regions of the country.) There is another rumor that regards that review as a lottery. It suggests that if you keep applying year after year you will eventually be successful. In reality, if your work is not growing and strengthening there is not likely to be a fellowship in your future no matter how persistently you reapply. Still another aspect of the lottery notion is that decisions will be made without a serious look at the slides you send in. It would be a mistake to believe that. The slides are the most important part of your application.

THE REVIEW PROCESS

Consider how your application is reviewed. As soon as it arrives at the Endowment, it is logged in and checked for completeness. It is given a number and placed in a separate file folder together with supplementary material that you may want to include. It is not a bad idea to send in catalogs of recent solo exhibitions you have had. Reviews of your work by critics, on the other hand, are not useful. When your slides come up for review, particularly after several viewings, the panel will begin referring to your file folder for more information about your career and your circumstances. The most telling part of your presentation, however, will be the ten slides you submit. (Or in the case of artists working in video, conceptual or performance areas, video tapes.) The images are projected on a wall, five at a time, and shown in chronological order from left to right. It often helps to include a few details among the ten. Generally speaking, the panelists get a better idea of what you do if you select work from a period of a few years. That is preferable to showing only the things that were included in your most recent exhibition. You have to decide what best represents your work and the direction it is taking.

The staff here prepares all the material for the panel review sessions, trying to anticipate any questions the panelists might have as they view the slides. As the panelists are narrowing their choices, they begin to take into account some of the circumstances of the artists under review. It is difficult to be more specific since the nature of the discussion among panelists varies with each set of slides.

The panel that will be looking at the material will be made up of three to six people. They sit together and watch the slides, and they rank each presentation according to how strong they feel the work is. When the score is tallied, applications that received high ranking are brought back to be shown again. At that point, discussion begins to get lively, especially if the panelists differ in their perception of what they are seeing. With each round of viewing, some applications are dropped and others are brought back for more viewing and further discussion.

THE IMPORTANCE OF SLIDES

It should be clear now how important the slides are in this process. You would be surprised at how many artists send in transparencies that are badly shot. Often the exposure will be so badly off that you cannot tell what is on the screen. Sometimes there will be so much glare on the surface of a painting that you cannot see the paints. Also, all too frequently, the slide will show the painting propped against a porch railing and a bicycle, and it gets lost in the clutter of the background.

Artists who have not yet learned to photograph their work would do well to find out how, if they plan to continue using slides to represent what they do. If you find that you cannot take good pictures, you would be well-advised to find someone who can and who would be willing to do it for you.

While Visual Artists Fellowships do not require a statement describing what you plan to do, there are other types of grants that artists can apply for from other agencies where a proposal is requested. (Many state and city arts councils now offer fellowship and project support for individual artists, as well as opportunities for public art commissions.) In that case, that applicant should be aware that simple, concise writing will be greatly appreciated. If the proposal meanders for paragraphs without getting to the point, no panelist will take an interest in it. It is a good idea to use the opening two sentences to lay out precisely what the project is about. After that you can go into details without worrying that the reader will get lost.

In case of grants that require a project description, make sure that what you are applying for is actually something you yourself want very much to do. Some people are clever at thinking up attractive proposals, but few of them have the kind of experience that is needed to do the project well. It is better not to waste your time gambling for grants or the time that panelists have to put into reading and evaluating them.

THE REVIEW PANEL

Who are the people who sit on panels and make decisions that affect artists? For the most part, they are artists who are known for having a particularly keen eye and who in the normal course of events see a great deal of artwork. They are selected by the staff. Usually the coordinator of an area for which a panel must be chosen submits a list of possible candidates. That person and the Program Director compare names from many lists, aiming for a group who will be knowledgeable and compatible.

Their final recommendations must then be approved by the Deputy Chairman in charge of Programs. Aside from having had long experience in the field, panelists are also chosen for their openness to a broad spectrum of aesthetic approaches. In addition to that, considering how many hours and days go into the deliberations, it is essential that the panel have considerable stamina and a sense of humor. Frequently we look for panelists among curators of museums as well as artists, or directors of artists' organizations who work closely with practicing professionals and who understand their lives and their work.

The composition of the grants panels changes continually. With a rotation system, it is possible to bring many points of view to the evaluation. The way that a panel views work one year may be completely different the next. The rotation system also allows many more people to take part in the responsibility of making decisions that affect the development of art in this country. Only occasionally will a panelist serve a second time for the sake of continuity.

Receiving a fellowship makes a number of things possible for an artist. It basically means that an artist can drop everything and concentrate on artmaking for a year. It means being able to work without interruption and with as few distractions as a person can manage. It also means getting hold of materials and whatever else may be needed. To put it another way, the fellowship provides a chance for an artist to devote his or her time to doing major work at a point when that person is ready to take it on.

WHEN TO APPLY

It has been the policy of the Visual Arts Program to let the artist decide when s/he is ready to submit an application. Too often an artist applies before being anywhere near ready for the heavy competition that exists in such a review. Most applications that are sent in are, in fact, submitted prematurely, when the work largely reflects the thinking and stylistic approach of another more experienced artist. All too frequently, applicants will try to compete even though their efforts fail to go beyond the obvious. In the past, the panels have not responded favorably to work that simply restates what is already known, or lacks fresh, original insight.

Artists who are considering submitting their material for a fellowship review are advised to take timing into account and apply only when they feel they are ready.

Artists who are associated with an arts organization may want to consider other categories of funding that are described in the Program Guidelines. There are opportunities for communities to get assistance in commissioning works of art for public places. Assistance is also available for organizations that provide artists with facilities for producing new art or for exhibiting work. There is also a category whereby artists' organizations can get matching funding for their publications, for seminars, short-term workshops, or visiting artists' programs.

Other sources of funding that you may find helpful are local and state arts commissions. They too will have information and guidelines that you can get by calling them directly or by writing.

10

Understanding Financial Resources for Artists: Art in Public Places

by

Patricia Fuller

◆◆◆◆

PATRICIA FULLER, formerly the administrator of the Art in Public Places grant category in the Visual Arts program at the National Endowments for the Arts, is currently a consultant in the area of Public Art at the University of Minnesota's Center for Art and Environment. While at the Endowment she also advised other federal agencies, including the Veterans Administration and the General Services Administration, in their Art-in-Architecture programs.

◆ ◆ ◆ ◆

During the past 15 years interest and activity in public art have grown dramatically across the country. At the national level, the National Endowment for the Art's *Art in Public Places* grant category and the General Services Administration's *Art-in-Architecture* Program have heightened the visibility of art in public places and have broadened support and stimulus for increased activity at the state and local levels.

PROGRAMS THAT SUPPORT PUBLIC ART

The concept of percent-for-art as a legislative strategy, which insures the inclusion of artwork in public construction projects, has gained broad acceptance, and many public agencies have set aside funds for art in major building projects as a matter of policy—even where legislation does not require it. Commissions for art in public places continue to be initiated and supported through the efforts of private organizations and citizens' groups as well.

The result has been a broadening range of opportunities for artists to work in public contexts—at sites ranging from major downtown revitalization projects to parks, transit facilities, public buildings and public school, college and university campuses. As experience has been gained, an even greater range of media has been opened up for exploration. Light, sound, and a variety of non-traditional materials have been used by artists in public settings as contemporary extensions of public art.

This proliferation of activity at many levels and through various agencies has led to some confusion both in gaining information about, and in distinguishing among, the various programs. What follows is a brief guide to the major areas and types of support for art in public places, as well as identification of some of the more important points to consider in undertaking public commissions.

ART IN PUBLIC PLACES

The Art Endowment's Art in Public Places grant category, located in the Visual Arts Program, was initated in 1967. Grants of up to $50,000 are made to organizations so that they can sponsor public commissions in their communities. Eligible grantees include state and local governments or their agencies (such as arts commissions, housing and redevelopment authorities), or private nonprofit agencies (such as ad-hoc citizens' committees, universities and colleges). Grants are given to match dollars that are raised, or that are set aside through percent-for-art, to support the local commissions in the fabrication and installation of works by living American artists. Applicants are responsible for selecting both the site and the artists prior to requesting matching funds; applications are reviewed by a national panel of experts from the field for decisions on funding. The projects are carried out locally, each grantee being responsible for all the aspects of implementation once the grant is awarded.

For further information, see the Visual Arts Program's guidelines for the current fiscal year, available from the National Endowment for the Arts, 2401 E Street, N.W., Washington, D.C. 20506.

ART-IN-ARCHITECTURE

The General Services Administration's Art-in-Architecture Program was begun in 1963 by administrative directive, and it has continued without legislation, subject to periodic suspension, to the present. The GSA policy calls for setting aside ½ percent of the construction budget for each new federal building built by the agency. (Not all federal buildings are under GSA jurisdiction. Post offices generally are not; whole federal office buildings and courthouses generally are.) The architect is encouraged to plan for works of art in the design, and when GSA is ready to bring an artist in (usually when the building is well into construction), the Arts Endowment is requested to convene a panel to nominate artists available for selection. The Visual Arts Program has the responsibility of appointing a three-member, ad-hoc panel of experts in contemporary art—such as artists, critics, educators and curators. The architect sits as the fourth member of the panel. The group meets at the site and nominates between three and five artists, who are chosen on the basis of their past work and ability to deal with the site within the given budget. The GSA then makes the final selection and invites the artist to visit the site—at the artist's expense. If the artist accepts the commission they negotiate a contract; otherwise the second-ranked artist is offered the job, and so on, until a contract is signed. The artist is then responsible for all costs—travel, expenses, materials, fabrication and installation of the work. He is not, however, responsible for site preparation.

All GSA commissions are negotiated and administered by its Art-in-Architecture program staff based in Washington, D.C. The program maintains a registry of slides and biographical material of artists interested in being considered for these commissions. The registry is reviewed by the program staff prior to each on-site panel meeting, and slides of work by artists who might be appropriate are presented to the panel for consideration.

Further information on this program is available from the Director, Art-in-Architecture, General Services Administration, Washington, D.C. 20405.

VETERANS ADMINISTRATION ART-IN-ARCHITECTURE PROGRAM

In 1979 the Veterans Administration, which constructs and operates medical facilities across the country, instituted a similar Art-in-Architecture program. Again, ½ percent of the construction budget—up to a maximum of $50,000—is set aside, and similar procedures for the selection of artists and commissions are followed. A registry of artists is also maintained at the Veterans Administration.

For further information contact the Director, Art-in-Architecture Program, Veterans Administration, 811 Vermont Avenue, N.W., Washington, D.C. 20402.

Other federal agencies which do not generally undertake construction projects but fund them at the local and state level, such as the Department of Transportation and the Department of Housing and Urban Development, have encouraged the inclusion of artwork as a local option. The Department of Transportation has published a guide to assist in planning for public art in such projects as transit facilities, airports and highways: "Aesthetics in Transportation." It is available from the Superintendent of Documents, U.S. Government Printing Office, Washington, D.C. 20402.

Generally, the plan for including artwork must be part of the initial application and budget submitted to the federal funding agency by the local community. Therefore it is the responsibility of local arts groups and interested citizens to become involved in the planning of such projects and to insure that artwork is included.

PERCENT-FOR-ART PROGRAMS

Percent-for-art legislation has created more than forty continuing programs at the state and local level to commission art for public places. The actual percentage of construction funds set aside and the procedures that are followed vary widely among jurisdictions. Access to information about these programs and current commissions has been difficult to obtain, although better dissemination of information to make more artists aware of such programs and commissions seems to be the trend. Many of these programs maintain registries of interested artists, and advertise commissions regionally in arts publications. Some limit eligibility to artists within the jurisdiction or the surrounding region.

A current list of percent-for-art programs can be requested through the National Assembly of State Arts Agencies (NASAA), 1010 Vermont Ave., N.W., Washington, D.C. 20002. (NASAA provides information for programs at the state level.)

For programs at the local level, information is available through the National Assembly of Community Arts Agencies (NACAA), 1625 I Street, N.W., Washington, D.C. 20006. After receiving the information, you can then write to the individual programs and ask to be put on their mailing lists.

PUBLIC COMMISSIONS

Public commissions offer the opportunity to work on a scale, and with materials, that might otherwise be impossible. They also give artists the chance to explore new possibilities for the chosen sites, as well as the relationship of the work to the matrix of the built environment. Commissions also bring the process of creating a work into a public context, and this entails considerations and restraints that are not encountered in a studio, museum or gallery, or in situations involving private and corporate patronage.

The procedures for selecting artists vary considerably among the different programs, but three basic methods are in general use:

(1) open competition, (2) limited or invitational competition, and (3) direct selection. Many publicly legislated programs use open competition, and some use open competition exclusively. Usually a prospectus announces the competition and describes the site, the amount of the commission, and the parameters of the project. The announcement also invites proposals from artists. (If specifications for proposals are not given, it is important to check what restrictions may apply to size and materials, and whether models are expected.)

Open competitions are generally used on the assumption that they will reach the broadest possible range of artists and therefore offer the widest choice to those who make the decisions. Many artists, however, have pointed out drawbacks to the process. Only artists living near the site of the proposed project can actually visit and become familiar with its limitations and possibilities as the basis for a considered and feasible proposal. There is also no compensation for the time and materials an artist invests in the proposal. There have also been problems when proposals have been returned damaged, and in many cases proposals have not been returned at all! (It's a good idea to make sure your submissions are insured.) For these reasons, many artists are unwilling to make the speculative investment repeatedly required by the open competition process.

The limited or invitational competition presents fewer such drawbacks. Normally, between three and five artists are initially selected for the commission. Many sponsors advertise and invite the submission of slides to be considered by the selection panel. This system provides the same access to artists without requiring the speculative investment. Each artist is paid an honorarium—plus expenses—to cover the costs of visiting the site and developing a proposal. It may also be possible for the invited artist to renegotiate the requirements named in the proposal by requesting, for instance, the elimination of maquettes and the presentation of only drawings. Hidden costs can make what seems like a generous fee less than adequate. It is important to make clear at the outset whether developing the proposal will require such things as an engineering analysis of the site. In many cases necessary information, such as architectural plans and engineering drawings, already exists. In that case, it is the responsibility of the sponsor to supply such information for the artist's use. Otherwise, the proposal development fee should include those costs. Even if documentation of engineering and cost feasibility is not required, it is a very good idea to have those analyses made to insure that the work, if commissioned, can be executed within the budget. In the long run, it will be worth the extra expense.

Direct selection is the third method of choosing artists that is commonly used. Normally the selection committee meets at the site and considers a number of artists, finally agreeing on the one who seems best suited for the particular project. As with the invitational competition, sponsors may first invite the submission of slides by artists for the consideration of the panel, or they can draw on available slide registries. The chosen artist is then invited to the site at the sponsor's expense. If the artist accepts, a contract is negotiated for the commission.

NEGOTIATING CONTRACTS

Once the artist agrees to accept the commission, a written contract should be negotiated between the artist and the sponsor. While some public agencies have developed their own standard contracts, the important points can usually be covered in two or three pages and need not be phrased in complex legal language. The important function of a contract is to make clear and equitable the responsibilities and expectations of each party. Contracts usually remove the possibility of misunderstanding and prevent disputes which could jeopardize completion of the project or lead to costly legal proceedings. In all cases, the advice of a lawyer is recommended in the design of an equitable and workable agreement. Presented here are some major points to consider in contracting for a public art commission:

Budget

Usually the artist's commission must cover the cost of materials, fabrication, transportation, installation, and the artist's fees and expenses. The sponsor is usually responsible for preparation of the site (foundation, landscaping, water supply, etc.), and in some cases the sponsor may provide or arrange for donation of materials, fabrication or labor and equipment for installation. These responsibilities should be clarified at the outset and set down in the agreement.

Proposal

A preliminary proposal is generally required as the first step, if it was not already used as the basis for selection. Usually a portion of the commission amount is allocated as the proposal fee and is paid on submission by the artist of the proposal. As with the invitational competition, it should be adequate to cover costs of travel to the site and the materials and time invested.

The process for review and the agency or individual(s) responsible for approval of the proposal should also be designated in order to avoid later confusion and delay. A time limit can also be determined. The parameters of the costs involved should be spelled out too, as should be the steps to be taken in the event of rejection. In some cases the artist may want to reserve the right to submit an alternative proposal or retain ownership of the proposed materials. In such cases the proposal fee might be adjusted.

Timetable

All parties should agree upon a timetable and set up a procedure for extending the deadlines if problems should arise. Construction schedules should be consulted if the commission site is under construction. Difficulties in locally obtaining materials and labor, and construction delays are typical problems, and should be taken into consideration.

Schedule of payments

Normally payments to the artist are made sequentially, and often a substantial advance is required to purchase materials. The final payment is usually made on completion of the installation. Intermediary payments should be linked to stages of completion, not to dates.

Dealers' fees

The National Council on the Arts (the Presidentially appointed advisory committee to the National Endowment for the Arts) has approved the policy that a dealer's fee should not exceed 10 percent of the artist's fee for commissions funded in part through the Endowment's Art in Public Places grants. This is widely used as a guideline in the field, although agreements between artists and dealers vary widely. Most often, if commissions are covered in such agreements, they are handled differently than are gallery sales. In fact, many artists act independently in the area of public commissions. It is important to agree on the dealer's role at the outset, particularly if it has not been previously established. Other matters between artist and sponsor which should be clarified at the outset and which may become part of the agreement include:

- *Access to information and cooperation,* if the commission is part of a site under design or construction. Coordination with architects, engineers, contractors and others becomes critical in planning and executing the work. It is the sponsor's responsibility to facilitate this coordination and to make pertinent plans and documents available to the artist.
- *Care and maintenance of the work.* This is also the long-term responsibility of the sponsor, and procedures should be established at the outset. The artist may in turn be required to address problems of maintenance in the design of the work and provide detailed specifications for proper care of the work.

The contract itself cannot cover all aspects of a project, and there are certain broad responsibilities that are difficult to define but equally crucial to the success of public commissions. Public information and relations with the community at large must be effectively handled to avoid any misunderstandings or controversy that might jeopardize or delay the project. Like fundraising, this is the responsibility of the sponsoring group. A project for which an effective strategy for fundraising and public information has not been adequately planned is a risky undertaking. While the artist should not be placed in the position of soliciting funds or defending the project, participating in a dialogue with the public is important to inform and develop support in the community. Sponsoring agencies may plan activities, such as symposia or lecture series, which involve the artist, or they may ask the artist to exhibit some of his work. Expectations as to the nature of these activities should also be discussed early on, and the artist and sponsor should be in agreement. The assumption is not that public discussion is negative or should be avoided; quite the opposite—this dialogue is an important aspect of art in public places. It is clear that destructive controversy can be avoided by those sponsors and artists who work to inform the community about the planned piece of artwork, and who invite discussion of it.

Included here is a sample contract designed by the Seattle Arts Commission for art in public places, which has been used successfully several times. As you can see, it is not a complex document. It is included as a possible model for use by other sponsoring organizations.

Also available is a publication surveying the projects that have been carried out with support for the Endowment's Art in Public Places category since its inception in 1967. It is distributed by Partners for Liveable Places, 2120 P Street, N.W., Washington, D.C. 20037.

Sample Commission
Agreement Used by
The City of Seattle

AGREEMENT

THIS AGREEMENT is entered into by The City of Seattle (hereinafter referred to as "The City"), acting by and through the Seattle Arts Commission and the Executive Secretary thereof, and_____ (hereinafter referred to as the "Artist").

WHEREAS, the City is implementing a public art program pursuant to Ordinance 102210, as amended, by allocating certain funds for the establishment of artworks in public places and authorizing the making of payments for the design, execution and placement of works of art and the support of an artist-selection process; and

WHEREAS, Seattle_____Department 1% for Art funds have been allocated for the selection, purchase and placement of artwork (hereinafter referred to as the "_____Project"); and

WHEREAS, the Artist was selected by the City through procedures duly adopted by the Seattle Arts Commission; and

WHEREAS, both parties wish the integrity and clarity of the Artist's ideas and statements in the artwork to be maintained;

NOW THEREFORE, in consideration of the mutual covenants hereinafter contained, the parties hereto agree as follows:

1. Description of Work. The Artist shall design, fabricate and install the following work of art:

The above work of art hereinafter referred to as the "Work."

2. Scope of Work. The Artist shall accomplish the following:

3. <u>Price and Payment Schedule</u>. As payment for the services of the Artist and for the completed Work and subject to the conditions herein, the City shall pay the Artist the total sum of _____
_____($) upon invoice from the Artist as follows:

      a) 30 percent upon signing of this Agreement;
      b) 30 percent upon commencement of facrication;
      c) 30 percent upon commencement of installation
      d) 10 percent upon completion and acceptance of the Work
         by the Arts Commission.

4. <u>Sales Taxes</u>. Sales taxes shall be payable by the City in addition to the actual final cost set forth above.

5. <u>Non-Discrimination</u>. In carrying out the performance of the services designated, the Artist shall not discriminate as to race, creed, religion, sex, age, national origin or the presence of any physical, mental or sensory handicap, and the Artist shall comply with the equality of employment opportunity provisions of Seattle Ordinance 101432 as presently existing or hereafter amended.

6. <u>Review</u>. The City shall have the right at reasonable times to review the Work while in the process of execution and to receive progress reports.

7. <u>Protection of Premises</u>. The Artist must take all reasonable precautions to protect City property adjacent to the installation site of the Work. The Artist will be responsible for securing adequate protection of the public during installation.

8. <u>Liability</u>. The Artist shall indemnify and hold the City harmless from any and all loss, claims, actions, or damages suffered by any person or persons not a party to this Agreement by reason of, or resulting from, performance or alleged lack of performance under this Agreement. In the event that any suit based upon such loss, claims, actions, or damages is brought against the City, the Artist shall, upon notice of the commencement thereof, defend the same at its sole cost and expense; and if final judgment be adverse to the City, or the City and the Artist jointly, the Artist shall promptly satisfy the same. The liability described in this Section shall not be diminished by the fact, if it be a fact, that any such death, injury, damage, loss, cost or expense may have been contributed to, or may be alleged to have been contributed to in part, by the negligence of the City, its officers, employees or agents; Provided that nothing contained in this Section shall be construed as requiring the Artist to indemnify the City against liability for damages arising out of bodily injury to persons or damage to property caused by or resulting from the sole negligence of the City, its officers, employees or agents.

9. Compliance with Laws. The Artist shall comply with all applicable federal and state laws, the Charter and ordinances of the City of Seattle, and rules and regulations of the administrative agencies of all such governmental units.

10. Notice. A public notice, including the Artist's name and mention of the City's ownership, shall be publicly displayed and identified with the Work, and shall be designed, fabricated, installed and paid for by the Artist.

11. Guarantee. The Artist shall guarantee to repair or replace any defects of material or workmanship in the Work for a period of up to one year from installation.

12. Non-Destruction/Alteration. The City shall not intentionally destroy the Work during the Artist's lifetime, without the Artist's written consent. Alteration of the Work other than restoration or maintenance shall not be done during the Artist's lifetime without the Artist's written consent. The City has the right to restore and maintain the work as it deems necessary.

13. No Waiver. No waiver of full performance by either party shall be construed, or operate, as a waiver of any subsequent default of any of the terms, covenants and conditions of this Agreement. The payment or acceptance of fees for any period after a default shall not be deemed a waiver of any right or acceptance of defective performance.

14. No Assignment or Transfer. The rights and privileges granted by this Agreement are not subject to assignment, or transfer in any manner whatsoever, without the prior written consent of the City. The giving of a consent to an assignment or transfer shall not authorize a further assignment of lease or transfer without further prior written consent by the City.

15. Excuse and Suspension of Contractual Obligations. The parties hereto shall be excused from their affected contractual obligations when their performance is prevented by acts of God, war, war-like operations, civil commotion, riots, labor disputes including strikes, lock-outs and walk-outs, sabotage, governmental regulations or controls, fire, or other casualty. Failure to fulfill contract obligations due to conditions beyond either party's reasonable control will not be considered a breach of contract; Provided, those obligations affected shall be suspended only for the duration of such conditions. During the existence of any such condition, both parties shall use a reasonable effort to protect each other's property, equipment and inventory.

16. Documentation. As documentation of the Work, the Artist shall provide one unmarked 35 mm. color slide, accurate in color and detail, and the information to complete the catalogue worksheet (Attachment A).

17. Records. The City shall maintain on permanent file a record of this Agreement and of the condition and location of the Work as long as the City is the owner of the Work.

18. Reproduction. The Artist shall retain the copyright and all other rights in and to the Work except ownership and possession; Provided that the Artist grants to the City an irrevocable license to reproduce the Work in any manner whatsoever, for non-commercial purposes.

19. Amendments. No modification or amendment of the terms hereof shall be effective unless written and signed by authorized representatives of the parties hereto. The parties hereto expressly reserve the right to modify this Agreement from time to time by mutual agreement.

20. Entire Agreement. This Agreement is all of the covenants,promises, agreements, and conditions, either oral or written, between the parties.

For Seattle Arts Commission:

_____
Karen A. Gates
Executive Secretary
Date:_____

_____
Date:_____
Address:_____
_____

Marketing

11

Career and the Artist

by

Henry Geldzahler

◆ ◆ ◆ ◆

HENRY GELDZAHLER is Commissioner of Cultural Affairs of the City of New York. Prior to his appointment, Mr. Geldzahler served as curator of the Department of 20th Century Art at the Metropolitan Museum and Director of Visual Arts at the National Endowment for the Arts.

◆ ◆ ◆ ◆

Picasso, as he so often did, said it best: An artist must be two people—one who knows how to paint, one who knows when to stop. We all know the old anti-abstraction anecdote about the chimpanzee who, given paper and colors, does a creditable "painting," which is subsequently entered in the local art show and wins a prize. What is less well known is that, left alone, the chimp will continue to apply color to the paper until he gets restless, then will roll the paper into a ball and eat it. What of those chimpanzee paintings the popular press loves so often? Ah, they were snatched away from the chimp by a curator at the moment he or she thought they were most ripe and ready. Who then is the artist?

Picasso was one man who knew when to paint and when to stop. The chimp knows how to paint; the curator when to stop. Picasso is alone; the other two form a team, the nucleus of what in European and Latin American art of the 1960's and 70's was called an *equipe* or *equipo*.

The artist must often feel like a chump, dependent on the whims, commercial sense, altruism and general apathy of others— dealers, curators, deans. The system works, of course, but not well and not for everybody.

The question broached by this publication is this: can a handbook on artists and career be useful? The answer is *yes*, when it comes to such technical matters as taxes, materials, apprenticeship programs, and legal rights. *No*, if the question is how can I make better art. The answer still lies in the private sector, in fact, with the artist. No semigovernmental tract can possibly help.

THE REAL QUESTION

All technical questions such as what laws govern the establishment of a cooperative gallery and when artists can be held liable can be addressed by specialists. Even such quasipersonal matters as how best to present my work, whether to make appointments with dealers through their secretaries, and with which ones is it better to drop in, unannounced, before rather than after lunch, can be answered. But in my opinion all such considerations are rococo frippery compared to the bare and basic query: how good is my *art* (not my career), how original, to what extent is it consonant with my intention, what is my ambition for it, and does it have (this must be asked as diligently of abstraction) redeeming social value, does society have any need of it or use for it? These are the questions that hurt.

THE INFLUENCE OF THE ARTIST

The influence of the artist on American life and style goes far beyond his work as seen in the art gallery and museum. In the past hundred years the artist, particularly the visual artist, has been the pioneer in many things other than the world of depicted forms; most obviously he has led the real estate developer by pointing out to the wealthy that poverty and disuse can make a stretch of coast or a deteriorating neighborhood romantic and desirable. We need only list St. Germain des Pres, the Hamptons, Provincetown, London's Chelsea, Sausalito, Cuernavaca, St. Migel Allende, and in New York the West Village and most recently and dramatically, SoHo and Tribeca.

In each case a hardy group of artists saw beauty and practicality in buildings and prospects invisible to others. In the case of SoHo, from the early nineteen-sixties, artists lived and worked out of abandoned spaces in loft buildings increasingly emptied of their light manufacturers. Some few had enough vision or cash to buy their buildings, or as sophistication grew, their co-op. With the growth of social and peer pressure to live and work in this geographically restricted area, prices rose, and landlords began to encourage artists to rent and renovate. Art galleries, boutiques, and restaurants came next. By the early nineteen-seventies prams, often with fathers at the helm, became common in this so recently light manufacturing district. The career of the artist merged insensibly with that of the minor real estate entrepreneur.

Something similar and, after the fact, equally predictable, happened in the blocks that surround the Lincoln Center complex, a project that was completed by the middle of the nineteen-sixties. Once again cultural activity became the lodestone for real estate development. Apartment houses, restaurant rows, and gentrification followed in much the same way as, a decade later, the Marais, a seventeenth century neighborhood in Paris around Beauborg, began to be rehabilitated and renovated.

For the artist, even one who interests himself only in what goes on in his own studio, alertness to the ways in which his neighborhood, or one he is contemplating moving to, is likely to change can save him the anguish of sudden surprise and displacement. The signs are apparent and easily noticed; count the fancy delis, and if there is more than one, buy your loft or start looking elsewhere. You don't want to fix up yet another place for a landlord or for the next owner.

On mature reflection I withdraw my earlier scowling attitude toward the subject of artist and career. While it is true that I feel altogether too much energy is wasted these days on the careerist and therefore is unavailable to the artist, there clearly are areas in which guidance of the kind available through experts, handbooks, and panels can be helpful.

I have however observed that it is not the cunning careerist who wins in the end. It is the careful nurturer who tills his garden daily and grows the most natural, organic, and unforced flowers—the most beautiful ones and those most esthetically "necessary" and satisfying. A successful career is, most often, the result of countless decisions made along the way, decisions that always intuitively support the art and, without ignoring life-style, give it the weight it deserves. Success is a reward. Making honest art is the goal. In the short run, career strategies can appear successful. In the long run, only the art remains as witness to a life.

12

The Integrity of the Artist, Dealer and Gallery

by
Tibor de Nagy

◆ ◆ ◆ ◆

TIBOR DE NAGY escaped from Hungary in 1948 and came to the United States via London in 1949. In 1950 he established the Tibor de Nagy Gallery in New York City. The gallery deals with contemporary painting, sculpture, and works on paper.

◆ ◆ ◆ ◆

Art is a personal expression no matter how much or how little it covers of the universe. Whatever it encompasses, it has to be a sincere vision. The technical skill with which it is created is essential for its success. I see, in every artist, a priest of his own religion who wants to deliver his sermon in order to collect his believers. The places where he exposes his beliefs are art institutions and galleries. There are many priests but hardly any saints within a given epoch.

I believe in complete freedom of expression. You have to choose your own god and interpret him in your own way. But you have to be sincere about it if you want your prayers to be appreciated and remembered.

The brilliant mechanisms built in our heads are glorified computers. The creator must have constructed a great variety of such computers to try them out on so many animals. They registered only what was needed for their survival and reproduction. It was only when he attached to the computer a channel that had a direct spiritual contact with him that the human brain was completed and he announced, "Ecce Homo!"

Once this computer is fed with the history of art and absorbs the influences of numerous works of art, soaks in beauty and horror, past and present circumstances and experiences, the result may be a mixture that is an intellectual production—or there may be only a copy of something that has been done before. When the artist is capable of associating with the spirituality of the universe—that is to say when his soul feeds the computer as well—then the miracle happens. A striking balance of intellectual and emotional experience makes a great artwork. An original artwork will delight the responsive viewer.

THREE GALLERIES

Then the priest starts looking for a temple that would expose his sermon. He will have to face three types of possibilities:

1. The pioneering galleries, of which there are very few because they are rarely self-supporting.
2. Galleries that work only with well-established artists because they are out to make money.
3. Interior decorator galleries, of which there are many. They deal in pretty paintings with pleasing subject matter, or else with art that is very much in fashion. Often they will exhibit only with payment of a fee.

My gallery—although in existence 31 years—still belongs in the first category and always will. It is, therefore, more interesting in my case to write about the coming-out period of the debutantes, than to concentrate on the high-geared business activities going on in the other two categories. The "Jus Prime Noctis" is a rather exciting experience. The virgin is so modest and yet so full of hope that one feels embarrassed even to talk business. The artist-dealer game starts!

THE ARTIST-DEALER GAME

The dealer-artist relationship is a rather complex one because it does not involve just commodities. It is rather like bringing up and exposing one's own daughters to society and then marrying them off as successfully as possible. Both parents will work together just as artists and dealers do for the best possible result.

Often even between the parents there are conflicting opinions as to what would be the most advantageous set of circumstances for solving the future of their offspring. Is the financial angle the most important? Or is it the moral standing and social position of the future husband (the place where the artwork finds its final home)? Should they expose and promote their daughter in a discreet, disciplined and most dignified way, or just do it without restriction and hesitation?

When an artist ties himself or herself down with an art gallery, its reputation should give a clue about the handling practice of its artists. The artist can then decide whether or not it appeals to him or her.

The real and most common danger that threatens a lasting good relationship is where the two parties' mutual interest drifts apart; where the sharing of the burden of expenses and the dividing of sales price is at stake—who pays for what and how much and how to split up the money received for the artwork.

Agreements and legal contracts may help the relationship over a short period, but a lasting and good relationship depends on the basic philosophy and integrity of the matched parties. If the artist feels that the amount the dealer gets as his share from the sale is not a "necessary must," but a well-deserved cut for the services the gallery renders, the relationship will be pleasant and will flourish. The artist has to be convinced that for all the dealer's promotional work, advertising, printing expenses, exhibitions and placing of artworks in other shows, and—last but not least—the tremendous expense of the overhead needed to keep the gallery going, he has to take such a cut.

The artist has to see clearly that, once his name is becoming known and a demand is established for his work, it would become more and more difficult to decide whose merit it is when a sale or commission comes through in the artist's studio. It is no doubt the result of previous combined efforts. It happens because customers and agents think that, through a direct purchase from the artist, they may get a better bargain because the percentage to the gallery in commission is avoided. This is often the key factor in the breaking-up of relationships. It can be avoided only if the artist refuses to sell from his or her studio and directs the party to the gallery, or else gives an agreed-upon share to the gallery of every studio sale. If that procedure is carried out with honesty, the relationship will not suffer and no paranoia will start poisoning the atmosphere.

ART ADVISORS

It has been interesting to see how our rapidly growing art market has brought along with it a new profession which has squeezed itself in between the art dealer and corporations, banks and even smaller business offices—the art advisors. Some of them are well qualified; some of them quite ignorant but charming people. Some of them have established in the course of time a good vision but some can not help remaining interior decorators. The quality of the corporations' art collections depends on them. Some of the art advisors are daring and ambitious and will want to educate the taste of their employers. But unfortunately the majority want to please unlettered executives with pretty, happy artworks—works that best fit the space and colors of the surroundings, just like a costume.

They not only take away business from dealers but also bring in much business which would not have happened without them. Whether they are salaried or not, they want a discount. Such discounts vary between 10 and 30 percent, thereby adding another problem to be worked out between the dealer and artist. Unfortunately, it is mostly the poor, not yet successful artist who has to share most of this added expense—not the rich ones who are in a position to dictate their terms.

Greediness will ruin a relationship. Therefore, in the long run, it will not benefit either the artist or the dealer. Sometimes marriages survive crises when adultery is confessed and the relationship gets back to normal. It is easier to forgive than to tolerate.

As a rule, artists are difficult—to say the least! Their emotions are more intense. Their egos are either enormous, or just the opposite, but they are never well balanced. Artists love and hate, and hardly ever feel neutral. Their enthusiasm is exaggerated. They recognize beauty faster. They are more sensitive in connection with other peoples' suffering. Their intellect keeps them from ever being boring to other people. Their jealousy tortures them day and night. They give more than they consume. In short, if you want a smooth existence, keep away from the art world. But if you want to really live—meaning suffer and burst out of joy—become involved with artists! You will never fade away; you will just die of exhaustion.

Generalizations are like statistics. They very often distort or even lie. The truth of the matter remains expressed in Goethe's *Faust*:

> He wants from the sky the fairest star, from earth the highest joy that's to be had: everything near and everything far can never satisfy his deeply stirred desire.

13

Promoting Yourself and Your Art

by
John E. Dowell, Jr.

◆ ◆ ◆ ◆

JOHN DOWELL is a painter, printmaker and performance artist. He is a professor of printmaking at the Tyler School of Fine Arts at Temple University in Philadelphia and also teaches a course on the business aspects of art.

◆ ◆ ◆ ◆

So you've decided to be an artist. You've already discovered you have the talent, the ability, to create art. What do you do with your artistic talent and your stack of canvases, once you've finished art school?

Today, art schools are filled to capacity. At this writing, in Philadelphia alone at some 20 art schools, more than 7,500 are enrolled. Many will graduate and promptly retire from the field. Why? Simply because they are not prepared to make a living as artists.

This chapter is about survival—how to succeed financially and support yourself as an artist. If you've got the determination and drive to "make it," here are some suggestions and techniques to consider.

SURVIVING AS AN ARTIST

Begin by realizing that you are really three persons wrapped up in one personality: (1) the creator of poetic visual statements, (2) the provider, who assembles the equipment, puts skills to work and uses the tools of inspiration and "artistic light" to create; and (3) the promoter who must take the products of his ideas and concepts and market them. You've got to get your work out there, whether you're doing it for fame and immortality, personal achievement, or simply for the money.

How does the artist pay for his studio, his equipment and life support system while he's in the creative process? In the past, there was a support system—the church, the wealthy, and academia served as patrons of the artist. Throughout history, the artist has been faced with a stigmatic duality: On the one hand, he is the manifestation of culture, providing status and immortality, making a few people very rich. On the other hand, he is the ward of a whimsical society, expected to conform to the old-saw work ethic of "suffer for success."

In the 1960's, the colleges and universities emerged to provide a support system for the artist: instructors were needed for the boom of art students. Today, the art department as a support system for the artist is virtually closed. Thousands of M.F.A.s are graduated each year with only several hundred new job openings in art departments of educational institutions.

If you want to survive as an artist, you've got to realize that *art is a business* and it must be conducted as such. No one is going to come banging down your studio door, there are few art-related alternative sources of employment, and in order to be successful, you've got to get into the art establishment—the Network.

UNDERSTANDING THE NETWORK

The Network consists of the dealer—gallery, agent or private consultant; the curator—museum, corporate collection, private collection and university collection; the art critic; and the collector. These are the components of the system with which you must learn to deal, on one level or another, in order to survive.

THE DEALER

The main wholesaler of art is the gallery/dealer, but there are several types of dealers. The agent serves as your representative to the business world. He negotiates everything, including details for exhibitions or gallery shows. He gets your work to collectors, to museum personnel, and to private dealers. In short, he is the artistic godfather, promoting you, selling your work and handling all the time-consuming details so you can be free to create. An agent receives a retainer fee and/or a percentage of all sales and, if you can arrange it, may take back some of your artwork as payment for his services.

A good agent is an artist's dream, but is very hard to find. If you can't train your spouse, you might consider training someone else to serve as your agent.

Private dealers sell by appointment only. They arrange sales presentations and parties in their homes or offices and sometimes on the premises of their clients. Some private dealers will rent gallery space for exhibitions and shows. The private dealer has an excellent mailing list of collectors, businesses, and corporations to whom he regularly sells.

Next is the art gallery with exhibition space for shows open to the public. There are all sizes and types of galleries. Few large galleries make sales solely from walk-in trade, but rather tailor their marketing to a specific clientele. Galleries also work with museums to arrange exhibitions and engineer purchases for museum collections. They deal with corporations and provide work from their stable of artists for corporate offices as well as for the corporate collection of art for investment. Galleries maintain lists of collectors to whom they regularly sell work; they also develop new collectors. Galleries receive a commission from the artist for work sold.

THE CURATOR

Museum curators play an important role in the art establishment because they are often looked to for the validity stamp of an artist's worth. Museum curators decide what art will be seen by a large segment of the art-interested public and, in the process, help to build a reputation for the artist. The viewing public often feels that if your work is in a major museum, it must be good. Curators of university museums, libraries, public collections and corporate collections are usually less influential in helping to establish a reputation for an artist; but they do buy art and give needed exposure to established as well as developing artists.

The art consultant falls into two categories: the project consultant, hired by a firm to provide art for a new building, and the classic consultant, who has access to much artwork by many artists and who offers these, for a commission, to the project consultant and to collectors. Both deal with large quantities of work and will sell a lot of work, but the art consultant is not generally looked to for extensive promotional efforts on behalf of the artist.

THE ART CRITIC

In the Western world, we are impressed and influenced by the printed word; in the art network, the art critic plays a paramount role. He serves as the intermediary between the artist and the viewing public by reviewing shows and exhibitions and explaining the whys and hows of your work as well as providing a summary of your background and achievements. In addition to writing reviews, the art critic also writes catalogues and, from time to time, may even serve as curator for major exhibitions.

THE COLLECTOR

Completing the Network is the collector—an individual interested in acquiring art not only for enjoyment and aesthetic fulfillment but also for investment and, in some cases, for social advancement and recognition as a patron of the arts.

If your ultimate goal is recognition and volume sales, you've got to learn to approach one or all members of the Network. For years, the traditional approach for a young artist to use in developing and gaining a respectable reputation in the art world was via the art gallery. Today, unfortunately, there are more artists than the galleries can effectively support. Artists must compete with each other for the limited number of stalls in the gallery stable. Finding an effective gallery becomes a difficult task.

FINDING THE RIGHT GALLERY FOR YOU

In searching for a gallery to represent you, at first you should find out what services the gallery will provide. Equally important is determining what you want from the gallery. If you are doing performance or conceptual art, it would probably be a mistake to approach a gallery that exhibits only figurative or realistic work. If you do photography, you probably wouldn't try the gallery that shows only drawings and paintings. If the gallery only deals with mid-career and known artists and you are just out of art school, look elsewhere. Check art magazines, gallery guides, and other artists to find out which galleries will fulfill your needs.

How about the services? When a gallery takes you on, what will it do for you? Will it take your work on consignment, make you sign an exclusive and then stash your work in the storeroom? Will there be an opening reception, announcements, advertising, news releases, catalogues? If so, who's going to do the work and who's going to pay for it? Will the gallery insist on framing your work and then present you later with a bill? Do you have to have work insured while it is at the gallery? Are the owners asking you to sign an insurance waiver? Do they want you to gallery-sit two days a week, address all the mailers, and will you then have to hand over 60 percent of all sales? How much is this show going to cost you, anyway?

You've got to do your homework. Some galleries are interested only in established quality. Whether they sell a lot or a little, once they discover an artist they consider strong and superior, the gallery will support him, go to bat for him and provide him with a firm commitment. Many galleries will deal only with artists whose work they know they can sell. You may or may not fit in. The gallery owner may have a feeling for your work, but if you're doing drawings and he's into selling paintings ... you'll have to look elsewhere.

HOW TO GET EXHIBITED

You've done your investigation and have located the pie in the sky. How do you get a bite? Your best method of getting into the gallery is to enlist the aid of the gallery's major artists with whom you are friendly. An influential member of the Network—collector, curator, consultant—can also provide a successful entrée. You can get to know members of the Network and gallery dealers by attending openings and art-related social functions. One New York gallery dealer suggests you "hang out in the right bar." Whatever works for you—develop your own style.

If you want to make contact with an out-of-town gallery, write a letter; if you know a name, use it and mark the letter "personal." Write the dealer about a month in advance. Let him know you are going to be in his area on two or three specific days (that way he will have a choice) and say in the letter that you will be calling (in about two weeks) on a specific day for an appointment to show your work. Give some brief biographical information and, if possible, mention the name of someone in the Network who has suggested that you contact him. Locally, you should also write a letter stating you will telephone on a certain day for an appointment. If you are not an established or well-known artist, avoid making "cold" telephone calls for appointments.

Most galleries which still actively look at the work of new or unknown and mid-career artists have a viewing policy—one day a week or month when they look at work, either by appointment or on a first-come, first-viewed basis. If you want your name on the schedule for a particular time, write ahead and include a resumé, some promotional material and slides.

PRICING YOUR WORK

One of the questions frequently asked by students and artists just starting out is this: How do I price my work? You've got to intelligently investigate the market to ascertain what the going rate is for work done in a similar medium, style, size, degree of complexity in execution, done by other artists in about the same stage of career development. Check out galleries and ask other artists about prices so you will have a feel for the range. If you have not sold before, opt for a price that lies between low and middle of the range—this, so that you can start moving your work. Once it begins to sell, then you can start raising your prices. And for the oft-heard phrase, "I'm going to lower my prices so I can sell more"—forget it. Never lower your prices once they have been publicly established. There is no faster way to anger a collector. Imagine his ire when he has just paid $300 for one of your prints and then sees the same a week later for $200! Any gallery interested in your work will be willing to assist you in determining prices.

ORGANIZING YOUR PORTFOLIO

If you have a confirmed appointment with a gallery owner or dealer, you're going to need a well-organized portfolio with all the contents lined up according to how you will make the presentation. Along with your slides and transparencies, you should include actual pieces of your work, if this is manageable. You should also have your resumé with you, which should state your name, address and phone on each page; your educational background; scholarships, fellowships or grants; a list of exhibitions (note juried/nonjuried), commissions, inclusions in any major private or public collections; and any jobs you have had which relate to art.

The size of the entire portfolio is important: bigger is NOT better! I have seen artists walk into galleries with portfolios that measure 40 X 110 inches and paintings ten feet long. They have to put them on skates just to roll them in the door. The dealer is trying to conduct a business. When he sees you walk in with a gigantic portfolio and three friends carrying your work, terror is written all over his face. Your portfolio should be a size you can handle comfortably, yet big enough to accommodate work—22 X 30 inches, no larger.

Pick some samples of your work that reflect the chronological progression of your career, preferably in similar sizes. I have often found that viewers have difficulty going back and forth from large items to small ones. If you feel that some of your stronger pieces are 2 X 2 inches and you have others 20 X 30 inches that work very well and illustrate your progress, include them despite the size difference.

When I meet a dealer for the first time, I like to show a few pieces from my early career, done perhaps five years ago; something from two years ago, and maybe six or eight of my current work, plus one I have just completed to telescope what I am planning to do in the future.

Your work should look as though you respect it. It should be fresh, not dog-eared, bent up, folded, with footprints in the center. Your work should be "dressed up." If you yourself don't care for and respect your work, how do you expect a dealer to respond positively? You've got to set the stage.

Decide whether you want to have your work matted, dry-mounted, matted with acetate over it or with slip sheets between pieces. I don't mat my prints, but if you choose to, make sure the mats are clean and cut straight. When you're putting your portfolio together, make sure you have finished the juicy submarine sandwich and cleaned your fingers before you handle your work. I also don't use acetate because the shine may cause a reflection, making it difficult to properly see the work. You may want to use envelopes made of mylar, taped shut, with one side left free for insertion of prints or watercolors, and with a support board between two pieces of work.

I also include a few extra sheets of clean paper so that if I have to lay my work down on the floor, I can put it on the paper to keep it clean. A large piece of cardboard, preferably chipboard, is also useful for displaying the work vertically during presentation.

You should have a maximum of 15 pieces in your portfolio. You can show 10; if the dealer wants to see more, you have the few extras. If he is really interested and wants to see more, you have your slides.

The main thing to remember is that you want to walk in looking organized. You don't want to have to go in and out three or four times carrying a lot of things. Polish your approach. Make it easy for the dealer to like you and to do business with you.

WHAT YOU SHOULD KNOW ABOUT SLIDES

It's impossible to generate interest in your work if no one can perceive what you do. Slides are the means by which you show your work, so good slides are important. Hire a professional, if necessary, to do the job right. Your slides should have no visual interferences. Leave your mother's hand, the bedroom wallpaper, and the back door out of the slide; show just the actual artwork. A black, white or gray background shows the work most advantageously.

You should have slides of your latest work—as well as the chronology of what you've been doing in the last several years— prepackaged in an easy-to-view arrangement.

Each slide should be labeled with your name, address, the media (acrylic, oil, watercolor, etc.), and the date of execution. The size, height, and width of the work should also be indicated, along with the notation of "top" of the slide.

Select between 10 and 20 slides, each very representative of your style and as close as possible to the actual work. Be sure the color and subtle tones are accurate. Include some detail close-up shots of particular areas or sections of some works.

Once you've chosen the slides, arrange them in a definite order in the sheet or box and number them accordingly so the viewer can follow the sequence. Attach a reference sheet, listing each numbered work. This sheet is also helpful if the dealer misplaces some of the slides you may leave with him. If you mail slides or leave some for further consideration, don't count on getting them back immediately, even if you have included a stamped, self-addressed evelope.

If I have landed an appointment with a dealer, I arrange my slides a little differently than if I'm mailing them. The continuous chronology is less important, because I can talk about my work and I might want to jump ahead to a specific work for emphasis.

I bring a portable slide viewer with a hand advance lever so I can show one slide at a time as I remove them from the prearranged box. The viewer should be clean and have good batteries (searching for an electrical outlet can waste valuable time and leave a bad impression). If the dealer wants you to leave your slides for further consideration, remove them from the box and insert them in a slide sheet. It will be easier to file in his folder along with your resumé.

For the appointment, choose your slides very critically; they should show work you feel good about and which you can discuss enthusiastically. If your work has delicacy and many intricate aspects, consider having a few 8 X 10 transparencies made. A 2 X 2 inch slide can hardly convey the majesty of a 5 X 7 foot work. The giant transparency can be handled easily and the viewer can hold it up to a window and see the work clearly, without squinting and without a machine. Smart shoppers may be able to find old 8 X 10, 5 X 7 or 4 X 5 cameras at auctions or secondhand shops, saving the $40 to $150 fee charged, per transparency, by a professional photographer.

Your "kit" could also include some black and white photos so the gallery owner will have some idea of how your work will appear in promotional material sent to newspapers and magazines. For those who work in three dimensions, black and white photos, with some absolute blacks and absolute whites and all the tones between, tend to show the form more truly than slides.

When you go for that first tête-a-tête at the gallery, bring along some actual pieces of work. Even if sculpture is your field, bring a small piece—something actual and three-dimensional.

One effective technique is showing the gallery owner a slide of a piece of work you've brought to the interview. As you describe the comparison between the actual painting (watercolor, sculpture, etc.) and the slide, the dealer will gain confidence in what your slides represent.

I can't impress on you how important it is to have something with you for the dealer to touch. Something believable. Something to hold in the hands. It is essential for the dealer to have an intimate experience with your work without going through another medium (slides). If you're a painter and you do big paintings, do a couple of small ones for the presentation. If you don't paint small, bring in some drawings or watercolors.

KNOW YOUR GALLERY

The first rule in going to the galleries is DO YOUR HOME-WORK! Know the gallery's specialty and its size. Huge sculptures or paintings will hardly be welcome in a postage-stamp-sized gallery. If you don't know the basic facts about the gallery you're courting, *ask*—or have a friend call and do the digging for you. And you should know which show is currently hanging in the gallery. This will indicate that you are interested in the gallery—just in case the dealer asks.

DEVELOPING A WINNING PRESENTATION

The presentation at a gallery, to a curator, or to a collector is your ten seconds in the sun. You've got to know your work so you can converse intelligently about it and deal with any negative reactions. Many artists, fearing rejection, procrastinate in setting up the gallery interview. You are about to share something that is a part of your existence and you may fear that if, for one reason or another, the gallery turns your work down, it is also putting you, as a person, down. How do you handle this?

Develop an honest self-critique. Every morning, you should look in the mirror when you brush your teeth, saying, "Why of course, there lies the genius." Reinforce this positive feeling by being aware of your visual ideas, by understanding what your work is about, by knowing that it is composed, painted and constructed well. You want to be able to walk in with confidence, knowing that there are no aesthetic or visual holes in your work and that it is based on a firm foundation of understanding—that it is excellent and "out-of-sight" and you know it.

You must deal with the presentation objectively, not emotionally. You have to learn to detach yourself from your work, which is difficult; they are dealing with your blood, sweat and tears—and all your insides. If someone does not like your work, that does not mean the work has no value. It could just be a matter of taste. I may like French shirts; you may prefer Italian ones. If I were making good French shirts, the fact that you opted for Italian ones wouldn't mean mine were of no merit.

Just remember, if you have developed a good self-critique, you can walk in and deal with confidence, be charming, be enthusiastic about your work, and sell it on its merits. You won't be sitting there, insecure; you will know exactly what you are about, your intents, what you are attempting to achieve, and how you are getting there.

A trick I use to build confidence is setting up several appointments for the same day so I won't feel that any one gallery is my last resort. You can't deal in "life and death" terms; people spot it and will wipe you out because they sense you have relinquished to them that additional power. True—they have the power to show or not to show your work, to bring you fame and put you in the Network. But if you know what you are about, you also know that there are other galleries.

Accept your nervousness and use it to get "up"—to be aware of what is happening, to talk about your work while being sensitive to what is being said. By having several sets of appointments lined up for different days, there is never that "bottom line"; you always have something to look forward to in case you bomb out on the first presentation.

You're ready to make your presentation. When you walk into the gallery, immediately look around for a suitable location to "do your thing" (if you haven't already cased out the gallery in advance).

First off, look for a section of the gallery with some free wall space and good light. You can't see artwork in the dark. Normally, two-dimensional work is meant to be experienced vertically on the wall, not flat on a table, so try to avoid the desk situation. Find a place to stand your work up. If it is not matted or framed, you can use the extra pieces of cardboard or chipboard in your portfolio to lean against the wall or on a chair so you can show your work as vertically as possible and as close to a viewing distance as you can. If you have to put your work on the floor, the dealer will have to bend over; propped against the wall, a desk or chair, the work will be closer to eye level. The dealer can't really appreciate your work if his feet are hurting or if he is getting a backache bending over. Make it easy for him. You may even want to use a portable easel, but it should be small enough to fit into your portfolio and you should be able to set it up in less than three minutes. If it takes any longer, leave it home; you don't need the hassle.

Your presentation should be a continuous flow. While the dealer is looking at one piece, you should be getting the next one ready. You want to show your work without breaking the dealer's concentration, so establish a flow system and practice it at home until you can do it blindfolded.

Eye level and eye contact are crucial. There is something psychologically negative about being on a lower eye level so try to be on the same level as the dealer. If he is sitting, try to stand, and you'd better be standing if he is.

Watch their eyes. The dealer's eyes will tell you exactly what he is looking at, when he is having a problem with the work and when he has finished looking. Track him. You don't want to whisk something away too soon, and you don't want to leave it up too long either. You have to develop the right rhythm so that interest will not lag.

If you have shown a few pieces and the dealer hasn't made any comments, start asking questions: "What do you think about this piece? the color? the movement?" If the dealer seems to have any problems, attempt to clarify things. You've lived with your work for a long time, he hasn't. It's up to you to alleviate any problems.

The interview with the gallery owner is an excellent opportunity for feedback. You will be getting valuable information about your work if you can sit still and listen to a dealer's objective statements.

Another question frequently asked by students is this: "What do you say when the dealer tells you he doesn't like your work, and he just is not interested?" Remember that you have been asking questions throughout the interview to find out where the dealer is having problems with the work, and you have done your best to resolve any conflicts. When you are hit with the final negative— "Sorry, you can't hang"—be sure you understand why you are being turned down before you walk out the door.

Is the rejection based on the dealer's judgment that your work is not up to snuff? Or are you being rejected for other reasons over which you presently have no control? For example, the dealer may like your work, but already have a number of artists that fall into your category—five years out of school or in mid-career, work of the same price range or of similar images. Perhaps he feels his clientele will not respond to your work. There are numerous reasons, including the gallery's budget situation.

Many times, despite problems with the work, the dealer may still be interested and suggest you come back in six months or a year. Don't take that as a put-off; the dealer may honestly want to see what you are doing in six months. He has just seen your work for the first time and often will want to wait and see if you are going to continue to grow. So run right home and mark your calendar to call the dealer in six or eight months.

Above all, maintain your dignity and avoid your natural inclination to mutter obscenities while stomping out. The art world is small, and although this dealer may not have appreciated the calibre and outstanding message of your work, he *is* a member of the Network and you never know when you may encounter him again.

GETTING REFERRALS

If the gallery is not interested, ask the dealer to suggest a gallery that may be. Ask for contact names. There may be some gallery you haven't heard of or considered. *Always* ask if you can use the dealer's name when you call the gallery he suggests; this gives you a little edge. And if the dealer is enthusiastic about your work but can't use it for reasons discussed above, ask him if he will phone the other dealer. What better introduction than from a member of the Network?

KNOWING THE GALLERY SYSTEM

What happens if, after looking at your portfolio, the dealer says, "I love it"? Here is when you have to know how to deal with the system. Ideally, you will say, "Buy it. Purchase me. If you believe in me, do it to death."

Galleries have varying policies. Some will buy outright; others will want the work on consignment. It is up to you to find out the gallery's policy and what the dealer intends to do for you. Does he want your work on consignment? If so, is he just going to sit and look at the work for a while to see if he really likes it? Or does he have clients in mind to whom he wishes to show the work? Is he considering including you in a group show? A new talent show? A group presentation to corporations? Is your work so fantastic that the dealer wants to give you a one-man show?

If the dealer decides on an exhibition of your work, is this going to be a one-shot deal, or will he handle your work for a defined period of time? Will this be a trial run to see if your work sells and is he going to let you know after the show whether or not he will take you on?

Many times, a gallery will want to give you a show and then wait to see what happens. The gallery will arrange an exhibition of your work, bring in people to view it, maybe spend some money on advertising, and then want to keep the work for awhile. You've got to find out in advance exactly what the game plan is and what the rules are.

Know your own situation. If you have more art than money, deal with the artwork if you can. Shows and exhibitions involve expenses. You might try to make a deal with the gallery to trade work for some of your obligated expenses. Be sure to get a receipt for these expenses so you can deduct them from your income tax and list artwork traded as income. If you have more money than artwork, then deal with the money. The point is that when necessary, you should look for alternatives and know your bottom line.

You must ask questions. If the gallery likes your work and wants you to leave it on consignment, find out for how long. Before you leave any work, fill out a consignment sheet describing the size and title of each piece and the value of each. Other pertinent terms of your arrangement should be stipulated: Who will pay for insurance? What rate of commission will the gallery receive? How will payment be made to you and how long will you have to wait for your money? Be sure to have the dealer sign the consignment sheet and then tuck it away in a safe place.

Keep in mind the fact that the work you leave behind is being taken out of circulation. If you have no other prospects at the moment, you can afford to have it tied up for a while. A dealer should know after two or three months what he is going to do with your work. If the gallery is going to represent you for a certain period of time, you might make arrangements to pick up work and replace it with other pieces. Within six months, the gallery should have been able to show your work to most of its clients interested in your style; if nothing has sold, you might want to bring in new pieces or even pull out and look for a new set of walls, a storage room or a paper bin.

I can't overemphasize how important it is to discuss all details of whatever arrangement you will have *before* you leave the work. If you talk about things first, you can negotiate. After the fact, you have less control.

Above all, get everything in writing. People forget what they have said in conversation. Make a habit of taking notes. When I was beginning to make the gallery rounds, I would be so excited or so nervous when a dealer wanted my work—when I found out I was going to get wall space instead of drawer space—that I would go home and forget all the details. Now I go back to my studio and compose a letter, reiterating explicitly the obligations of both parties. I keep a copy and send one to the dealer with a return receipt to make sure it has been received. People rarely back up from the written word.

THE CONTRACT

I am always cautious when a gallery brings out a contract. I go over it carefully before taking it to my lawyer. Once you sign a contract, that's it. There is no room for negotiation. If a dealer wants you to sign an exclusive contract, find out how many shows he will have of your work. If he does not sell a certain amount of work, will you be put on stipend whereby the gallery will purchase so much of your work? You need to know how much money you can count on monthly or yearly. If the gallery is not going to provide the income you require, you might do just as well to take your work and hustle it yourself.

GRANTING TERRITORIAL RIGHTS

Many times, when you are dealing with a gallery that is representing you in a certain area of the country, the dealer will ask for territorial rights; he doesn't want you dealing with another gallery in the area. There is nothing wrong with giving a gallery these rights—provided the dealer is going to guarantee to do specific tasks to promote and sell your work. A gallery should earn territorial rights. If the dealer promises at least one show every two years, to promote you in announcements and brochures, to get you into group shows, to make sure you will have some reviews by art critics and to get shows for you at other galleries ... then it is worthwhile to grant territorial rights to the gallery. But if you have to give him *exclusive* rights and he does nothing, your hands are tied and you can't do anything for yourself.

There is a gray area when it comes to the situation where a gallery is representing you and doing promotion. You may get a call from someone who wants to come to your studio to buy work. Is the gallery entitled to a percentage of the sale?

I believe that if I have developed a client on my own and he did not hear about me by going to a show at the gallery, and if I meet the client, do a sales presentation, and the client purchases a piece of work directly from me, then the gallery is not entitled to a cut. If I develop a client and he later goes to the gallery and purchases something, then, of course, the gallery is entitled to a share. If the gallery sends a client to my studio, then the gallery deserves a portion, but not a full cut because I am performing the sales function. If the dealer brings a client to my studio to see work not shown at the gallery, and a sale is made, the gallery is entitled to a proportion of the normal commission, but not the full amount, because I have taken time to show the work and I am assuming the costs for storage of the work.

COMMISSION RATES

Commission rates to galleries vary. In some rare instances, you find a dealer who will accept one-third of the price of the artwork (33⅓ percent). Forty percent seems to be the norm, except for New

York, where 50 percent is average. Some European galleries take 75 percent, but they provide an extraordinary amount of promotion and public relations. In some instances, it may be more advantageous to pay 75 percent to a gallery that is going to promote and move your work, than 33⅓ percent to one that may sell only one small piece, or worse, nothing at all.

COMMISSION ARRANGEMENTS

There are three types of commission arrangements: (1) the gallery has the work, it is stored there, and the gallery sells it; (2) the gallery brings someone to your studio and sells something you have stored in your studio; and (3) the gallery sends someone over and you do the selling. If the regular commission rate is 40 percent of the sale, I feel that in the second instance cited above, the gallery is entitled to 33⅓ percent; in the third instance, 20 or 25 percent. This should all be worked out in advance and spelled out on a consignment sheet.

If the gallery works through an art consultant or sells to an interior decorator, you may be asked to give up an additional five or ten percent so that the gallery can give a discount to the consultant or decorator. I have had bitter battles over this. Why should I give up more of my share when the gallery chooses to enlist the aid of someone else in the sale of my work? The gallery owner is supposed to be selling my art and I have nothing to do with how he chooses to sell it. If, however, the gallery deals almost exclusively with decorators, art consultants, and certain corporate groups to whom a discount is normally given, you may want to consider giving up one-half of the ten or 20 percent discount, especially if the gallery is turning over a lot of your work, thereby bolstering your reputation.

SECURING PAYMENT

Another item you as an artist must face and conquer, besides fear or rejection, is the reluctance to discuss money matters: how you will be paid; when you will get your money. We all know we want to make money to buy paint and to pay rent.

Often, dealers will use the artist's money to sponsor other projects. Some dealers will sell your show and, faced with expenses for the next show, be tempted to use some of the money due you to set up the new one. Expenses for the gallery are ongoing and must be covered, but should this be done with funds due you?

If method of payment is spelled out in the consignment sheet, you will have something to fall back on. My consignment sheet states that I expect payment within 30 days after the gallery/dealer receives his money. If the dealer accepts partial payments for installment sales, I insist that the work remain with the gallery until the client has paid at least one-fourth of the sales price. This money, paid to the gallery, should be distributed pro rata to the artist.

Some galleries pay immediately; some pay once a month; some have to be hounded. You have to check and see what has been sold and then ask for payment. There are a couple of dealers in New York who take a year to pay their artists. I am a marginal businessman and I have to have cash-flow because I put everything I earn from my art back into it. If a dealer holds up my money, then I won't be able to do new projects. I am not doing art as a nonprofit adventure. This is my bread and butter, and I don't want to wait for money rightfully due me.

My consignment sheet also establishes that the work belongs to me until it is sold. If the gallery goes bankrupt, its doors are closed; you will have a tough time proving that the work there on consignment was actually yours and did not belong to the gallery. Your work could be held up for seven years through litigation which won't do you any good. Your consignment sheet should state up front that you are the owner of the work and that it does not belong to the gallery.

Once you are dealing regularly with a gallery, you may ask for a statement of account, either monthly or quarterly. Definitely, you should know at the end of each year where you stand. You will want to know to whom the work was sold so that you can add the names to your list of collectors interested in you. You will also want the names so that when you are considered for a museum show, you will know how to locate works you may wish to borrow for the exhibit.

Keep your own set of records of where your work is and how long the gallery has had it. After a year or more passes, you will have difficulty remembering all these details. Good record-keeping is crucial.

As you iron out all the details and confirm them in writing, consider your responsibilities and what you are going to have to pay for.

INSURANCE, SHIPMENT, FRAMING, AND OTHER MATTERS

Will the gallery insure your work during shipment and while it is at the gallery? Some artists ask to see a copy of the gallery's insurance policy; this is not always easy. One gallery I know of asked its artists to sign an insurance waiver that was absolutely absurd. The gallery would cover items it purchased, but those on consignment would not be covered. Some artists would put up with this balderdash and try to get their own insurance, but it is very expensive.

If the gallery is out of town, who is going to pay for shipment of the work? Some galleries will pay, others will not. If the gallery is taking a 50 percent commission, it usually pays the shipping. Negotiate this.

Who is going to frame the work and who will pay for the framing? Will the gallery frame it and then assess you at cost? Will you be expected to pay for the framing in advance of the show? If you do sculpture, will you be responsible for the bases? If you frame the work yourself, will there be someone at the gallery to help you do it? Some galleries may want you to do all your own framing; at $50 to $80 a frame, that adds up. Will this cost be tagged onto the sales price? Many galleries have "quick-change" frames your work can be slipped into. But if they want the work glassed with welded mould or welded steel framing (expensive) and you want pre-cut channel frames (cheaper), you will have to get this settled in advance.

How will your work be stored while at the gallery? Ask the dealer about his storage methods. You won't want to get a print, watercolor, or painting back after a show and find it all bent up or with a dent in the middle. Remember, buyers will be asking for "fresh"work.

PUBLICIZING YOUR SHOW

What about an announcement of the show—do you design it and pay for it or does the dealer? If a photograph of your work is needed for the announcement, do you have to provide one? In most cases, the artist provides the photo; in some, the gallery will hire the photographer. Announcements can be as simple as a postcard, or as elaborate as a fold-out containing a color reproduction of your work and biographical information. The gallery may ask what you want, so have some ideas ready.

Will there be an opening reception? If so, will there be refreshments and who will provide and serve them? I am beginning to believe that very little artwork is sold at openings that tend to be more social than business. But if you want to invite your friends and have a little bash, do it. Just remember that the point is to get exposure and sell your work. If the show opens in Minneapolis in the winter and it's snowing and 50 degrees below, you're probably going to get your friends and interested art-lovers out only once—so you'd better plan to greet them with a cool head. This may be the one chance you and your dealer have to sell something to them.

Don't be disappointed if nothing sells at the opening. Artwork is sold to people coming into the gallery by appointments arranged by the dealer; it is sold by the dealer getting on the horn and calling his collectors, sending out information to those on his mailing list, and using his other resources to bring people into the gallery.

What about a catalogue? Catalogues of your show provide good promotion for you and for the gallery. Many galleries have neither the budget nor the inclination to risk the cost of a catalogue, even though it might help to sell more work. Some will be interested in doing a catalogue if you agree to pay for it.

What kind of promotional and advertising program does the gallery adhere to? Will press releases be sent out in advance of the show and, if so, who will write them or pay to have them written? Will photographs of you or your work be submitted with each press release and, if so, who is to provide the photos? Will these releases be simple statements that an exhibition of your work will be shown at the gallery? Or will the release contain biographical information and a synopsis of your career development and appear more like a feature article?

In terms of publicity, you must always be thinking about what you have and how best to utilize it. An example: recently, a New York gallery had a show of an artist whose conceptual work featured animals. The exhibit opened a few weeks before Thanksgiving. A corner of the gallery was fenced off for two live turkeys to strut about, and the turkeys were to be given to the children's zoo after the show closed. This was a perfect set-up for a feature article, but it wasn't even mentioned in the press releases. You've got to realize how to get the most mileage out of what you have to offer.

It is important to understand the word "deadline" and to know, in advance, exactly when a gallery needs something from you. Galleries are known for calling and wanting something yesterday. If you can't read minds, find out in the preliminary discussions what they will need and when. If the dealer has said he will prepare and send the news releases, check to make sure they have gone out. If the gallery needs help, you might offer to do some of the releases. The more exposure you get, the more chance there is of enhancing your reputation and increasing sales.

What about television and radio? There are numerous talk shows, especially on public broadcasting (educational) stations. If you can get your image on the tube, you're in. People buy what they see on TV. You must be persistent and willing to make a few calls. Come up with a "hook"—an idea that will make for interesting listening. If you do landscapes, get on the air and discuss land conservation. If you do seascapes, you might talk about saving the penguins.

What about paid advertising? If the gallery says you are going to have to pay for a little notice in a magazine or newspaper, forget it. Take the money you would spend on an ad and hire someone to make calls to people on your mailing list or the dealer's list, informing them about the show.

What does the gallery dealer expect of you? Are you to be available while the show is up, to attend promotional events and parties for collectors? If you have alternative employment, how much advance notice will there be before you have to take off from work for radio or television interviews and similar events? Most artists are their own best salesmen because they are enthusiastic about their work. When some people buy art, they also like to buy biography. They enjoy an opportunity to speak with the artist so that later they can say, "Well, David said this about his work … he's concerned about these issues … and he's such a wild guy!" They talk about everything except the artwork. If that's what they need to buy your work, then you will want to provide it. A number of people are really curious about artists and the creative lifestyle. They want to become "experts" on an artist, his life and his work. Most are buying more than just the artwork … they are buying a part of you. The more they know about you, the more comfortable they feel when someone asks them about that painting hanging on the wall. Those who have purchased your work will, indirectly, be acting as your representative. The more information you can provide, the easier it will be for them to discuss your work with their friends and business associates who may become future collectors of your work. If, however, you are one of those artists who has a propensity for putting his foot in his mouth, work on changing, or avoid promotional events.

What do you do if, after the initial hoopla and sales, a year down the pike, sales start to lag, interest drops and the monthly or quarterly checks peter out? You may think you should move to another gallery, but the same situation could occur again. What can you do to help the gallery stimulate interest in and sales of your work?

Continue to show an interest by stopping into the gallery occasionally. Don't call every week, but it's not a bad idea to show up once a month. If the dealer is really interested in promoting you, there may be critics you can meet or collectors you can talk to. It won't hurt to sit down every so often with the dealer and discuss new game plans. You can offer to provide slides or photographs of newly completed pieces, or names of additional collectors you have met. You might suggest some projects you are considering that would stimulate additional publicity through news releases.

What happens if you are not one of the gallery's hot numbers, even though the dealer is doing all he can to stimulate sales? You are going to have to think about taking matters into your own hands.

Self-promotion takes time. You must examine your priorities. If you are content to sell one or two pieces of work now and then, fine. But if you want to create more demand for your work so that you can escalate your prices, increase sales, and gain the opportunity to realize more of your creative dreams, you're going to have to develop the concept of self-promotion. I know an artist in Chicago who, on his own, sold $40,000 worth of his work in one year by persistently pursuing contacts and tenaciously adhering to a rigorous program of follow-through.

So you've got your artwork all ready, and you're going to try selling it on your own. If you are right out of art school, even if you don't have a mammoth amount of work ready to sell, you can begin with the quality work you do have. You have a product and now you need a market for it.

STARTING OUT

Where do you start? Here's an analogy to consider. Say you have just moved from the country or suburbs into a large city for the first time. To avoid being mugged or robbed while walking the city streets, you soon develop an automatic street-wise attitude—you know to look behind you, to watch alleys—and this self-protective sense becomes a part of you.

MAKING THINGS "HAPPEN" FOR YOURSELF

And so it is with creating a market for your artwork. You must develop a second sense of watching everywhere for those who may be interested in purchasing your work. When you get up in the morning, remind yourself that you are an artist and you want to sell your work. No matter whom you meet or where you go, keep in mind that each encounter is an opportunity to further your career. If you're taking the train to New York, carry along your slides, you never know who might be sitting next to you. If you go to the theater or ballet, be sure you have your business card, you don't know whom you might run into during intermission.

You want people to know you are an artist and that you are selling your work yourself. There are a lot of people out there interested in art but not yet into acquiring original works of art. If you have a good sense of timing, you will know when to approach these people to gently bring them into the fold of your collectors. Your doctor, lawyer, boss and even the lady next door—all are eligible candidates. When someone buys a piece of your art, he will be joining your support team. He will be telling friends about you and your buying base will broaden.

As you attend art functions and openings, you will be meeting prospective buyers. They wouldn't be there if they weren't interested in art. The more of these functions you can get to, the more familiar you will be with the people who attend. Let them know you're an artist. You can have great artwork, but if you're off standing shyly in the corner, you're not going to sell any of it. And if you go to openings looking as though you just dropped your brushes and ran, don't be surprised if the prospective buyer runs the other way.

If you meet someone who expresses an interest in your work, whip out one of your business cards, ask for his card, tell him you will add him to your mailing list, and run right home and mark your calendar so you will remember to follow through on the lead. I consider it gauche to show slides or transparencies of my work while at the opening of another artist. But it is quite acceptable to contact these people later for presentations, either at your studio or at their homes or businesses.

You might ask, "How can I act as my own agent, running all around town, and still get my work done?" One method is to form an organization with a group of artists to promote each other's work. This may be difficult to work out—getting together a group of egos, each wanting to be THE genius, not one among other geniuses—but with a little effort, you can find a workable group.

YOUR MATERIALS

Develop a promotional packet of articles and reviews written about you, a resumé, slides and photographs and any other promotional material. If you can't write, find someone with a good command of English and sense of creativity who can help to put together your "kit." If you're working on this with a group of artists, you can split the expense of hiring someone. Packets can be sent out individually or as a group package.

Develop a subscription-type letter to introduce yourself. Include a statement describing your work and some current projects as well as those you plan to undertake.

Once you have a promotional pack put together, you can start sending it around to collectors, curators, art consultants, interior decorators, architects, and governmental agencies that commission art.

If you're considering taking matters into your own hands, I want to emphasize the importance of developing a system of follow-through. You can't just send out promotional material and expect the phone to ring the next day. You've got to keep in constant contact with those who may be interested in your work. After you have sent out material, make a telephone call to see if the package was received, if there are any questions. And by all means, continue to send announcements of where your work can be seen and any press releases you have developed. (I get copies of news articles and features reproduced offset for mass mailing.)

KEEPING YOUR MAILING LIST CURRENT

One of your most valuable tools will be your mailing list. In making one up, start with your relatives, your dentist, doctor, lawyer; add art consultants, curators and collectors who have bought your work. You can purchase lists of people (like doctors and lawyers) who are presensitized to the idea of investing in art. If you are a sculptor, you may want to subscribe to the *Architectural Record* (which lists construction projects) so you can submit proposals for sculpture commissions. You can also procure a list of corporations that acquire art and names of the individuals responsible for corporate collections.

Art consultants can be valuable sources of sales. They make presentations to large corporations, to architects and project directors. If the art consultant likes your work, he may be willing to take it on consignment, for he is constantly seeking to develop new markets for himself.

The name of the game is getting your name around and keeping the buying public aware of your achievements and progress. Collectors may be aware of you, but they will want to see what you can do. Although you might not do anything major for a few years, if the public has seen your name, a curiosity will build and the energy and effort required to lay this advance publicity will be well spent.

One method many artists use to make contacts and keep in the art-world limelight is serving on boards of civic organizations and cultural institutions or volunteering to work on various art-related community projects. I know of some artists who go from board to board, collecting names. By getting into the public eye in this fashion, you will be demonstrating your interest in the art world as well as receiving publicity for your endeavors; any positive "ink" you can get won't hurt you. Be sure to follow through with any leads. When you meet people on boards or at events who may be interested in your work, add their names to your mailing list.

ORGANIZING YOUR OWN STUDIO SHOW

Once you have your list set up and your promotional package all organized, if you can't find a gallery that will show your work, consider having a studio show—provided you have a decent studio or can borrow a friend's. This takes planning and lead time, but it does not have to be overly complicated.

Plan a studio sale for a Saturday and Sunday on two consecutive weekends. This way, you can divide your mailing list and not have too many people at one time. Make up a small announcement, as simple as a black and white postcard, and send it to those on your mailing list. Quite a few artists I know have sold a lot of work at studio sales. Art-lovers and collectors enjoy meeting the artist and seeing his or her studio and creative space.

The logistics of a studio sale are simple. Have a friend tend the door so that only those invited are admitted. You may want to include "Guests Welcome" on the announcement so that you can augment your mailing list. Have a guest book at the door so you can pick up new names for your list. You can have your work hung around the studio and bins set up with matted work. Rope off any areas you do not wish to have disturbed. After a few practice sales, you'll have the mechanics down pat and will find you can have a studio show for less than it costs to have a show at a gallery.

Another method to procure space for a show without the sponsorship of a gallery is to take advantage of recently passed legislation which permits the use of government owned buildings for exhibitions. Usually, five or six artists get together and work out a proposal to submit to proper authorities. This may require as much as six months' lead time. The group either writes its own press releases or hires someone to do so, creates the announcements, and makes use of all the members' mailing lists. Members may wish to take shifts to be on hand during business hours to answer any questions and to write up orders.

A group of artists, or individuals, can look into having shows at banks and libraries, restaurants, shopping malls, and lobbies of apartment buildings and hotels. Often, the library staff or bank personnel will do the publicity for the show. One thing to remember is that libraries do not always carry insurance to cover work on display, although they will permit you to have a show if you sign a waiver.

Having a show in a public building will generate good publicity for you because today we are all responding to the theme of "pulling ourselves up by our own bootstraps." You will be trying to do something on your own, you are not "the establishment," no one is making a profit off you, and there is sympathy for those trying to survive on their own.

Getting publicity for these types of shows is important. Be sure to include decent photographs with the press releases; contact local art critics and members of the media. If you can manage five seconds on the evening news ... score city!!

Another alternative is to contact colleges, universities, and art schools. You will have to submit slides with your proposal for an exhibition of your work. In some cases, you may also be invited to speak—about your work and medium (print-making, glass-blowing, paper-making, or whatever your specialty). You may even be asked to conduct a workshop. Do not expect a large sum for speaking engagements or workshops. Always find out in advance what the remuneration will be, which department or office will handle payment, and when payment can be expected.

SPECIAL PROJECTS TO AROUSE INTEREST

You may also want to consider special projects that will stimulate interest, spread publicity, and generate sales. The idea is not to change your concepts, but rather to expand them into larger projects. Perhaps you can come up with an alternate style of executing your ideas—switch from traditional lithographic techniques to offset lithography, from small paintings to murals or objects done in relief. Rather than doing individual prints, paintings, or watercolors, you might do a series on a particular subject. Collectors may be lured into investing in a series of prints, sold by advance subscription at one-third of the retail value. (You cover the cost by deciding your edition size and then making a set of artist's proofs for the backers so that you are giving them something special outside of the edition.)

In dealing with the cost factor of a large-edition project, if it takes you 20 hours to make a print on your own, will you have time to make enough prints to sell so that you can have a cash-flow system? Rather than investing in your own press, you might consider taking your work to a printer. Or instead of doing lithography, maybe you can do silkscreen faster without sacrificing quality—or go to original hand-drawn offset prints.

If you can involve some of your collectors in the project as backers, they will feel that they are not only purchasing art, but are also actually helping to "make it happen" by supporting you.

After a year or two of actively "doing your own thing," you will want to assess your progress. If the picture looks bleak, don't give up. Find the weak link and replace it with another approach.

MOVING UP

If you have managed to develop a positive cash flow, consider purchasing art supplies by volume, moving to a larger studio, or even hiring studio assistants to do some of the more menial tasks (like cleaning prints, matting, wrapping work for shipment), and hiring someone to do your public relations and keep your books. At this point, you may be ready to relinquish a source of income from part-time alternative employment so you can concentrate on creating art full-time.

Take a good look at your goals. Determine how much work you can and want to produce in a year, how much you think you can sell, and how much money you can and want to make.

You will now be in a position to determine whether you are better off following the traditional gallery/dealer route, or functioning in the Network on your own.

You must grasp an understanding of the nature of self-promotion, develop the tools, and utilize them to your fullest advantage. Whichever avenue you choose, it is important to be constantly cognizant of the fact that today, you, the artist, are not only a creative genius, but also a businessperson.

You've done enough reading—now it's time to go out there and shake a tail feather!

14

Preparing Your Portfolio

by
Kate Keller and Mali Olatunji

◆ ◆ ◆ ◆

KATE KELLER is the Head Fine Arts photographer at the Museum of Modern Art in New York City, where she has worked since 1973. She earned her degree in photography from Ohio University.

MALI OLATUNJI has been a Fine Arts photographer with the Museum of Modern Art for seven years. Previously he studied photography in New York City for several years.

◆ ◆ ◆ ◆

Photographing works of art is not a magical process whereby one can produce, on photographic material, an image that is intrinsically akin to an original work. It is a resemblance—a clue to the original. However, much of the way we see art today is through photography in magazines, books, and lecture slides. It is a primary vehicle for showing one's own work to other artists, dealers, grant juries and editors. Thus, in a sense it has become a substitute for the original in the eyes of many viewers. This change of perspective of photography's inherent role makes it necessary for the photographer to go beyond mere documentation. The special qualities of a particular work of art must be presented to their best advantage. To obtain this one must excercise both understanding and control over the photographic medium.

This does not have to be an awesome task, but it is one that does require practice. To help your understanding we will give some background information on equipment and materials, as well as discuss a variety of shooting situations: the how, when, and what to use. It is impossible to cover all aspects of the process in a few pages. Therefore, we have focused on essential information and techniques to use as building blocks from which to expand your own working patterns.

EQUIPMENT

When buying equipment, whether used or new, do not rely solely on the salesman's word. If you are unfamiliar with the model or manufacturer, check with someone who has had practical experience with the equipment. In purchasing used equipment, be sure that there is a satisfaction guarantee. Conduct your own tests to insure that the equipment is working properly. When dealing with rentals, familiarize yourself thoroughly with the equipment before leaving the store.

Aside from the basic equipment of camera, lens, meter, tripod and lights, there are other necessary accessories which are useful in handling a variety of photographic situations:

a. level
b. timer
c. cable release
d. grey card
e. color patch
f. white boards, sheets, newspaper
g. black boards, black cloth
h. diffusing material.

At the end of this chapter is a list of catalogue addresses to which you can refer in comparing prices and equipment.

CAMERA

Most slide presentations are designed for a 35mm camera. For that reason and because of general popularity we will concentrate on its use. If you do not have a camera and intend either to buy or borrow one, the single lens reflex is preferable to a rangefinder or automatic camera. Single lens reflex (SLR) cameras are more adaptable to situations that might be encountered when photographing art, but this does not mean the others cannot be used.

Automatic cameras are primarily intended for candid outdoor photography. The camera automatically correlates the light intensity with film speed to properly expose the film. In a fully automatic camera the photographer knows only if there is adequate light, not specific exposure information. The photographer cannot determine the f/stop or shutter speed that is necessary for consistently good results. There are automatic cameras that have manual overrides. The type offering manual f/stop control is best for obtaining depth of field, which is necessary in photographing three-dimensional works.

Light travels through the lens of a rangefinder camera and directly strikes the film plane. There is no mechanical apparatus that translates this exact image to the photographer. The photographer looks through a separate lens that gives a close visual approximation. Because the subject is viewed and photographed from two positions, there is displacement from the image that is seen and the image recorded. This is referred to as parallax. The closer the camera moves to the subject, the greater the displacement. With practice this problem can be minimized. There is a wide variety of rangefinder cameras with interchangeable lenses and accessories, which gives versatility in handling various situations.

With the single lens reflex cameras (SLR) you see the subject as the lens sees it at all times. This is accomplished by the placement of a mirror inside the camera body which directs light entering the lens to the viewfinder. You are able to get as close to the subject as your lens permits without having to compensate for parallax. When long exposures are necessary, movement of the mirror can cause vibrations in some cameras. This can be compensated for. After the lens is focused you can use a device that prevents vibration by locking the mirror during the exposure.

As with the rangefinder camera there is a vast assortment of accessories for SLRs. Lenses and viewing screens offer greater flexibility when photographing art with an SLR.

LENSES

Inherent defects or aberrations in lenses can, in a variety of ways, distort the images they produce. Most lenses made today satisfactorily compensate for these problems. The degree to which they have been corrected is often reflected in price. It is better to have a reasonably good camera body with an excellent lens than the reverse situation.

35mm cameras generally come equipped with a 50 or 55mm or "normal" lens. This lens gives you an angle of view similar to that of the human eye, which is about 50°. It is a satisfactory all-purpose lens.

A 35mm lens on a 35mm camera is considered a "wide angle," with a 70° angle of view. A subject can be photographed at a much closer distance when using a wide-angle lens than when using a normal lens. This would seem the ideal solution when shooting in a small area, except that the edges of the image flare out and become more distorted the closer the subject is to the camera.

A long focus, 85mm lens for 35mm cameras has an angle of view of about 35°. When looking at a subject at the same distance with both normal lens and long lens, the long lens will see only part of what the normal lens sees. In order for the long lens to cover what the normal lens sees, the distance between lens and subject must be increased. A long lens is not generally used for photographing art, because of the greater space needed. However, it can be used to reduce the glare from a painting, since its increased distance from the object being photographed will result in fewer rays of reflecting light striking the lens. It can also lessen the distortion when photographing three-dimensional work. Do not use a lens longer than 135mm on a 35mm camera for photographing artwork, because other characteristics of the lens will affect the quality of the image.

Macro lenses are made for SLR cameras and are designed and corrected for close-up photography. We use a 55mm macro lens, which gives the versatility of a normal lens plus the ability to photograph at close range without adjustments. It is a very sharp lens which is also designed to photograph flat surfaces. It is an excellent lens for photographing art.

Note of importance: lens shades should always be used on lenses. Their use prevents extraneous light from entering the lens and causing a dulled, light-flared image.

METERS

Light meters assist the photographer in making sure a work of art is lighted correctly as well as giving the information needed to properly expose the film. There are two types of meters: (1) a reflective light meter, which measures the light bouncing (reflected) off the subject; (2) the incident light meter which measures the light falling onto the subject. The latter is most useful in photographing art. By its readings one can tell if a two-dimensional work has the even lighting it needs, or in the case of three-dimensional works, the correct lighting ratio.

Incident meters are hand held, which enables you to take a reading near the subject. Care should be taken not to let your own shadow interfere with the reading. Meter readings give proper exposure to a medium grey. In most cases all other tones or values will fall into place. However, if you have a work with dominant dark values, extra exposure is required to retain detail. One half to one stop is the necessary adjustment. Work that is light in value needs less exposure. The correction here is one half to one stop less than the given meter reading.

To lessen the risks of improperly exposed film, further exposures should be made in addition to the one indicated by the light meter. This is called "bracketing." To bracket black and white film, take three shots in all: (1) your indicated exposure, (2) one stop more exposure, and (3) one stop less exposure. Example: if the meter reading is f/22 at ¼ of a second, the additional exposures would be f/22 at ½ of a second and f/22 at ⅛ of a second. Because color film is more critical, the brackets should be one-half stops in both directions.

Meters located inside the camera itself are reflective meters. These meters can be adapted to check and correct the amount of light falling on the work of art. Readings are taken by placing a Kodak grey card in front of the work and parallel to the lens, then moving it to various positions in front of the work. Consult the owner's manual for particular instructions on how close to the grey card one must be in order to get an accurate meter reading.

TRIPODS

When the shutter speed is below ¹⁄₆₀ of a second, a hand-held camera can blur the image. This effect, caused by both mirror (SLR cameras) and body movement, can be lessened somewhat by holding one's breath during the exposure. However, this measure is not a satisfactory one for producing the quality needed when photographing art. Therefore, a tripod is a necessary piece of equipment.

A tripod needs to be sturdy; usually, the heavier the tripod the more stability it will have. Look for a tripod which can be adjusted to allow movement of the camera in any direction. This allows parallel alignment with the work of art.

LIGHTS

The advantage of indoor over outdoor lighting is the ability to control the direction and distance of the light source and to maintain a near constant color temperature.

Changes of height, distance and angle from the subject are easily made when lamps are mounted on movable light stands; while lamps can also be clamped onto ladders, chairs, boards, etc., their mobility is somewhat limited.

The choice of photo lamps depends on the type of film. The choice is not critical when using black and white film, but is with color. Photo bulbs are available with color temperatures of 3200°K (Kelvin) and 3400°K. Most indoor color film is compatible with 3200°K. The exception is Kodachrome A, which requires 3400°K. The relatively short time some bulbs can maintain constant color temperature makes it important to keep a record of how long each bulb has burned. Use bulbs of similar age together. Once these bulbs have gone past their recommended life for color they can be used for black and white photography, where color temperature is not crucial to the image quality.

There are three basic bulb designs: (1) the standard bulb, which looks like an ordinary house bulb with a long neck; (2) bulbs with built-in reflectors; and (3) the narrow tube quartz light. Regular photo lamps do require aluminum reflector bulbs to reflect their light. Reflector bulbs have a metallic coating which acts as a reflector, making the aluminum bowls unnecessary. However, reflector bulbs can fit into bowls for additional control of the beam. Quartz bulbs require special electrical fixtures.

There are advantages and disadvantages to each bulb. The quartz bulb is the most expensive, with its price being three to five times as high as that of the other two types. The standard and reflective bulbs range in price from $3.00 to $6.00. However, the life of a quartz light is 100 hours compared to four to six hours for the other lamps. The quartz light is very mobile because of the light-weight construction of the fixture head. Quartz lights do require stands. While the quality of this light source is rather harsh, it can be compensated for by bouncing the light or using a diffusion screen. There is a wide range of prices on quartz equipment. It is possible to buy complete set-ups containing several lights and stands at very reasonable sums.

When buying reflectors for standard bulbs, remember that the diameter of the bowl should be the same for each bulb. It will standardize the light beams, making it easier to attain even light. Clamps can be used for securing the lamps either to light stands or to their substitutes. This is an economical set-up, since 10″ reflector bowls and sockets with clamps are about $5.00. The quality of light from these lamps is softer than from the quartz.

Standard bulbs are available in different wattages depending on electrical capacity. Most bulbs used are 500 watt, although there are also lower wattage bulbs. In the list below, figures in the "bulb life" column indicate the hours we feel we can safely use the bulb without color change. They are slightly lower than the manufacturers' recommendations.

Name of Bulb	Description	Watt	Color Temp.	Bulb Life
EAL	Reflective bulb	500	3,200 K	5 hrs.
FCX	Quartz	650	3,200 K	100 hrs.
ECA	Frosted inside	250	3,200 K	15 hrs.
EVB	No. 2 frosted	500	3,400 K	4 hrs.

Having the best equipment does not guarantee the best results. To a certain extent the capacity of the equipment does affect quality, but the important factor is the person behind the camera. Understanding the limitations and possibilities of the equipment vis-a-vis the work being photographed is essential. We find the following accessories useful:

ACCESSORIES

Level	—used to insure that the camera is parallel to the surface being photographed.
Timer	—used to time exposures longer than one second.
Cable release	—used with long exposures to prevent movement when the shutter is manually released.
Grey card	—used with reflective meters to insure proper lighting.
Color patch grey scale	—used to determine proper filtration of color film or prints when necessary.
White boards, sheets, newspaper	—used for bouncing light from its source to a work for proper exposure or lighting ratio; also to cover reflecting colored objects.
Black boards, black cloth	—used to cover objects that reflect.
Diffusing materials	—used to create soft light from a harsh light situation.

FILM

The choice between black and white or color film should be based on aesthetic as well as practical factors. A three-dimensional work that is primarily concerned with form can lose its impact if the element of color is brought into play. In much the same way, the shades of grey in a black and white photograph cannot relate the visual intentions of a work whose color values are its distinguishing characteristics.

Final costs are a practical consideration in choosing between the use of a color negative or a transparency film. Although the initial expense in the use of transparencies may be greater, the printing process is eliminated. With the use of negatives that cost less, finding a good reliable printer who has reasonable rates can be a problem. Most commercial labs do not have the necessary experience to deal with the special considerations of reproducing art work. There are exceptions; try to establish a a good rapport with your lab.

BLACK AND WHITE FILM

Film emulsions are made with light-sensitive silver halide crystals. The size of the crystal determines the characteristics of the particular film. An emulsion with small uniform crystals produces a film with low sensitivity to light, fine grain when developed, and the power to record fine detail with maximum sharpness. In comparison, larger crystals produce a film that is faster in its response to light with grain that is noticeably larger and that loses acuteness in the recording of fine detail.

Speed	Grain	Contrast	Detail/Sharpness
Slow Film	Very fine	High	Maximum
Fast Film	Large	Low	Good

A.S.A. is the term used for film speed. The higher the number, the more sensitive the film. Films with an A.S.A. of 8 to 50 are considered low; 64 to 200 medium; 320 to 1600 fast.

The subject of the photograph and the conditions under which you are working determine the speed of the film. Works of art require careful rendering. Therefore, a slow, fine-grain film is usually used. When the need to stop motion is a factor, a faster film must be considered. A shutter speed of $\frac{1}{125}$ of a second is the threshold at which motion is stopped. Often fine-grain emulsions are too slow even under high illumination. A high-contrast range, either within a work of art itself or the way in which it is lighted, can be reduced by using a film with a medium or high A.S.A. rating.

All brands of film have about the same degree of quality and constancy. The choice of a manufacturer is a personal one, which can be made only through trial.

AGFA

AGFA-Pan Professional-25	ASA 25
AGFA-Pan Professional-100	ASA 100
AGFA-Pan Professional-400	ASA 400

ILFORD

Pan-F	ASA 25 (changes with
FP 4	ASA 64 developer)
HP 4	ASA 200
HP 5	ASA 400

KODAK

Panatomic X	ASA 32
Plus X	ASA 125
Tri X	ASA 400

Kodak's pamphlet S-23 describes direct positive films and processes for making black and white transparencies. Satisfactory slides can be made with Panatomic X developed in Kodak's Direct Positive Film Developing Kit. Black and white slides can also be made with color film. One thing to remember: since the film will respond to the dominant color of the medium used in the work of art, what the eye sees as black might record as another color on the film. To correct this response, use a correction filter.

COLOR FILM

All films are sensitive to heat and humidity, and should be stored properly before and after exposure and processing. This is particularly true with color film, since improper storage can alter color response. It is necessary to eliminate as many variables as possible when using color materials. By referring to the following list, you will help maintain color constancy and, in the long run, save time and money.

1. Read manufacturers' information sheets; use as guide for initial testing.
2. Buy film in quantity. A "brick" containing 20 rolls of film will cost less than buying 20 individual rolls.
3. Store film in refrigerator with low humidity. This keeps film stable and prevents color shifts.

4. Warm film to room temperature for one hour before using to prevent condensation marks and change in film speed.
5. Test film under the same conditions that will exist where actual photography will occur (lights, camera, medium). Determine correct A.S.A. and color filtration, if needed.
6. Bracket exposure. Once A.S.A. has been established through testing, it is advisable to expose film both ½ stop over and ½ stop under the given light meter reading.
7. Use a reliable lab. Processing should remain constant without any drastic color changes.
8. Check color with original. This should be done under the same color temperature source. In the case of slides, a white board is held under the slide at a short distance away with the same light illuminating both the original and the slide.
9. Correct color with cc filters. After the tests have been compared to the original, and if there is an unsatisfactory color change, cc filters can be used for correction. Kodak's book E-77 explains the theory and use of cc filters.
10. With color negative film, place color near work without interfering with the image. It is used as a guide by the printer.

Remember: color film responds to color with varying degrees of accuracy. This is due to the particular sensitivity of the film in relationship to the medium used in the work and how it is applied. For instance, pinks tend to be paler than other colors present in a slide. Undercoatings not visible to the eye often show up in color film. In some of these cases cc filters can bring the colors into acceptable balance. All colors will not record perfectly at all times, and a compromise is often required. Generally, the compromise will not greatly affect the overall quality of the slide.

The correct film and light source combination is essential when photographing in color. A color slide of an art work, when illuminated simultaneously with an incandescent light and daylight, will render false color. Color film cannot compensate for mixtures of light as can the human eye. Manufacturers make three-color emulsions, each responsive to a different color temperature (°Kalvin) light source. The sources and temperatures are daylight 5600°K, Tungsten 3200°K, and Photolamps 3400°K.

If an incorrect film/light source combination is used, the results are usually unsatisfactory. Tungsten film used outdoors will produce a blueish cast over the image. Deep yellow will dominate when daylight film is shot indoors under tungsten light. With the use of color conversion filters, a film that responds correctly to one color temperature can be converted so as to record accurately in another. This is not generally recommended, however, because it means the light must travel through another piece of glass, thereby lessening the overall sharpness of the image. It also means additional exposure is required.

It is possible to photograph works outdoors, but a variety of problems arise. Daylight is a variable source of light, making it difficult to maintain the constancy needed for color work. Its quality depends on the amount of direct light from the sun. Altitude, haze, and time of day are all variables and must be considered. Because there is less blue in the sky after sunrise or just before sunset, all colors will be warm. When photographing in open shade on a clear day, the reflected light from the blue sky will cast blue on the image. Objects bounce color when photographing outdoors so the work must be carefully placed. For instance, green foliage will reflect green onto the image. It is much easier to control light in a studio.

It is possible to obtain acceptable slides of gallery installations under existing lighting conditions. Find out the types of bulbs that are used. Consult a Kodak Professional Photoguide to determine color balance of the light, what filter to use, and the required additional exposure. Low light levels generally exist in galleries, and tripods are rarely permitted. To compensate, the A.S.A. of Kodak's Ektachrome film can be increased by one stop without noticeable contrast or color shift. It is important for proper processing that you tell the lab if you have increased the film speed. When shooting in an area with fluorescent lights, the same procedure is necessary. Because heavy filtration is needed, Kodak's suggestions for filtration are guides, but your tests must be made for accurate results.

The same relationship between film speed, sharpness and grain applies to color as well as to black and white. The choice of manufacturer for color is more dependent on what film the lab is able to process. For this reason Kodak is used when it is important to get results quickly. Ektachrome is primarily used because of the convenience of obtaining results from the lab within the same day. Now that there are a few local labs that have begun to process Kodachrome, check labs in your area. Due to the special processing, which is usually done by Kodak, it will take several days for the film to be processed and returned. Again, the choice of film should be made by testing and by your particular requirements. The following is a list of some possibilities:

Film	ASA	Type	Color Temp.	Processing
KODAK				
EKTACHROME 160	160	SLIDE	3200°K	LOCAL LAB
EKTACHROME 50	50	SLIDE	3200°K	LOCAL LAB
EKTACHROME 64	64	SLIDE	DAYLIGHT	LOCAL LAB
EKTACHROME 200	200	SLIDE	DAYLIGHT	LOCAL LAB
EKTACHROME 400	400	SLIDE	DAYLIGHT	LOCAL LAB
KODACHROME II				
TYPE A	40	SLIDE	3400°K	KODAK
KODACHROME II	80	SLIDE	DAYLIGHT	KODAK
KODACOLOR II	80	NEGATIVE	DAYLIGHT	LOCAL LAB
VERICOLOR II				
PROF. TYPE S	100	NEGATIVE	DAYLIGHT	LOCAL LAB
AGFA				
AGFACHROME 64	64	SLIDE	DAYLIGHT	AGFA
AGFACHROME 100	100	SLIDE	DAYLIGHT	AGFA
FUJI				
FUJICHROME RD 100	100	SLIDE	DAYLIGHT	FUJI/LOCAL LAB

SETTING UP

Being organized is essential in photography. The following procedures should be kept in mind during the shooting session.

1. The shooting area should be clear of extraneous objects. Start with a minimum amount of equipment—two to four lights, tripod, camera, and light meter. Other equipment should be off to the side for safety reasons.
2. With one or two lamps lighting the work, carefully position the work in the viewfinder of the camera and focus.
3. Determine the lighting possibilities to stress or de-emphasize the particular qualities of the work. Experiment.
4. Save time by keeping a record of how a work is photographed. Make a small diagram of the set-up. Note angle and distance of the lights to the work. List camera, lens, film, meter reading, f/stop, and shutter speed (Illustration 1). If the results are good, this information can be a basis in photographing a similar work at another time. Or if the results are unsatisfactory, the mistake can usually be pinpointed.

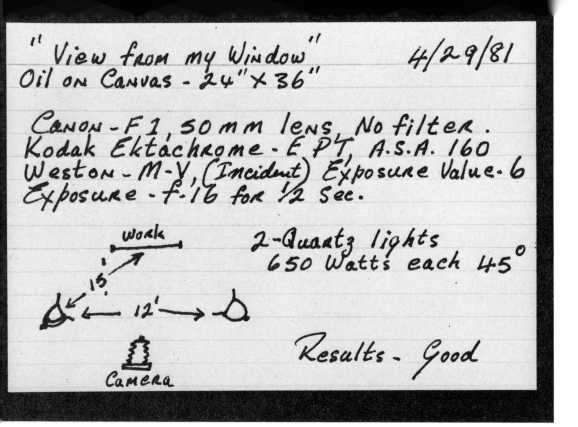

Illustration 1. *Note card with set-up information.*

LIGHTING

Surfaces, textures, shapes and colors alter their character in response to changes in the quality of light. For this reason and because of the uniqueness of each work, it is important to investigate various lighting possibilities. Most information on how to photograph works of art begins by saying, "Place lights at a 45° angle to the object being photographed." In principle, the surface reflection will be minimal at this angle. We have found this the exception, not the rule. We firmly believe there are no rules when lighting works of art—only guidelines.

TWO-DIMENSIONAL WORKS

There are two requirements for photographing two-dimensional work: (1) the camera should be parallel to the work, and (2) light must fall evenly on the work.

The camera must be horizontally and vertically parallel to the surface of the work. If it is not, the camera image will be distorted and unsharp. A level reading on both the camera and the artwork will help in achieving proper alignment. If the work is tilted, the camera must be at the same angle. The gridded viewing screen available to some SLR cameras can facilitate the necessary parallel alignment of the work with the camera (Illustrations 2, 3, 4, 5).

Even distribution of light is of critical importance. Varying light intensities will cause the film to record false information. This is particularly true with color film. A slight variation in intensity (½ stop) will cause a noticeable exposure change.

A hand-held incident meter placed and read at nine points near the surface of the work is the easiest way to insure even illumination (Illustration 6). Remember not to cast your shadow on the meter (Illustration 7). The procedure mentioned earlier, in discussing reflective meters (page 213), can also insure even lighting of a work. Place the 18% grey card near the work at the same nine points (Illustration 8).

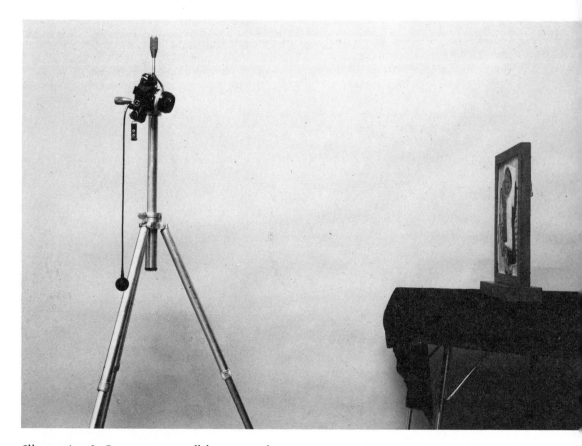

Illustration 2. *Camera not parallel to art work.*

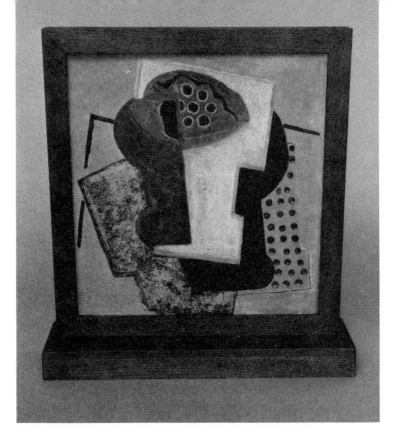

Illustration 3. *Result of Illustration 2. Note lines converging and lack of sharpness.*

Illustration 4. *Camera parallel to work.*

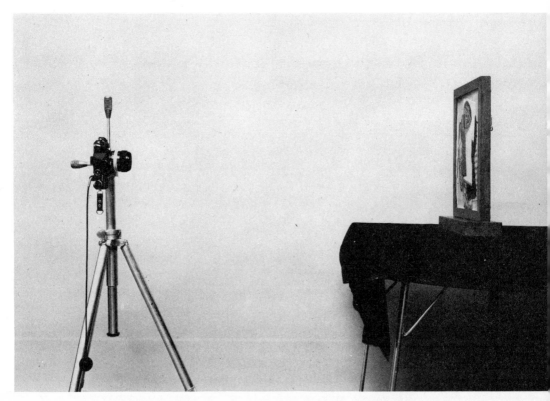

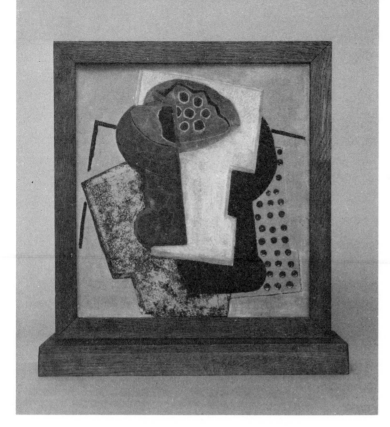

Illustration 5. *Result when camera is parallel to work. Compare with*
Illustration 3.

Illustration 6. *The nine points where light readings are taken. Note position of*
hand and body placement for accurate readings.

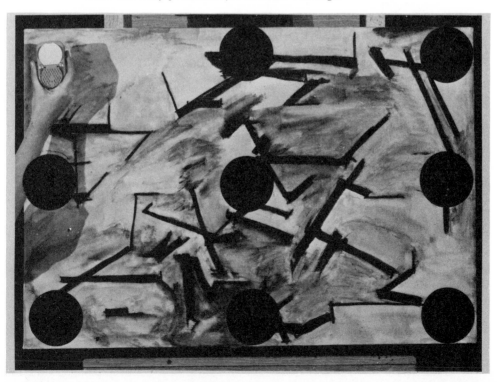

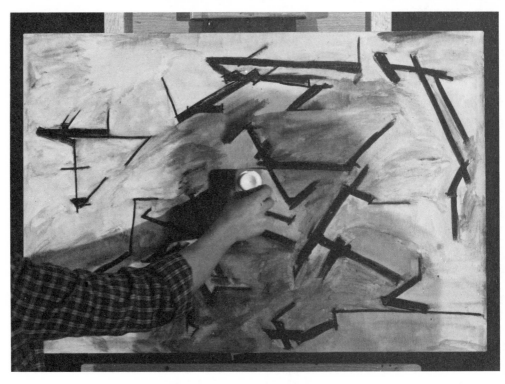

Illustration 7. *An incorrect incident meter reading will be obtained due to the body casting a soft shadow over much of the painting as well as a stronger shadow from the hand. See Illustration 8 for correct method.*

Illustration 8. *Convenient way to place grey card when taking a meter reading from a camera. Grey card is clipped onto light stand.*

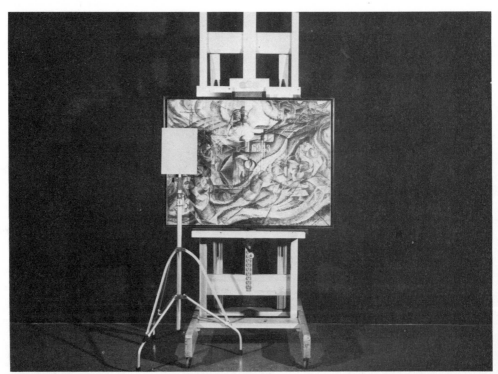

Conventional lighting set-up consists of lights placed approx-imately at a 45° angle to the art work (Illustration 9). It can be used when the surface of a work is not reflective, and when texture is not an important quality to emphasize. This is direct, harsh light. Although the characteristics of some work (water colors, drawings, etc.) generally lend themselves to this light, those works with delicate values may need softer lighting to delineate tones. Try bounce lighting.

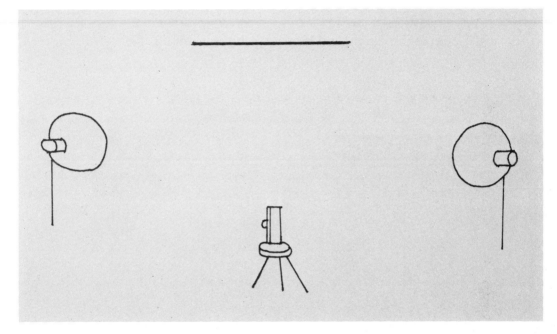

Illustration 9. *Diagram of conventional 45° lighting set-up.*

When photographing small works, it is possible to have even illumination with two lights. With larger works, four lights and sometimes more should be used. When trying to light a large area with only two lights, a "hot spot," or overlapping of light, will occur in the center of the image. The greater the distance the lights are from the work, the easier it is to obtain even light.

When even illumination exists on a work except at the very bottom—a problem with larger works—place a white board or cloth under the work. This will bring up the light level to match the rest of the work. This cannot be used with dark shiny surfaces, because the card will reflect its own shape onto the surface. A black board or cloth is placed under a work when the light level is too high, thus absorbing some of the light that would otherwise bounce onto the surface.

If you are working in a confined area it may be impossible to get the distance needed for even illumination. One solution is bounce lighting, which can be accomplished in a variety of ways:

1. Lights bouncing on floors, walls, ceilings (Illustrations 10, 11).
2. Light coming from one direction striking a wall or board (Illustration 12).
3. Lights facing each other (Illustrations 13, 14).

Illustration 10. *Bounce lighting set-up. Four lights bounced off ceiling and floor. The nine meter reading points are all equal.*

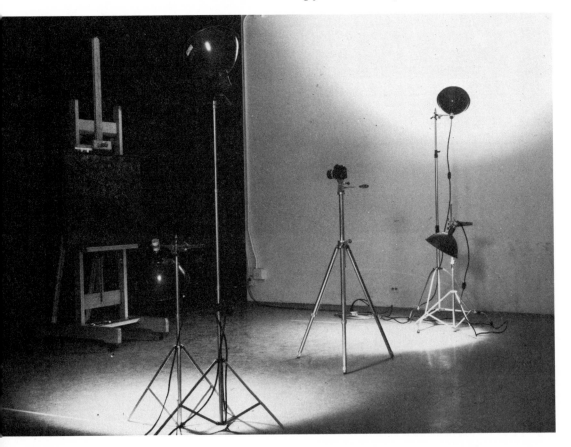

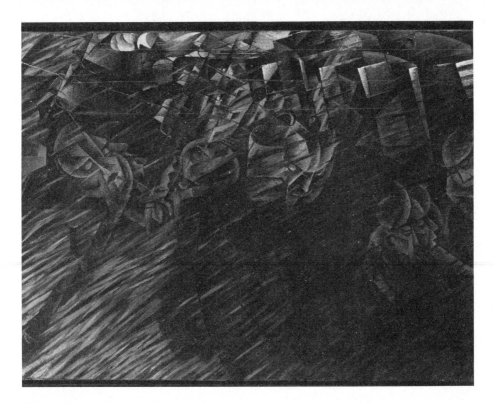

Illustration 11. *Result of bounce lighting.*

Illustration 12. *Set-up of light source coming from one side when bouncing off a white board.*

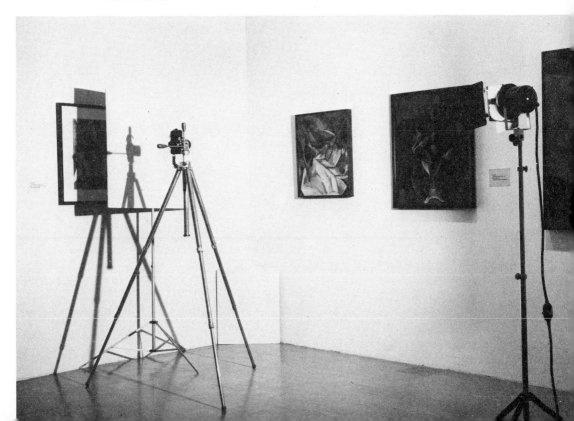

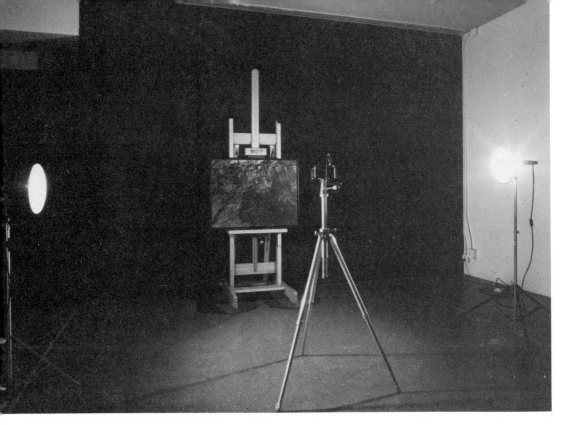

Illustration 13. *Set-up of two lights facing each other to obtain even lighting. Used to minimize glare.*

Illustration 14. *Results of set-up shown in Illustration 13.*

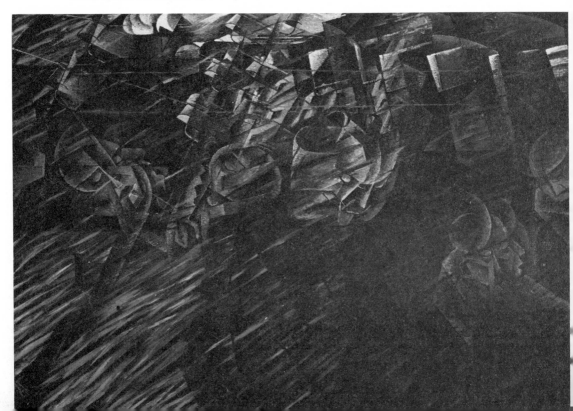

Lights bouncing around a room will cause environmental reflections and cast unwanted colors. Walls and boards should be neutral or white. Furniture, floors, walls and even the clothes you wear can affect color. Cover objects that might influence the color the film records. If a work is being photographed on or near the floor, place a newspaper under the work, making the floor neutral.

When you want to emphasize a strongly textured surface, use side lighting. Texture is exaggerated to convey the feeling of three dimensionality. The smaller the angle of light to the work, the greater the effect (Illustrations 15, 16).

It is often difficult to maintain even illumination with side lighting; a fill is then used. By using a wall or board near the darker side of the work, light will bounce from the boards back onto the surface of the work. If you use a board, note its angle, because this affects the density of the shadows cast from the primary light source. (Refer to Illustration 12.)

Illustration 15. *Side lighting for texture.*

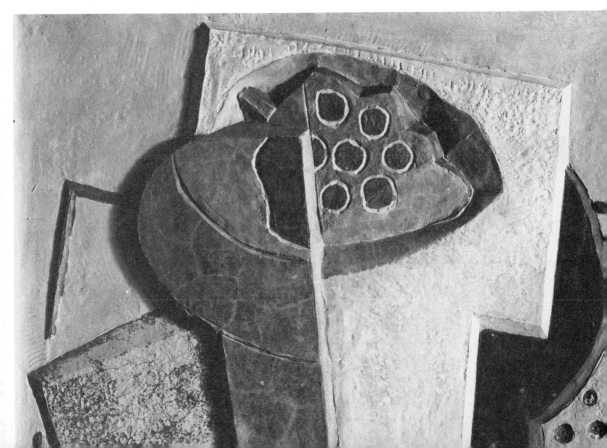

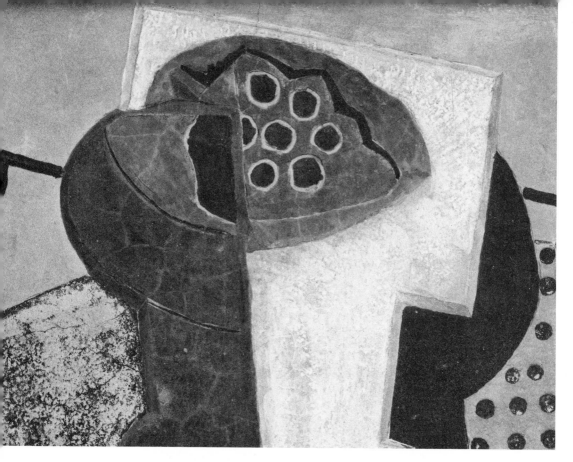

Illustration 16. *Same painting when lighted with lights at 45°. Note flat look.*

There is often a problem with reflection and glare when photographing two-dimensional surfaces. There are three ways to minimize this problem:

1. Bounce lighting.
2. Long lens.
3. Polarizing filters.

Conventional lighting can create glare, which makes definition of the image difficult (Illustrations 17 and 18). Bounced lighting helps to eliminate this problem. (Refer to Illustrations 11 and 13.) It is sometimes helpful when using bounce to place a black cloth over the camera. This cuts down further glare from the light bouncing off the wall opposite the work of art. A black cloth in front of the camera is also used when photographing a work under glass to stop reflection (Illustration 19).

Glare can be minimized to some extent with the use of the long lens. Compare it to the image produced by the normal lens (Illustration 20). Refer to Illustration 18.

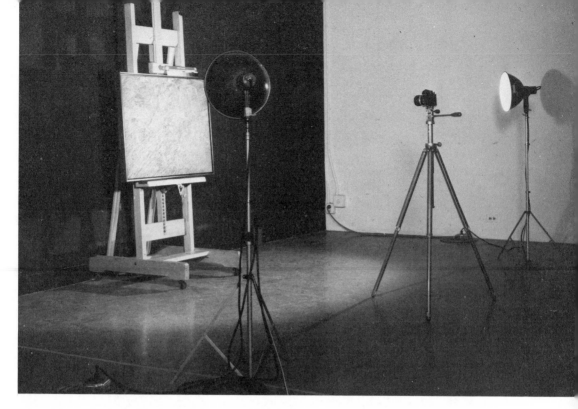

Illustration 17. *Conventional lighting set-up. Normal lens used.*

Illustration 18. *Result of conventional lighting set-up shown in Illustration 17. Compare painting with Illustrations 10 and 11, where bounced lighting was used. A normal lens was used.*

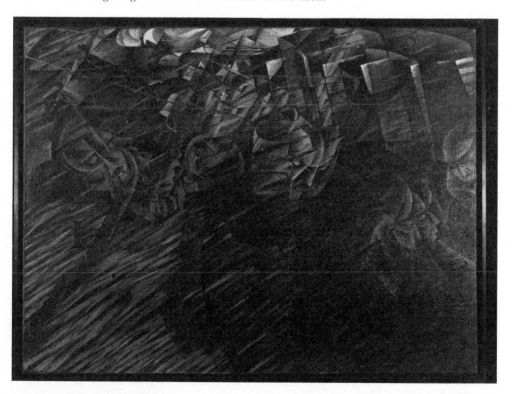

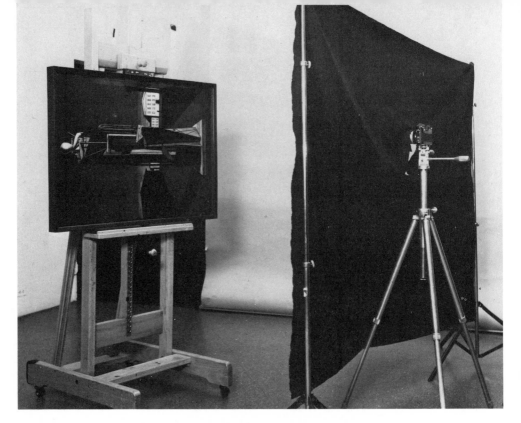

Illustration 19. *Set-up when photographing through glass or other reflective surfaces. Lights at 45°.*

Illustration 20. *Same set-up used as in Illustrations 17 and 18, but here a long lens was used. Note reduction of glare when compared to the normal lens.*

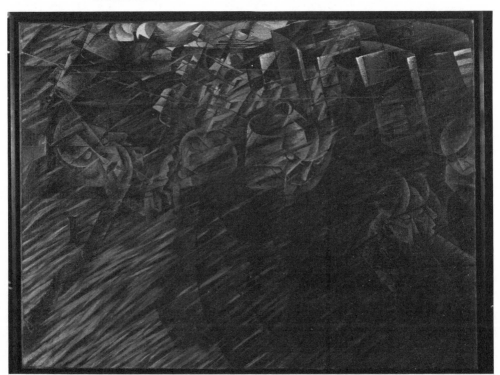

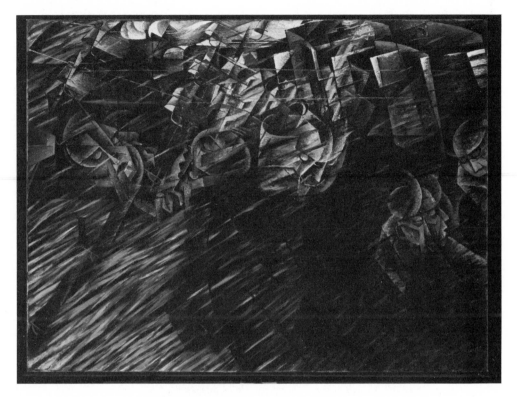

Illustration 21. *Same painting when photographed with polarizing filter. Note increase in contrast.*

Although polarizing filters can eliminate all reflection and glare, they are used as a last-resort measure; filters are needed on both camera lens and light sources; additional exposure of at least two stops is needed; contrast is also increased, which gives a false feeling to the work (Illustration 21). For these reasons we try to avoid using polarizing filters. However, there are materials that demand their use. For instance, graphite is very difficult to light since reflective problems cause part of the image to fade. Polarization in this case renders all details correctly (Illustrations 22 and 23).

THREE-DIMENSIONAL WORKS

The functions of lighting ratio, depth of field, and background all help to convey the feeling of three-dimensionality on the two-dimensional photographic surface.

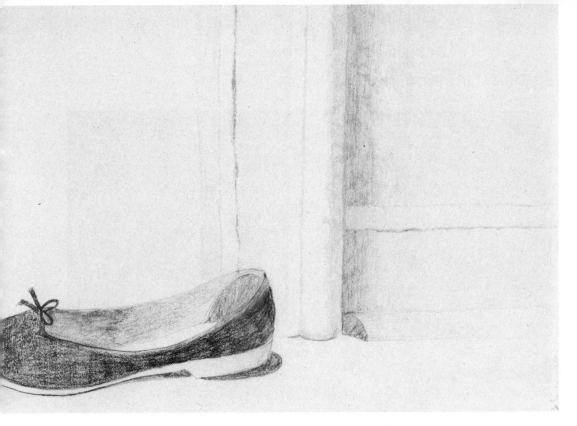

Illustration 22. *Graphite drawing with conventional lighting.*

Illustration 23. *Result when polarizing filters are used.*

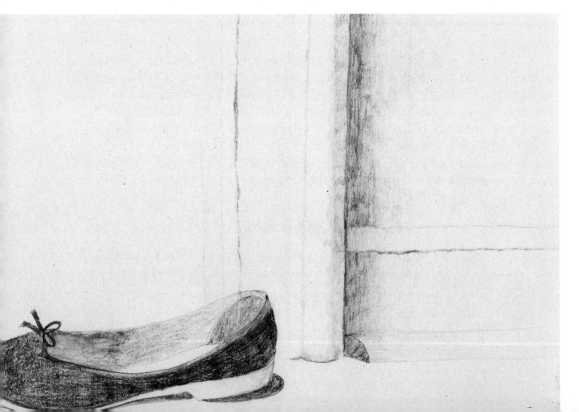

Lighting in a studio is the simulation of daylight. When looking at a photograph we unconsciously compare it with daylight and are aware of a dominant light source and its direction. If there are two light sources of equal strength casting their shadows on an image, there is a slight feeling of uneasiness. It upsets our viewing patterns, because we know it cannot exist in nature. Therefore, most three-dimensional lighting has one light dominating the subject.

Under most circumstances the use of one light creates too much contrast for the film to record all detail in both highlight and shadow areas. A second light must be used as a fill. The second light is placed at a greater distance from the subject. A piece of translucent material can also be placed in front of the second lamp to reduce the intensity of the light. A white card or cloth can also be used as a fill when positioned at the darkest side and held in such a way as to bounce the rays from the light source into the darker side of the work (Illustration 24).

The difference between the dark and light sides is called lighting ratio. To find the ratio, meter readings are taken from both the light and dark sides. If the difference is one stop, the ratio is 1:2, with the lighter area getting twice as much light as the darker area.

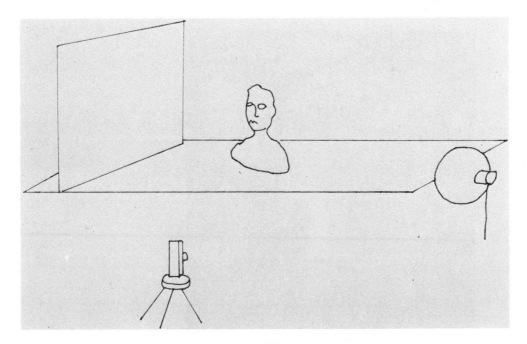

Illustration 24. *Set-up when using white card to control lighting ratio.*

The difference should not exceed two stops (1:4). Ratios above 1:4 will create a dramatic effect, but detail will be lost in the highlight and shadow areas (Illustrations 25, 26, 27).

The exposure is determined by taking the average of the two readings. If, for example, the meter reads f/16 at 16 seconds in the lighter area and f/16 at four seconds in the darker area, the correct exposure of f/16 at eight seconds will be used.

When the camera is focused on a particular point of a three-dimensional piece, every element of the piece at that distance will be in sharp focus. Part of the background and part of the foreground will also seem to be in focus. The distance from the nearest point to the furthest point in acceptable focus is called "depth of field." Depth of field is controlled by f/stops. The higher the f/stop number, the greater the depth of field that is obtained. The numbers generally assigned to a 35 mm camera are f/1.8, f/2, f/2.8, f/4, f/5.6, f/8, f/11, and f/16. The higher f/stop number has greater depth of field because the size of the aperture decreases as the number increases. Example: f/16 is capable of greater depth of field than f/8.

Illustration 25. *Using a ratio of 1:1.*

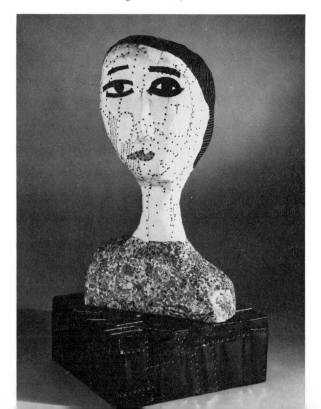

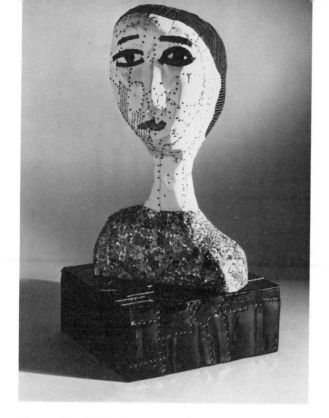

Illustration 26. *Using a ratio of 1:2.*

Illustration 27. *Using a ratio of 1:4.*

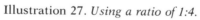

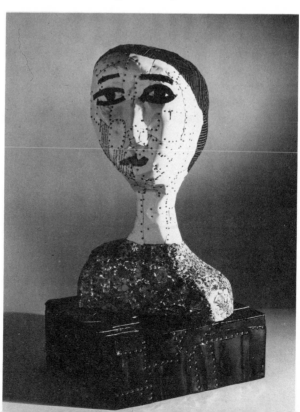

The depth of field of a lens extends further into the background than into the foreground. To insure sharpness in the foreground, the point of focus should be measured ⅓ into the work. Do not use the midpoint (Illustrations 28, 29, 30).

Normal lenses can be used to photograph three-dimensional works; however, the use of a longer lens can eliminate distortions. Photographing at a high or low angle can also cause unwanted exaggeration, so beware of the angles you choose.

Background is a consideration with both two- and especially three-dimensional work. In both cases keep your background clean. If working with paper or cloth, make sure there are no creases or wrinkles (Illustrations 31, 32). Dark backgrounds bring the work to the foreground but can destroy the three-dimensional feeling by absorbing the shadows of the work. In cases when a light background is preferred but the shadows are unwanted, place the work far away from the wall or background paper and close to the camera. Bounce lighting can also eliminate shadows. The placement of a small spotlight on the background of a work helps to separate the work from its surroundings (Illustrations 33, 34, 35, 36).

Illustration 28. *Depth of field. Lens wide open at f/1.8. Note tape measure; the focus is at ⅓ the depth. Focus falls off noticeably at 4" in the front and at 10" toward the back.*

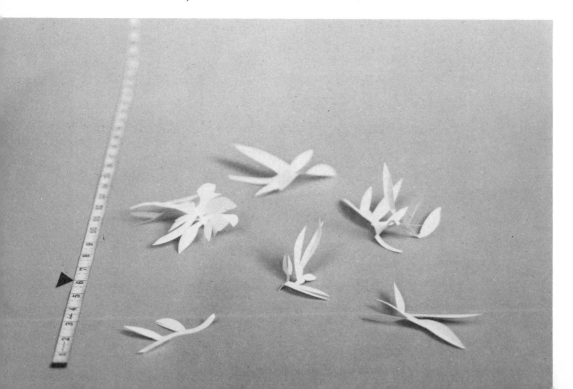

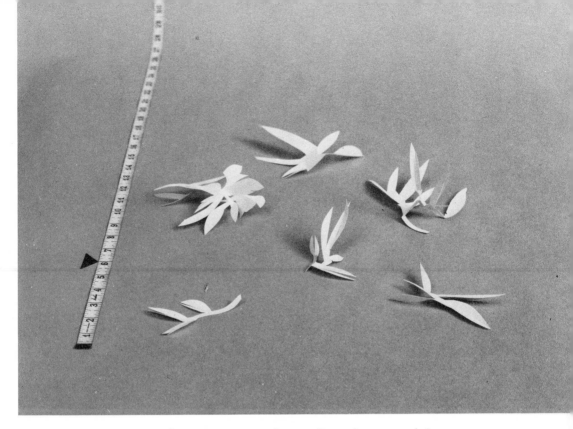

Illustration 29. *Lens set at f/5.6. Tape measure focus still not sharp toward the far rear or front.*

Illustration 30. *All areas in focus when f/16 used.*

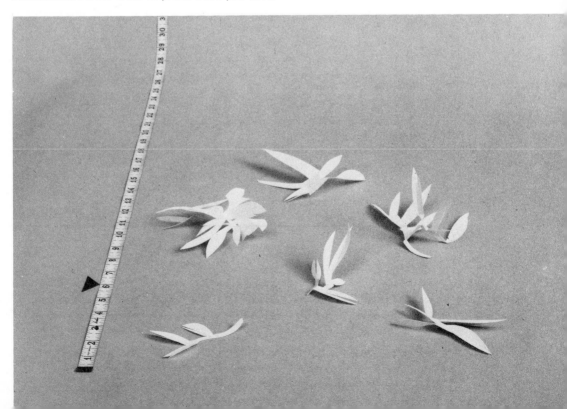

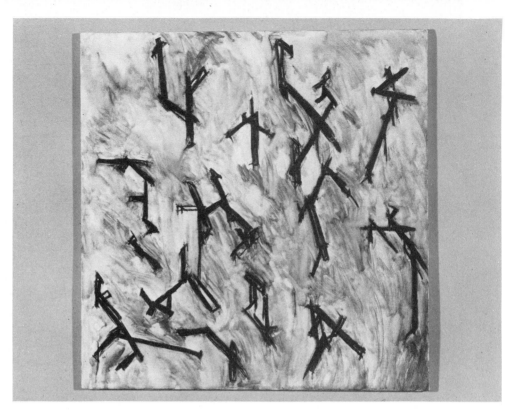

Illustration 31. *Painting on light background.*

Illustration 32. *Same painting on dark background. Individual taste will dictate best background for work.*

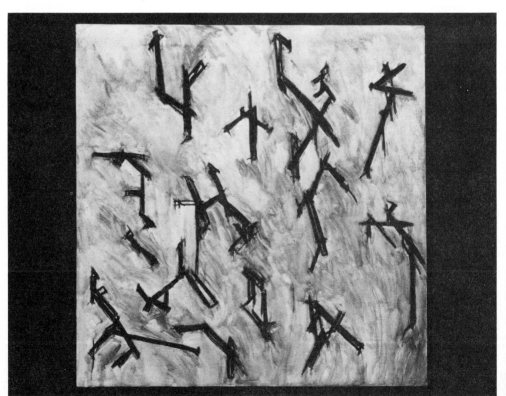

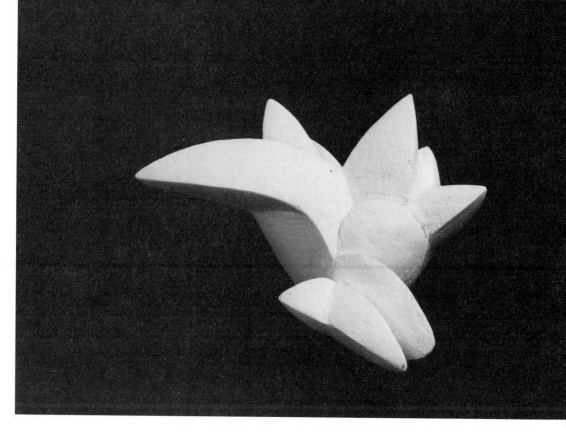

Illustration 33. *Sculpture on dark background loses some three-dimensional feeling but can look dramatic.*

Illustration 34. *Same lighting set-up with sculpture placed on grey background.*

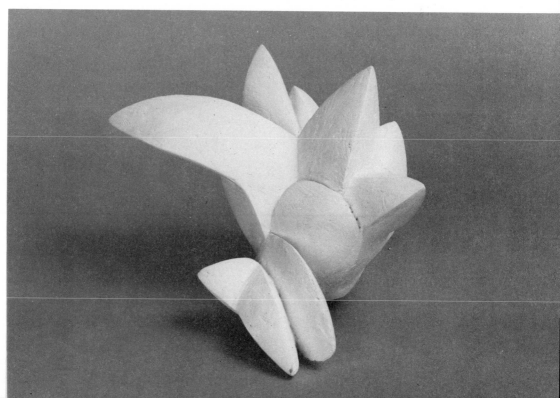

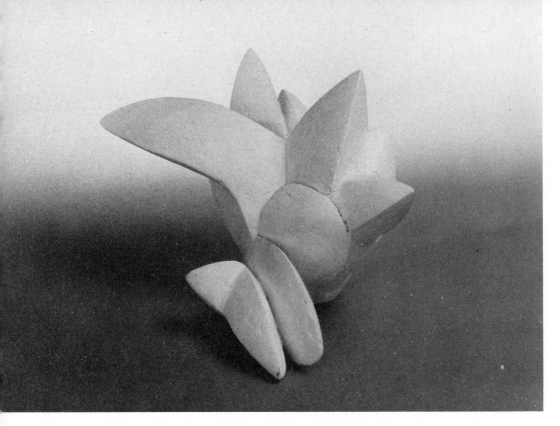

Illustration 35. *Same set-up as Illustration 34 but with background light added to create more separation.*

Illustration 36. *Diagram of set-up for Illustrations 33 and 34.*

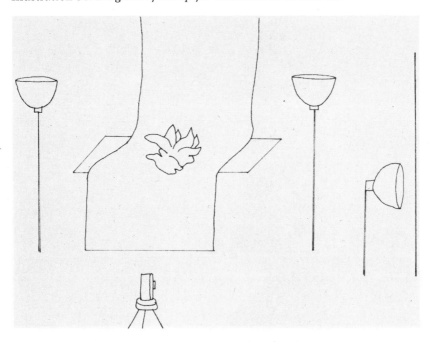

Lighting various materials used in sculpture can be challenging because there is usually more than one satisfactory way in which to represent a work. Again, it is best to experiment to see what is possible and then determine which situation has worked best. As an example of the choices to be made we have photographed a translucent vase two ways. First, we emphasize the form by placing white cards on either side and bouncing light off them. The forms of the cards are reflected onto the vase. Further definition of the form is accomplished by placing a small spot on the background. Stronger representation of the internal design is seen in the second example. A light in the background is the primary light source, with bounce light as fill (Illustrations 37, 38, 39, 40).

Illustration 37. *Set-up for photographing translucent piece. Light bounced from two white cards at the side.*

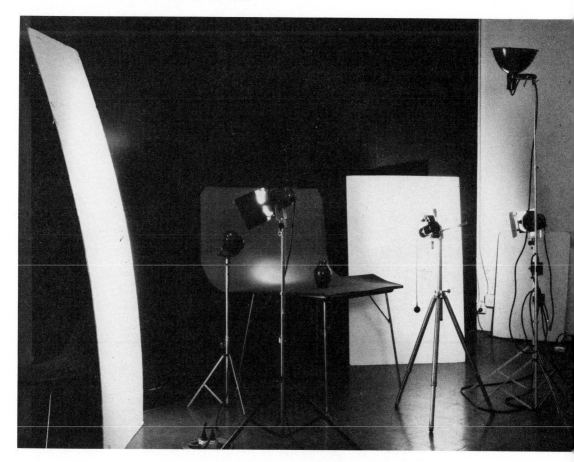

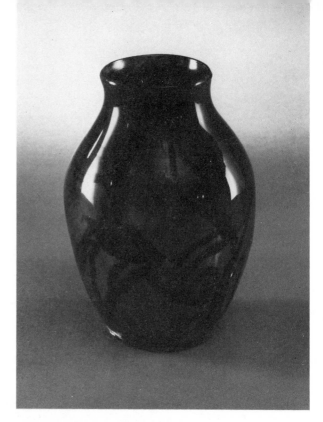

Illustration 38. *Result from light bounced from two white cards.*

Illustration 39. *Light bounced from the background through the work.*

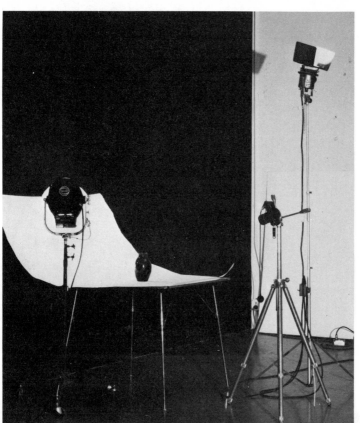

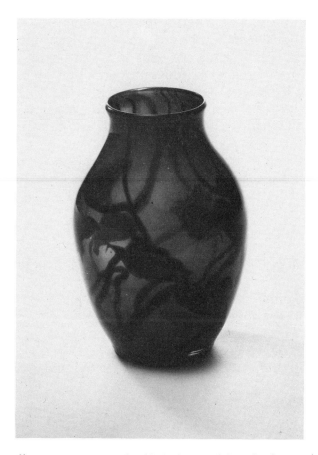

Illustration 40. *Result of light bounced from background.*

PRESENTATIONS

Slides are made when viewing is intended for more than one person and enlargement is necessary, as in classroom or art jury situations. They are also used when approaching galleries, because it is expedient to have a number of images neatly fitted together in one pocketed 11 x 9 transparency sleeve, ready to view on a light box. Each viewing situation needs a different slide density. Because of a projector's strong illumination and the enlargement needed, slides for projection should be slightly darker than those that will be viewed on a light box. When using transparencies for publication, printers prefer a denser image to work with, because it is easier to retain detail in highlight areas. However, the density should not be so great as to change the color or character of the artwork.

Prints are also used to show to galleries. Paper and emulsions are fragile, however, and prints should be kept in protective transparent sleeves. Black and white prints are often used for opening invitations and publications because of lower reproduction costs. Generally, prints with a little less than normal contrast but with separation in all tones are the best for reproduction. Whenever possible, check with the printer beforehand and ask for his specifications.

In general, trust your common sense about what looks good and right to you, and simply do the best you can with what you can afford.

SUGGESTED BIBLIOGRAPHY

Hand Book for Contemporary Photography, 4th Edition, Arnold Gassan
Artificial Light Photography, Ansel Adams
Basic Photography, M.J. Langford
Color Photography in Practice, D.A. Spencer
Craft of Photography, David Vestal
Photography for Artist and Craftsmen, Clause-Peter Schmid
Kodak Color Guide
Kodak Professional Photoguide
Kodak Copying M-1
Kodak Color Films E-77
Kodak Black and White Transparencies S-23

PHOTO CATALOGUES

47 Street Photo Inc.
36 East 19 Street
N.Y.C. 10003

Camera Barn
148 West 32 Street
N.Y.C. 10001

Competitive Camera
157 West 30 Street
N.Y.C. 10001

Arkin-Medio
131-27 Fowler Ave.
Flushing, N.Y. 11355

Olden
1265 Broadway
N.Y.C. 10001

ACKNOWLEDGMENT

A note of thanks to Robert Kobayashi for his help in preparing the manuscript.

The following works of art have been used as illustrations through the courtesy of the Museum of Modern Art and with the help of Richard L. Tooke:

Boccioni, States of Mind: Those Who Go, 1913, oil on canvas.
Illustrations 10, 11, 13, 14, 17, 18, 20 and 21

Laurens, Bowl of Fruit.
Illustrations 2, 3, 4, 5, 15, and 16

Lois Comfort Tiffany, Vase, c. 1900, Faurile Glass.
Illustrations 37, 38, 39 and 40

Braque, Road near L'eataque, 1908, oil on canvas.
Illustration 12

Boccioni, States of Mind: The Farewells, 1913, Oil on Canvas.
Illustration 8

The following works have been used through the courtesy of the artists:

Robert Coats, Blue Fat Line, 1980, oil on canvas.
Illustrations 6 and 7

Robert Coats, 2nd Fat Line, 1980, oil on canvas.
Illustrations 31 and 32

Nancy Fuller, Nature Study, 1978, plaster.
Illustrations 33, 34 and 35

Nancy Fuller, Leaves, 1977, paper.
Illustrations 28, 29 and 30

Robert Kobayashi, Martine, 1980, tin on wood.
Illustrations 25, 26, and 27

Donna DeSalvo, Untitled, 1980, graphite.
Illustrations 22 and 23

15

Selling Art Under Contract

by

Tennyson Schad

◆ ◆ ◆ ◆

TENNYSON SCHAD is the founder and owner of LIGHT Gallery, a New York gallery dealing in fine photographs. Mr. Schad is also an attorney specializing in intellectual property.

◆ ◆ ◆ ◆

How an artist achieves a relationship with a gallery is the stuff of which seminars are made. The fact that a thousand or so artists would spend the better part of a day in New York recently to hear artists and dealers expound on that issue underscores the depth of the concern on the part of the artistic community. All of us, in search of insights, have spawned an entire industry of seminars and "how-to" books, and we are still left with ourselves to deal with. To be cynical, how does a young woman make it to the top in Washington? How does a young actor achieve fame and fortune in New York City? The analogies are manifold.

The idealist in us says that success for artists is based upon excellence, new ideas and insights, and in some measure that is true. But it is also true that those artists are few and far between. The pragmatist knows that when everything else is equal other factors come to bear. Society being what it is, there are, of course, other factors. Visibility is a big one, as is being in the right place at the right time and knowing the right people. But I've said nothing new. Dealers receive calls all the time on behalf of the shy and retiring artist. That sort of reticence is perhaps endearing, but it's also self-defeating. While the dealers, to survive, must be on a constant search for new talent, at the same time someone has to be back in the gallery selling your work. In short, you must take the initiative. Don't hunker down in Moose Jaw, Saskatchewan, and wait to be discovered.

If you want to exhibit and sell your work, you must work at your craft, develop a coherent body of work, and take whatever steps are necessary for that work to be exhibited as often as possible, in museums, universities, cooperative galleries, wherever. There is no substitute for exposure. A word of caution, however. Nothing reveals a thin body of work faster than multiple exhibitions.

Dealers are always interested in adding new artists to complement their gallery roster. Even though you may not be an established artist, you should not hesitate to explore with a gallery the possibility of representation or exhibition. Galleries are always looking for new talent even if you do not have an established market.

To many artists, an association with a gallery is a sign of self-affirmation, a metaphor not unlike the Tinman's testimonial or the Scarecrow's diploma. But there are, on the other hand, a number of successful artists who prefer to represent their own work, and personally arrange their exhibitions at galleries and museums throughout the country. I admire these vagabond artist-entrepreneurs, but it takes a person of considerable stamina and self-possession, and one who loves to travel. The style is particularly suitable for photographers, not tied to a studio, who enjoy mixing it up with dealers and museum people and who often can use the travel time to their own advantage as working artists or to satisfy their wanderlust.

Others have agents and work not on a consignment basis but with hard cash. An agent, however, is no substitute for those who seek the exposure of a prominent gallery to build a national reputation.

If you wish to establish a relationship with a gallery, you must decide what kind of tie you desire and, of course, which gallery.

WHAT TO LOOK FOR IN A GALLERY

Before you sign with a gallery, you should be satisfied that (1) the gallery understands and feels a sense of commitment to your work; (2) your work fits in with that of the other artists represented by the gallery; (3) you feel comfortable working with the dealer or the gallery director; and (4) the gallery will enhance the visibility of your work and your reputation.

Your eagerness to align yourself with a gallery should not blind you to the realization that you may be better off without a gallery than with the wrong gallery or the wrong people.

SHOULD YOU HAVE A CONTRACT?

There are, as you probably have read, strongly divergent views on the question of whether artists and dealers should execute a written contract defining their relationship.

Much instructive material has been written about artists' dealings with galleries. The source books abound with legal clauses and authorities, but for the most part they appear to be concerned more with form than with substance. While the form contracts are useful checklists, they are not graven in stone and do not touch upon the heart of the artist-dealer arrangement.

Some artists, not wishing to be in the thrall of anyone, shy away from a written commitment. A number of dealers, too, find the contract an unnecessary burden on their autonomy and freedom. One could draw an analogy to a formal marriage contract, which also has its vocal exponents. But allocation between marriage partners as to responsibility for child care, washing the dishes, and watering the houseplants suggests a basic distrust or insecurity and lack of understanding. Many artists and galleries have flourished under long-standing commitments that have been cemented with little more than a handshake. They reason that the relationship will work only as long as both parties are content with the deal. It is that excitement that makes the marriage work. You can't force an artist to produce and you can't compel a dealer to get excited by and to push your work.

Where the ephemeral agreement suits the needs and person-alities of the parties, well and good. An artist-friend of mine produces one painting a year, and occasional drawings, and is represented by a single gallery. And he trusts his gallery. They see little need to set their mutual responsibilities in concrete. Neverthe-less, such a loose arrangement is not without its perils.

There is little need, it seems to me, for an artist and dealer to execute a written contract when the relationship falls short of actual representation, i.e., for a single exhibit or the consignment of a few works for a limited period of time. But that does not mean there should be nothing in writing.

WHAT TO PUT IN WRITING

Where works are consigned for a show or for a limited period of time to a gallery, a representation agreement is not necessary, but there should be in writing an understanding that states (1) the specific works received; (2) that the work is consigned for a specific period of time; (3) the prices at which the work is to be sold; (4) whether or not the work is insured while in possession of the gallery; (5) the commission to be paid to the gallery; and (6) when you are to be paid. These issues are discussed more fully below.

As you may have gathered, I do not believe that the contract is the essence of the artist-gallery relationship. You and your dealer must realize that your dealings with one another, with or without a contract, are determined by mutual understanding, trust, and shared commitment.

Nevertheless, I personally favor a contract with an artist because, if reasonably drawn, it informs the parties of their responsibilities and objectives with respect to each other. If you and the dealer work well together, the agreements will rarely if ever be referred to, for you will generally be able to reach a mutually satisfactory accommodation on most issues. The agreement should be little more than the skeleton on which you build the relationship. It should not be carried around in one's vest pocket like a road map. Contracts may identify problems, but only people solve them.

Your agreement with a dealer should be positive in tone and written in language you both can understand. As a lawyer, I am aware of my colleagues' passion for precision, but as a gallery owner I know how intimidating and incomprehensible a formal agreement is to many artists and dealers alike.

The contract should be short and sweet. If you need a lawyer to understand it, what good is it (unless, of course, you have a lawyer in the family)? I discuss below what I believe should be in the basic agreement.

POINTS TO CONSIDER

1. The parties

The agreement should obviously state the names and addresses of the parties. If your dealer is a corporation—and most are—then you should be so informed. (If you have any reason to doubt that a corporation gallery can live up to its financial commitments to you, be very cautious and feel out the possibility of having an individual personal signature as well.)

2. The term of the contract

Often the first agreement between an artist and a gallery will be for a relatively short period—a trial marriage. If you work well together, you will renew the contract as a matter of course. Often neither party gives formal renewal a thought, and both parties continue to abide by the original terms of the expired contract. I admire the mutual trust, but attention to the formal renewal is recommended. A term of two or three years seems most common in artist-dealer contracts. If you are an unestablished or less established artist, signing a longer term commitment may significantly interfere with your career in the future. On the other hand, your dealer may prefer a longer term arrangement. Negotiating renewals every one or two years is not high on anyone's priority list. Moreover, dealers spend considerable effort and money promoting the artists they represent and in making the public aware that their work is available through the gallery. A dealer is less likely to do so with enthusiasm if there is concern as to your staying with the gallery. Another material, although often unmentioned, consideration is that the longer contractual terms discourage poaching by opportunistic rival dealers with packets of promises.

3. Extent of representation

The extent of the representation of your work by your dealer can be restricted in terms of media and geography. For those bi- and tri-media types, it is not uncommon to have one dealer handle your paintings and another dealer carry your drawings or sculpture. The arrangement may make eminent sense, but it is the kind of issue that you should discuss with your dealer. Dealers don't like surprises any more than you do.

The limitation of a dealer's agency geographically is a more complex issue. Dealer preferences aside, whether you wish to be tied to a single dealer will be determined not only by your own personality but by the nature and quality of your work as well.

The advantages of regional representation are obvious, the disadvantages less so. The more dealers working to arrange for the exhibition and sale of your work, the better. It's a big country. But there are also drawbacks of which you should be aware. Unless the regional dealers work well with one another, there will be the usual disputes with respect to the timing and content of your exhibitions, the question of who gets what work and when. This is not a major consideration if your work is produced in multiples such as prints and photographs.

But having two or more regional dealers raises other issues as well. The need to keep track of inventory, accountings, payment, insurance, consignments to yet other dealers, and other record-keeping is only compounded by multiple galleries, particularly if you have a large amount of work. For that reason, you may prefer to deal with one trusted individual who can arrange for and coordinate relationships with other galleries on your behalf. This is particularly true where your dealer has a truly national rather than a regional clientele. A gallery with a national clientele may curtail its promotion of your work if its geographic area is limited and may affect its sales of your work. It undoubtedly would also affect the size of any guarantee the dealer would be willing to make on sales. Relying on your exclusive dealer to make arrangements with other galleries may require you to give a little on the amount you receive for your work, and you will have to determine whether such an arrangement is in your best interests.

I note that a number of form agreements specifically allocate territory to a dealer in terms of where the clients reside. That to me is an extremely difficult and troublesome way to handle this issue. Unless your regional dealers travel the country, posing the possibility that they may end up in adjacent suites in the Topeka Hilton pushing your work, it is much simpler to permit each gallery to sell from its location without regard to where the clients reside.

4. Exhibitions

The representation agreement should provide for periodic solo exhibitions of your work for a specified number of weeks. This is, of course, an important consideration. The frequency of the exhibitions will depend not only upon how productive you are but also, with some dealers, upon the relative marketability of your work. Whatever the provision, it must be realistically applied. As you know, artists are not machines. They work in cycles as do all other creative people. There will be times when your work merits more frequent exhibition and other times when the exhibition of your work as scheduled will do neither you nor the dealer any favors. I have seen instances where an artist insisted upon the exhibition of his work pursuant to the contract although the quality and quantity of the new work did not justify a show at that time. The exhibition was not only unsuccessful financially but was also an embarrassment to the reputation of a major artist. Avoid that situation if you can. If you trust the judgment of your dealer, be heedful in this respect.

Some of the form contracts you will encounter stipulate that the artists shall have a solo exhibition every year or every so many months, shall be entitled to a specified amount of wall space, etc.

Those kinds of provisions severely restrict an intelligent dealer's prerogatives. In most cases, your dealer is as interested in promoting and selling your work as you are, although it may never appear that way. The artist-dealer relationship is in many senses a partnership and you must work together for your mutual benefit.

I also note, from writings on this subject, statements to the effect that the artist should control the choice of the work exhibited and the manner of exhibition. Undoubtedly there are artists with sufficient clout to enforce these provisions, but, with an intelligent dealer, they are self-destructive. Of course, you should be consulted with respect to the exhibition of your work. That does not mean, however, that the dealer's wishes and instincts should be ignored. Artists are not always the best judges of their own work—and rarely of the gallery's clientele.

Equally objectionable to me are those form contracts that give the artist control over advertising and publicity. This is a matter between you and your dealer, and is rarely a trouble point. But since the dealer is the one who must foot the bill and who ostensibly knows how to market the work, the dealer should ultimately prevail on this issue.

The provision as to exhibitions should also deal with who pays for the preparation and installation of the exhibit, and for the shipping costs. The gallery should pay for matting and framing of photographs and prints, but, where standard materials are not used and substantial expense is involved, another arrangement may be necessary. To avoid unnecessary disputes, this issue should be dealt with either in the agreement or orally, well in advance of any exhibition.

5. Commissions

The percentage of the sales price retained by the dealer as commission varies considerably, dependent upon a number of factors, including the nature of the art work, its price and marketability, the size of the gallery and its overhead, and the services that the dealer renders to the artist. Obviously, a dealer who promotes your work nationally and provides innumerable additional services, such as handling and fulfilling requests for your work in museum and other shows, will require a larger percentage than those dealers who merely handle your show at your expense. It is quite possible for one dealer to do handsomely on a commission of one-third or 40 percent while another dealer will have difficulty maintaining its operation even with a commission in excess of 50 percent. The commission, however, generally will range between 40 and 50 percent. Within any one gallery, however, the commission to artists should be fairly standard, if the same kinds of work are involved, if for no other reason than as a matter of elemental fairness and to avoid the inevitable bickering.

Dealers usually give discounts to established collectors, to museums, and of course to other galleries. You should be informed as to what those discounts are. It is not uncommon for a dealer to request an additional commission on your work to offset discounts given to other dealers. Such a procedure should be spelled out. It is quite possible that your dealer may simply take a larger standard commission and absorb all discounts to other dealers and to collectors.

Also in connection with commissions is the sensitive subject of private sales. Some dealers will permit the artist to make private sales, especially where there is no competition between the artist and the gallery, but it often does place the artist in competition with the gallery. Your dealer may ask for a full commission, whether you or the gallery sells the work. A preferable arrangement, to me, is for the artist to remit to the gallery a diminished commission. I call this a sensitive area, because there is no doubt that many artists do not abide by these commitments and, if the gallery is not performing, I am not entirely unsympathetic. But, of course, the gallery cannot truly perform when the artist is dealing actively in his or her own work. The activity, unless acceded to by the dealer, can only undermine the artist-dealer relationship.

Commissioned work is a prickly area. The provision with respect to commissions should also stipulate that the commissions are payable only on sales of your work, not on lecture fees or honorariums. The agreement should provide as to works done by you on commission from a corporation or municipality. Whether any payment to the gallery is to be made often depends upon whether it was instrumental in obtaining the commission. In any event, the amount paid to the gallery should be less than that paid on gallery sales.

6. Guarantees and advances

The greater your bargaining power, the more likely it is that the gallery will offer you a stipend or a guarantee of annual sales. More enlightened dealers will on occasion offer young unestablished artists stipends as well, in the fond hope that they will become important and profitable artists. However, dealers, contrary to the perception of many, are not patrons of the arts and in most cases are not independently wealthy. Budgetary considerations often inhibit the most ardent and supportive impulses. In negotiating a stipend or a guarantee, ask for a sum that places reasonable expectations on the gallery. To require a greater amount can only lead to tension and to disappointment. One dealer I know gave a major artist a financial guarantee that the dealer could not possibly fulfill through retail sales. To meet the guarantee, the dealer peddled the artist's work at substantial discounts to personal friends and others. Such tactics are not profitable to the dealer and, perhaps more troublesome, undoubtedly affect the integrity of the artist's market for his work. Nevertheless, at last hearing, both parties appear to be ecstatically happy with the arrangement.

If you are paid an advance against income to be received, make certain that it is nonrefundable. It is not infrequent for dealers to satisfy unfulfilled guarantees by having the gallery purchase its artists' work at the end of the year. That is an acceptable solution as long as the gallery and the artist are not placed in a conflicting relationship. It would take the integrity of a saint to refrain from selling gallery-owned material rather than consigned works. Nevertheless, if the guarantee is reasonable, the problem can be minimized.

7. Price

Your agreement should stipulate the prices of your work, and who sets them. This is a matter of critical concern to you and to your dealer, and you both should mutually arrive at the prices to be set. You obviously wish to achieve the highest possible price—as a matter of income and pride; and the dealer will want to maximize your income—and his. There is, in the long run, little to be gained by overpricing work. On the other hand, selling it too cheaply only diminishes the importance of the artist in the minds of clients. Remember, your prices can always be raised, but seldom reduced. While a dealer's guidance is helpful, the decision must be yours. Price clearly affects the volume of sales, and it is not only a business but a personal consideration by the artist as well. Some artists can produce to meet demand while others, as a practical or philosophical concern, choose to produce less.

The agreement should also provide that if you make private sales you will do so only at established or gallery prices. Certainly this is to protect the dealer, but it also is to protect you and your market. If you sell at a lower price you are making it extremely difficult for your dealer to maintain your market. Artists are often considered "easy marks" by art patrons with a soft line and hard cash.

8. Accounting and payment

Your agreement with a dealer should also specifically deal with the ticklish issue of accountings. Every gallery seems to handle the issue differently. My personal preference is for complete openness in this respect. I would rather have you know that I am a scoundrel, than have you suspect I am when I am not. The agreement should specify when you are to be paid and, with payment, that you should receive a specific record of sales, including the names of the works, the purchase price, and the names of the purchasers. I've heard it said that certain galleries will not disclose the names of clients, presumably in the fear that the artist will subsequently approach gallery clients and deal directly with them. Such a fear does not, in my judgment, justify secrecy. Perhaps I am ingenuous, but I think it far more likely that a gallery client will approach the artist directly, in hopes of either wheedling a good price or finding an opportunity to obtain work that is not in the gallery. Again, these are matters that cannot be dealt with in a contract, but they are central to the underlying trust and respect between artist and dealer. If either you or your dealer undercuts the other's efforts, the relationship necessarily is a fragile one.

Galleries make accountings usually on a quarterly or a semi-annual basis, although I understand there are some that account once a year. Dealers, of course, are reluctant to alter their accounting schedules to accommodate the wishes of an artist. Where substantial sales are involved, preparation of periodic accounts can be costly and time-consuming. You should receive payment for the sales of your work a reasonable time after the conclusion of the accounting period. What is a "reasonable period" depends upon the amount of bookkeeping involved. Sixty to ninety days should be the limit.

You should also be aware that many clients and other galleries that purchase your work may take an unconscionable time to pay. The dealer understandably is reluctant (if not unable) to pay you for unpaid sales. If a substantial amount of money is involved, it is not unreasonable to insist that your work not be delivered to the purchaser until your dealer has received payment of at least your share of the proceeds. The slow-pay situation can be dealt with by requiring payment on all sales within a specified time after the sale. If payment is not received, it becomes the gallery's problem to collect. You will not, of course, endear yourself to your dealer with such an arrangement! Any dealer can regale you with sad tales of clients lost and work returned when they hassled clients for payment. Moreover, few galleries are in a position to be a bank, although such a provision does keep the pressures on your dealer to collect on outstanding invoices.

Artists will always be fearful of dealers in financial matters. The dealer has your work *and* your money. One way to ease some of the concern is for the dealer to furnish the artist with a copy of each sales invoice involving the artist's work. If your dealer is willing to comply with this seemingly reasonable request, you will at least know what is going on. Bulk invoices without breaking down individual sales should be avoided, as should the inclusion of the work of more than one artist on an invoice. Be cautioned, however, that a sales invoice is not money in the bank, so refrain from spending "proceeds" that haven't been collected. On all too many occasions, payment of the invoice is delayed or, worse yet, the sale is subsequently voided. Nevertheless, with copies of invoices you will be saved the anxiety of wondering how the sales of your work are going.

9. Insurance

Your agreement should indicate that your work is insured, at least to the extent of what you would receive on its sale. The policy should also cover you for the loss of your artwork or its damage in transit. Public carriers are not renowned for their reverence with respect to art. You should also be aware that not all damage is insurable. Many an insurance claim has been denied on the grounds that the nature of the damage constituted "ordinary wear and tear," and was not covered. This is especially true with prints and photographs. In that situation, the burden should not fall solely on the gallery, *if* those who handle your work do so intelligently and carefully. Some galleries and institutions to whom work has been consigned for exhibition have returned it in tatters, all the while denying any lack of care in handling or shipping.

10. Change of director or dealer

Finally, you may wish to provide for your right to terminate the agreement in the event circumstances change and you are no longer transacting business with the dealer or director with whom you have established a close working relationship.

THE ARTIST/DEALER RELATIONSHIP

So much for the formal aspects of the artist-dealer relationship. The artist should also be aware of certain other intangibles that play upon your relationship with your dealer.

The definition of the ideal artist-dealer relationship is as elusive as that of the perfect marriage. It is simply a matter of what works, given the extraordinary diversity of artists' needs and temperaments. Dealers, too, are a disparate lot. The relationship is often a deeply personal and subjective one. With artists' livelihoods in their dealer's hands, it is not surprising that many artists view dealers with guarded distrust, if not disdain. Some artists see dealers as primordial antagonists, insensitive bullies who employ their mercantile wiles to exploit artists and debase Art in their single-minded pursuit of commercial gain. It is a base canard, but, alas, few relationships can withstand such antagonism. In fact, however, artists and dealers share a mutual concern, displaying and selling artwork on a profitable basis for mutual benefits. On the whole, art dealers share with artists a passionate and sincere commitment to the medium they represent.

One reason for artists' concern is that dealers control the walls; they have the power to say yes and the power to say no. What is perceived as dealer "power" is, for the yet unestablished artist without ready access to galleries, difficult to accept. In reality it is a misperception. Dealers have "power" as long as they have a choice among artists. But talk to a dealer about "power" in terms of successful artists! When a William de Kooning takes a walk, for example, it's role reversal time. Paranoia is not the sole burden of the artist.

I don't intend for my remarks to read like a manifesto for the Society for the Prevention of Cruelty to Dealers, but it is important to understand the dealer's dilemma. Good artists make art for themselves, not for the "market," and dealers are wont to echo that sentiment. But the dealer's tastes, such as they are, must accommodate the need to survive. "Commitment," a favored word among art-mongers, is a cherished ideal, as long as the rent is paid. An artist once told me that paying the rent was "my problem"; true enough, but it was also his problem. No gallery, no shows. Some successful galleries are fortunate enough to be able to carry a number of promising artists who have yet to establish a market, but the grim reality is that many cannot. Galleries are not museums, although that role is often wished upon them.

A successful gallery, as opposed to a "profitable" one, requires more than wall space and artists; a dealer must have or develop a strong clientele that buys the work. The market is not limitless (have you ever watched dealers squabble over a client?) and the temptation to bend to commercial considerations is fairly overwhelming. It is a regrettable, albeit important, fact that there is a larger market for mediocre art, for post-post-post impressionist paintings and wall decoration, than there is a market for interesting but untried new work that has yet to find a market. The dealer succeeds or fails on his judgment as to what is good *and* what will sell—a very subjective matter. It is understandable that artists will, for their own reasons, fault the judgment of dealers in that respect and, from time to time, consider dealers to be uninformed and insensitive cretins. The decisions are not easy ones, and doubtless some of them are made for all the wrong reasons. The occasional practice of giving shows to "well-connected" but marginal artists, or to prominent art patrons who also dabble in painting or photography, is indefensible, but our contempt surely won't change it. And few of us are in a position to cast the first stone.

The frustration of "the competition" also, I believe, underlies the occasional but strident complaint that galleries exclude women and minority groups. While I do not presume to speak for all dealers, I find it difficult to believe that any gallery would discriminate on those grounds. Even were a dealer so disposed, which is unthinkable, good artists are simply too few in number to permit such a noxious luxury.

No apologies for dealers are necessary, but you should understand that they, too, have problems, and their judgments are based not only upon esthetic considerations but upon the everyday problem of survival as well.

Dealing

part four

16

Dealing from New York

by
Ivan Karp

◆◆◆◆

IVAN KARP is the founder and president of O.K. Harris Works of Art in New York City, and the unofficial Mayor of SoHo.

◆ ◆ ◆ ◆

Among those of us who care and who are constantly alert to fresh developments in American Art, it has been observed that since the mid-sixties and certainly throughout the seventies there has been a fabulous and fertile surge of mature and innovative talent in painting, sculpture, and the related arts. An explanation for this exciting evidence of a flourishing culture might well reveal that an increase in prosperity and leisure and the growth of enlightenment as to the importance of the artist's contribution to a sensible society has permitted persons of imagination to venture beyond the established outlines of labor and commerce so vividly described in our brief but robust history. Yet the subtle and myriad factors that generate a visual culture in a particular place and time are never totally apparent and remain a part of the very mystery of the creative process and the fabric that it generates.

All artists seek fame and fortune, preferably as soon as possible and hopefully before they are forty. It has become evident that the quickest method of achieving this wholesome ambition to begin with is to have your work exhibited in a clean, elegant space which is populated by rich intelligent collectors, enlightened art critics and museum officials, and presided over by a brilliant and generous art dealer. In order for you to have your work exhibited under these superlative conditions you should have some evidence that your work has achieved a high measure of technical maturity that has struck, to some degree at least, an innovative chord.

By "evidence" we mean that a majority of the "informed" have acclaimed your work and have included it in professional exhibitions or referred to it in the press or purchased it for a significant collection or awarded it a meaningful prize in a rated competition. If your mother, father, spouse, or lover celebrates your artistic achievement, this would not necessarily be considered competent appraisal. To qualify as one informed to make judgments of works of aesthetic merit, one would also have to have been adjudged to be so qualified. This is a rather mysterious process since there is no known instrument that can measure a person's visual perception or, for that matter, what constitutes a work of art. It is only a matter of opinion.

It is therefore important to understand that some owners of art galleries have felt obliged to develop credentials through scholarship, regular collecting, or simply intense involvement in the art community. But there are many other persons operating galleries who are simply burdened with leisure or money who commence an art dealership because the work is dignified and clean and may result in immediate community respect and invitations to colorful social events. However, the judgment they may bring to a new artist's work may be far from accurate, and you must try to understand this in advance. There is no state law that requires art dealers to take a test to prove their expertise.

WHERE TO EXHIBIT YOUR ART—NEW YORK

Assuming that you, the young, ambitious artist, have convinced yourself, or have been convinced by those alleged to be informed, that you are ready to present your recent production to an established art gallery, then we recommend certain cities as offering the best opportunity for a responsive audience. New York City has over five hundred galleries, of which about three hundred specialize in the works of living artists. Of these there are about seventy-five that are considered by the "informed" to exhibit work of a high professional standard on a regular basis. Of the seventy-five galleries so described, the majority have but one main exhibition area where ten or eleven one-person shows are given every year, and perhaps one group show or invitational where promising young artists are shown, with one or two works by each. If a gallery so described has a complement of fifteen or twenty "affiliated" artists it is unlikely to be assiduously seeking new talent. By "affiliated" we mean that the gallery expects to exhibit particular artists on a regular schedule— perhaps once a year if the artist is especially productive and certainly every other year if the artist provides a body of work for the occasion. It would therefore appear that only a handful of openings for new talent occurs during the exhibition season, and artists are wont to discover that many of the dealers will not even receive applicants to review their slides.

WEST COAST

As for the West Coast, Los Angeles continues to be an ever-sleeping giant as far as contemporary art is concerned. There is something about the climate or the mental life of the inhabitants that seems to inhibit passionate interest in the visual arts. A generous count of good galleries identifies about fifteen that focus on the works of living artists, and half of these dwell on the works of artists who have achieved major reputations. As for San Francisco and the Bay Area, it may be that life is too replete with grace, gentility and ease to have provoked a lively interest in what the native muses have inspired. Here we count about ten galleries actively engaged in promoting the lively visual arts. The several thousand artists working in this area report a constant struggle to get their work shown—or even looked at for that matter. The museums in the Bay Area make an effort to improve this situation, but their efforts can never replace the work of the adventurous gallery.

OTHER AREAS

Oddly enough artists have better opportunities for exposure in such places as Kansas City, St. Louis, Minneapolis, Atlanta, Toronto, and Seattle than they do in the great cities of the West. Chicago is a lively scene, thanks to the zealous efforts of a handful of dealers, an excellent contemporary arts museum, and some of the smartest collectors in the country. There is a special loyalty in Chicago to artists working in that area, and we find that many are content to be known as members of the Chicago school and survive and sometimes even thrive on local attention. Boston and Washington, D.C., are fairly lively places for the visual arts, and the local collectors in both places show special dedication to regional painters and sculptors. As for prosperous Houston and Dallas, there are splendid new museums replete with funds for all purposes, but the galleries and the collecting public are largely involved in something known as "Western" art, which has nothing to do with our culture.

PRESENTING YOUR WORK

When it comes to confronting the owner or director of a gallery for the first time, you must be in possession of the ability to survive repeated and not always tender rejection; in other words you must have emotional resiliency and some perfectly intelligible evidence of what your work is about. This means a packet of ten to twenty slides—or better still, large transparencies of current work—all properly marked as to topside, material, date of production and size. A voluminous body of slides presented to the dealer may fatigue him in advance or make him skeptical of your ability to sort out the significant portion of your work. Restraint in the presentation makes a good impression. It is sometimes permissible to show a painting or an object to clarify the images conveyed through photos. But most dealers will not enjoy your scattering a number of works around the exhibition area or in the private office, and he or she is likely to express physical or audible agitation if the work you show is remote from the gallery's exhibition concept. It is therefore imperative that you make a full survey of current exhibitions in the various galleries to try to determine from what is shown the approximate philosophy and style of art the dealer prefers. Documentation of your previous exhibitions, achievements, and criticism may be offered. But a dealer with strong convictions about what is significant in art is not likely to be impressed by such material.

There are less than a dozen dealers in all of New York who will grant an interview to inspect your work upon your unannounced appearance. In most places an appointment must be made by mail or on the phone. Slides or photos sent in the mail should always be accompanied by a return envelope with proper postage and packaging. Dealers of good conscience will review the work and respond with commentary. Others may be distracted or uncaring and return your photos without any evidence that they have actually seen them—or they may not return them at all.

Those who are made to feel utterly defeated by continued rejections should find a friend or relation to carry in evidence of their high achievement. The various dealers really don't care who brings in the evidence since they exhibit not the artists but their production. A dealer who finds the work engaging may ask to see it in person—that is, to visit the artist's studio. In most cases the dealer will not invite the artist to ship works to the gallery for various reasons—such as the lack of uncrating facilities. In this event, artists who are not residents of the city in which they have found some measure of interest in their work should find in that city a place to set up some of their work for the dealer to see at his or her convenience. Since it could be burdensome for an artist to make such an arrangement, it makes good sense for the artist to try to interest several dealers in his or her work so that the effort involved in showing them will be more likely to prove worthwhile.

As in much of human endeavor and in many professions, physical beauty and/or intense and repeated proclamation of one's ability may bring success of merit sooner than deserved. Fortunately the majority of prominent art dealers possess some subtlety of mind and are capable of resisting duress, if not beauty. There are also many artists who are identified by critics or curators as harbingers of a brave new vision whose work is shallow and merely fashionable. There is nothing for an artist of integrity to do about such injustice but to persist in his convictions that his work is of transcendant importance and to try to get it shown.

All of this may lead to nothing except an accumulation of praise and vague promises which may add to the artists' courage to persist or, conversely, to despair or to pursuit of endeavors removed from the arts. It has been suggested that creativity, surely an overused and often misapplied description of a singular human attribute, is its own reward, and that personal serenity results from its possession. However, as an art dealer with twenty-five years' experience I have rarely found this to be true. People who make things strictly to be seen are dedicated to the hope that these objects will be seen in their lifetime and eventually but certainly applauded. Fortunately there is currently a sufficient number of enlightened observers to prevent an artist of consequence from being totally ignored.

17

Dealing from Los Angeles

by

James Corcoran

◆◆◆◆

JAMES CORCORAN owns and operates the James Corcoran Gallery in Los Angeles, specializing in contemporary painting, sculpture, drawings, and graphics. Mr. Corcoran also is part owner of the Costelli, Feigen, Corcoran Gallery in New York City, specializing in the works of Joseph Cornell.

◆◆◆◆

Today the visual experience of painting has evolved into a complex business, the business of art. As Andy Warhol once said, "Business art is the step that comes after ART." So there it is, in just a few words; my business follows art. And business art concerns the artists (both living and dead) who create art, as well as the audience or market (nearly always alive) that desires and acquires art. My role, in terms of dealer and gallery, is to act as liaison between the artist and his audience.

The chairman of Twentieth Century Art at the Metropolitan, William S. Lieberman, has described artists as "the only superior beings of the art world." Obviously recognizing this, the contemporary artist Billy Al Bengston has further pointed out, "All great artists have sexual magnetism." Sounds awfully nifty, this role as artist, wouldn't you say? Quite exclusively, these superior sexual magnets create art. Yet it is easier for some than others: Robert Rauschenberg can, with some authority, proclaim, "It is art because I say it is." Statistics, however, show that in the state of California alone there are 50,000 art students who will eventually seek representation from a mere handful of dealers representing contemporary work in Los Angeles. Adding to this predicament, I have heard it said that at a generous estimate, perhaps one half of one percent of contemporary painting and sculpture made and sold today will have any market value at all in thirty years' time. Statements such as these point to the sad situation facing new artists today.

As for the dealers—well, it has been rumored about the best of them that they know the predilections of every important collector in New York and perhaps a half-dozen other cities as well. So the story goes, they can or should be able to tell you the whereabouts of seemingly every modern work in private hands. Whether this is in fact an accurate observation of the mass of us or not, it describes the role assignment. The dealer provides a perspective of the art market. His or her knowledge about collections, collectors, transac-

tions and the finances involved—particularly in the present infla-
tionary economy—must reflect a consummate day-to-day awareness not only of the art world, but of the international business
world as well.

THE "VALUE" OF ART

"Nowadays people know the price of everything and the value of
nothing." That was Oscar Wilde, yesterday. Today, specifically in the
art market, he might have said, "Nowadays people like the price of
everything new and the value of everything old." It is a fact that
dealers who exhibit the work of living, contemporary artists have
often subsidized these exhibits from transactions involving the work
of dead artists. In my experience, no contemporary dealer is going
to turn away a Rembrandt if one is offered to him. Such a reaction is
due primarily to the large profit margin involved. Few living artists
can generate enough profit to keep contemporary art dealers in a
robust business. Also, my clients who invest in art are not particularly interested in experimenting with the potential of the
younger artist. For the most part, they look for sound track records
and established names.

Is all this just a matter of finances? From one viewpoint, it can
appear to be. A successful businessman might insist that making
money is art, and working is art, and good business is the best art.
However, intrinsic to the good business of ART is the market's
appreciation of and desire to own art. A former chairman of
Sotheby's, in an interview for the BBC, noted, "Without covetousness you are not going to have an appreciation of art. And I think
that if covetousness by some magic was destroyed art would come to
an end. It's very rare to be able to appreciate art without wanting to
own it." It is quite true that those of us who are involved in the art
business do stand at attention in front of the art and covet it. This is
not all based upon the dollar. There is something more to all the
looking, evaluating, appreciating. As the market fluctuates, collectors and dealers do take note, but basically art retains a bottom line
of its own—beauty.

I believe it is what George Santayana called "emotional consciousness" that separates the ordinary from the exceptional viewer.
As Santayana noted, "Expression depends upon the union of two
terms, one of which must be furnished by the imagination, and a
mind cannot furnish what it does not possess. The expressiveness of

everything accordingly increases with the intelligence of the ob-
server." It is this aspect of expressiveness that keeps art a controversial commodity all its own, despite its value as an investment.

THE FUNCTION OF THE ART GALLERY

The fundamental qualities of art itself do not change. It is the
art business, in reflecting economic pressures and intense internal
competition, that has become increasingly more intricate as an
industry. Galleries function to confront this intricate business of art.
It is their job to set up shows, handle clients and inquiries, to
process, filter and organize miscellaneous data relevant to both the
art they sell and the business of selling it.

Although galleries exist to relieve the artists they represent of
these problems, in L.A. as elsewhere, there are simply not enough
galleries and collectors to go around. The existing surplus of art
school graduates and art initiates have no choice but to accept this
as part of their reality.

There are a few alternate support structures in Los Angeles: Los
Angeles Institute of Contemporary Art (LAICA), Los Angeles Contemporary Exhibitions (LACE), new galleries burgeoning especially
in the downtown area, and academic-sponsored exhibitions. These
developments provide a degree of exposure to the community of
artists. Contemporary art dealers such as myself do look for new
faces as far as our gallery is concerned, but we need artists who have
clearly demonstrated themselves over the years. Occasionally I have
been fortunate enough to encounter such new artists. But all in all,
it is a generous approximation to say that in Los Angeles we have
ten established galleries representing twenty artists each. That's
only two hundred artists receiving representation. And, supposing
an arbitrary law of attrition in California stipulated that between 10
and 20 percent of these artists leave the area each year, only 20 to 40
new names could be absorbed into the system. A depressing fact,
but that's the game.

I continue to be astonished at the number of artists who come
to me unsolicited. Politely, many of them bring slides in and leave
them overnight so I can take a look at them at my leisure. One artist
came to me with photographs depicting "Artist Undergoing Sur-
gery." She was having holes drilled into her head. Some enthusiasts
desiring to surprise me with examples of their work pounce on me
outside of my office. This cat-and-mouse aspect of the Artist in

Search of a Gallery is by no means unimportant for the artist. The need for representation, particularly among newer artists, is a real need. The problems are obvious.

> He was interested in my pictures, he said bring some more into the Marlborough, and I did, and they HATED them. Harry Fischer thought they were awful, and told Kas, 'These are dreadful; what are you doing with this junk?"
>
> —David Hockney

But this search for a commercial outlet plays a minute part in a bigger picture—the relationship between the individual artist and the process of creating his art. While I find this relationship impossible to evaluate in any precise way, I offer the following which may shed some light: In June 1943, Mark Rothko and Adolph Gottlieb, with the then unacknowledged assistance of Barnett Newman, collaborated on a now well-known letter (written in response to a negative review). It begins, "To us art is an adventure into an unknown world, which can be explored only by those willing to take risks."

It's not a simple situation to understand. If you're a superior being, a sexual magnet, the art world may be for you. If you follow art around and covet it intensely, you may qualify as a dealer. If you take risks, you might be the next Mark Rothko. But keep in mind the philosophy of Andy Warhol: "If you say that artists take risks, it's insulting to the men who landed on D-Day, to stuntmen, to babysitters, to Evel Knievel, to stepdaughters, to coal miners, and to hitchhikers, because they're the ones who really know what 'risks' are."

18

Dealing from Washington, D.C.

by
Christopher S. Middendorf

◆◆◆

CHRISTOPHER S. MIDDENDORF founded the Middendorf/
Lane Gallery in 1974. The gallery specializes in 20th century
American art and represents the work of outstanding artists
currently working in Washington, as well as the work of many
nationally known contemporary artists.

◆ ◆ ◆ ◆

I have represented and exhibited the work of contemporary artists for seven years. During this time I have made mistakes about artists, represented some of them rather poorly and others rather well. But during this period I have been keenly aware of what sort of relationship I wanted to have with artists, how I felt they should be promoted, and to what ends I wanted to reach for their work.

I have also been approached by many artists in ways that have been difficult and painful for both of us, although far more for the individual artist. In the following few pages I will discuss certain things the artist may do to facilitate the entrance into a commercial gallery, some of the pitfalls that may occur, and some of the things I feel are and should be the responsibility of the artist in the development of his career. I am speaking as a commercial art dealer, though, so I will discuss some of the things that I feel are part and parcel of the other side of the relationship. Together I hope that these pages will help to illuminate the fine balance in the relationship between the artist and the art dealer.

OBTAINING SLIDES

First and foremost, you as an artist must obtain a high quality set of slides or, even better, four by five inch transparencies. These should be accompanied by a complete list of what the slides represent: media, dimensions, date, and edition size if applicable. You should have slides of about ten of your most recent pieces, and have available a short slide history of your earlier work. Concentrate on this. A beautifully printed resumé means nothing, nor do reviews of your accomplishments. They may aid the dealer later in trying to promote your work, but keep in mind that the dealer is himself a promoter and a salesman, and is most likely not going to be sympathetic to a sales pitch from you. Remember, it is the work that counts, and presenting it in a clear and well-documented way is of the utmost importance.

You are now equipped and ready to begin the process. Unless you already have connections to a nationally known gallery, you must first concentrate on your own geographic area. There you will be able to most easily build a local following that will feed on itself and grow, as will your reputation. The important thing now is to learn everything you can about the local galleries. You should know the types of exhibits the galleries have, the artists they represent, and the kinds of people who work in the galleries. Follow the galleries for several months, being aware of the visibility of their shows in the community, their advertising, the size of their openings, and the sort of press coverage they get. However, the most important qualification as far as you are concerned should be the quality of the the artists represented by the gallery. The better the artists, the better the collectors frequenting the gallery and seeing your work.

CHOOSING THE RIGHT GALLERY

You should then choose the gallery that seems to best fit your work, so do your homework about what type of work each gallery exhibits. (Many galleries show a wide spectrum of work.) Try not to waste your time or the dealer's by showing your figurative work to a gallery devoted to abstraction. Also choose a gallery with space compatible to the size of your work. After you have made your choice of the gallery in which you are most interested, make a list of the other galleries.

Now you are ready to approach the gallery of your choice. You must first understand how rarely a dealer will take on an artist walking in the door with slides. "If he is so good, what is he doing out pounding the pavements?" You must be more subtle. Treat your own work as the dealer would treat it if he takes you on—as something special, something rare and important.

Begin by putting the dealer on the list for any shows in which you are participating. It is also a good time to slowly put together a mailing list of your own. At first this list will be mostly friends and relatives, but as you continue it will grow to include collectors, curators, and critics. Probably the dealer will throw away your announcements, but quite possibly he will remember your name.

Try to get to to know the artists in the galleries' stables. They are your best avenue for access, as dealers tend to listen to their own artists. As you begin to make these contacts, put them on your mailing list as well. Drop them short notes asking them to stop by and see your work if they get the chance. Try to build up a groundswell of enthusiasm about your work. Operate under the assumption that all galleries are booked two years in advance, so you have plenty of time to get the ball rolling. Of course schedules do open up, but you are best off if you are not in a hurry (another aspect of being subtle, since you certainly *are* in a hurry!).

But your main goal during this period is just to make the dealer aware of your work. Dealers are always in need of something new and good to sell, and if your work catches their interest, they will make the advance. It can also be beneficial during this period to get to know the dealer. Now this can be difficult and embarrassing, especially if you attempt to become friends at an important museum opening. The dealer will drop you like a stone if his best client walks by as you are introducing yourself, and you should try to avoid this situation. But getting to know the dealer can be a tremendous asset, even if he chooses not to handle your work. If the dealer respects your work, his contacts and knowledge may help you later. If the dealer does end up representing you, you will most likely be spending a fair amount of time together, and it helps greatly if you get along easily together.

Now you have reached the stage where you have been rebuffed and have gone on to the rest of your list or, through some of your subtle maneuverings, you have enticed the dealer to your studio. The first thing to realize is that although the dealer has been to hundreds of studios, he is just as uneasy as you are. First, he is out of his gallery, and second, he knows that his reaction to your work is making you nervous. You are the host, so do what you can to put both of you at ease. Try to have your best work hanging, as this may help to get the conversation going. Also have readily available five or six of your best works. Do not show the dealer thirty works, unless he asks. Showing thirty works will tire you both, and if the dealer has not responded to the first six, he is not likely to be swayed by the additional paintings. Make sure the dealer has time to really look at your best work, as most dealers will agree that first impressions are not always correct, and it is to your benefit to give the dealer time for careful analysis. Try not to talk about your work unless it is something pertinent to a particular piece; it rarely works, and most often will put him off immediately.

There are some dealers who will wax poetic right off the bat, but for the most part they will not say anything other than a few brief comments. They will want to let the work sink in, and if it is good work, they may want to go back to the gallery and savor it, and decide what to do about you later on. Do your best not to put the dealer on the spot by asking him how he feels about the work. If the dealer does not say anything about giving you a show, or getting back to you later on, then you have struck out. But it is at this point that you want to turn on the charm. The dealer may not be able to do anything for you now, but there is always the possibility that he may have a group show in the future that could include your work. Or he might be working with a client who may want something like your work. You want to leave these doors open. Do not ask for recommendations either. If the dealer feels your work is good, but not up his alley, he will make recommendations on his own. It is sad to say, but in this situation (the dealer coming to visit the artist), it is a dealer's market. Although it is potentially a humiliating experience, you must have confidence in your own work. You must realize that if the work is good, there will be a dealer who will appreciate it, and recognize the talent you have.

ALTERNATIVES TO COMMERCIAL GALLERIES

If you have been rejected with no open doors, in addition to moving down your list you should begin to look at the other types of shows besides commercial gallery situations. In most cities in this country, there are alternative spaces of all kinds. They will be the most receptive to your work as they are supported primarily by the community and should in turn be supportive of local artists. Also, be aware of juried shows at local museums. These can be great ways to gain local exposure to get other dealers to see your work.

Although it may be hard at this point, keep doing your own legwork and promotion. Although you may have a friend or relative who would love to take your work around to galleries and museums, this can often do more harm than good. For the most part these well-intentioned people correctly feel you are best off in your studio. But you must take responsibility for your own work and realize that although well meaning, these friends are often quite naive. The reaction they may cause with dealers and curators can do irreparable damage. Let them promote you to their friends, even let them sell your work to their friends, but if you are going to have an agent of any kind, it must be someone who knows what he is doing.

If the dealer has responded to your work and offers you a show, the relationship now changes dramatically. Suddenly you will be working together for the same goal: to promote you to the fame and riches you have deserved for so long! But you are about to enter a relationship that is very important, with a person whom you may see only three or four times a year. You must achieve a balance of proximity and distance, business and friendship, dependence and independence. This relationship will be based on responsibility—the responsibility that the dealer has to you for your work, the management of your career and promotion, as well as for the more practical things like sales and insurance. Your responsibility to the dealer is to continue to do good work and to support him in what he is trying to do for you. This will be hard to determine, but as you become accustomed to the way in which your dealer works, it will become clear.

SHOULD YOU HAVE A CONTRACT?

As the relationship begins, you must try to clear up as many of the areas of responsibility as you can. Certain dealers will present you with a contract. This should spell out exactly who pays for what, and when, who covers insurance, when you should be told if a sale has taken place, and how long you will have to wait to be paid. These contracts are usually pretty straightforward, but it is worthwhile to have an attorney look it over. On the other hand most dealers do not have any sort of contract. The art business is a business based on trust, and as things are drawn into a contract this trust can slowly change. It then becomes a relationship based on a contract, not a relationship based on trust. Contracts can be very effective, and do protect all parties mentioned above, but there is much more to the artist-dealer relationship than can be put down on paper and signed. In adhering to a contract, one tends to do what is required, and no more. But the promotion of an artist, especially a young or developing artist, takes much more time than most contracts require. It takes enthusiasm on an almost constant level, and you gain this most often by having a good relationship with the dealer, not necessarily by having a good contract. Contracts are basically irrelevant in this situation, as there is no way in a contract to spell out what a dealer really must do to promote an artist or to require how that dealer should feel about the work.

It is important to note, however, that there are dealers who take advantage of this no-contract situation and may cause you to lose your work without being paid for it. If you have done your research on the galleries, this should not happen to you. But if you are an artist from another town, with no way of keeping in easy reach of your work in a gallery, be advised to have some sort of agreement between you and the gallery. The artists who usually get themselves into this sort of bind are those who so hungry for exposure and for a gallery they do not think carefully.

With or without a contract, you should make sure always to get receipts for your work. You should pay enough attention to what goes on in the gallery to know if any of your pieces have been missing from the gallery premises after six months, and why you've not been told.

WORKING OUT THE DETAILS OF THE ARTIST/ DEALER RELATIONSHIP

The first thing you and the dealer will probably discuss will be the timing of your show. Although you are dying to have your work shown, it may take a certain amount of time to get the momentum going. Also, the lead time for advertising and other forms of promotion can be three or four months. Thus you are best off if you give the dealer and yourself plenty of time to get ready.

During this time the details of your relationship should be worked out. First and most important to both of you will be the setting of the prices and the commission for the dealer. However, here again it may seem like a dealer's market. If it is a good gallery—one that is respected in the artistic community for its exhibits of living artists, and one that has been in business several years—the dealer will know exactly where he wants to set the prices. This can be based on the price of your work in the past and also on the prices of work by other artists in the gallery and area. The commission the dealer will take will be around fifty percent. He may want even more if he is buying the work outright. This can be a mutually beneficial thing for the dealer to do. First, it exhibits his confidence in you in a significant way. Second, it may allow you the money to frame and present your work professionally.

This situation may also be damaging to you, since the dealer may buy all your great works for less than the going rate. You should be careful to protect your interests; in the long run you are best off keeping as good a selection of your work as you can. Thus the way to keep yourself and the dealer content is to sell off a limited number of pieces at a time, being careful to retain some of the very best for yourself. Another alternative to this situation is to set up a certain commission for the dealer if he takes your works on consignment, and a even higher commission if he purchases the work outright or mounts an exhibition of your work. The costs involved in putting on exhibitions are tremendous, and the extra percentage can be a significant difference in making certain it is done right.

Once the hurdle of the commission schedule is surpassed the other aspects of the relationship are fairly simple. Any works the dealer takes on consignment from you should be covered by his insurance against almost all forms of loss. The insurance coverage should be worded so that in case of loss you will receive your commission as if the work had been sold. You should take all precautions to protect your own work as well. It should be your responsibility to make the dealer and the gallery staff aware of any necessary special handling techniques. Also the quality of materials for your work and its frames should be the best you can afford. It is important to note that when a dealer sells one of your works, be it for $500 or $5000, he then becomes responsible for the lasting quality of your work—physically, not aesthetically. If the work falls out of its frame, or the stretcher is warped, or the paint chips off, the upset client will call the dealer, not you. Also, and more important, if the dealer is selling your work as something special, he wants it to last. As the price for good contemporary art rises, it is reassuring to a potential buyer to know that the work is made to last.

In addition to the quality slides you used originally in discussion with your dealer, you should supply him with the best master set of slides or transparencies you can put together. This, combined with a complete scrapbook of your reviews and catalogues, will be not only a valuable tool for the dealer in the promotion of your work, but also a valuable visual record for you. This sort of accurate documentation may seem like a tremendous hassle, but in the long run will be extremely useful to you and the dealer. The expense for this material should be borne by the artist, but any additional copies of slides or written material should be paid for by the dealer.

PROMOTIONAL EXPENSES

The gallery will also be responsible for several other expenses. The most costly of these is advertising. The budget for advertising should be discussed between you and the dealer. The amount of money that can be spent on ads is tremendous, but the artist should realize that the amount and size of ads should be balanced against the current sales price of the work. As the prices rise, so then can the budget for advertising. Also included in this budget will be the cost of invitations to the opening, mailing expenses, and the cost of the opening itself. These costs should all be borne by the dealer. At first, simple postcards and cheap wine will make economic sense to the dealer, but with luck, as time passes, catalogues, posters, and an open bar will be your standard.

The budget for ads and invitations, the costs of frames and openings all are part of the fine balance that has to be worked out. Resolution of these simple problems in an easy way without either party feeling he is getting the short end of the stick is very important; not as important as the quality of the artwork, or the quality of the representation shown by the dealer, but nevertheless something that can damage a relationship based on trust and responsibility.

The final link between the dealer and the artist must be respect. The dealer should sincerely respect the work he is handling, and if this changes in any way, then you as the artist are in the wrong place, and the dealer will probably have a difficult time selling the work. But if the dealer is sincere, he will continue to respect you and your work as long as he represents you. Also his respect for you will begin as soon as he responds to your work. The respect you show to the dealer will come much more slowly.

In the early stages of working with a dealer, it is quite easy to treat the situation as an adversary relationship. You hope your work will be shown and promoted in a certain way, yet you have to have these discussions about commissions and costs which are very difficult for you, especially since you may not understand how the gallery works. But as the relationship strengthens, framing costs, advertising expenses, and commissions will become less and less important. The more important issues will be placement of your work in the right collections and shows, and your gaining more national and international exposure. These are the areas where a good dealer will earn your respect.

GALLERY OWNER VS. ART DEALER

These are the types of issues separating what I call the gallery owners from the art dealers. A gallery owner will put on exhibits of artists every month and that is all. Of course they will try to sell the work as best they can and even promote you in a certain way. But an art dealer will do much more, and will always be thinking of much more. Someone once told me that being an art dealer is a terrible way to make a living, but a wonderful way to get rich. By this I have always assumed he meant that if you are able to support, show and purchase works by a group of artists who interest you, eventually, if you have done a good job, you will have a tremendous art collection. A good art dealer, although he will always be concerned with the short run, will more than likely be looking at your work as something he will be promoting for a long time. For this reason there will be situations where he may sacrifice a sure sale in order to be able to do more with you and your work. An artwork is not something that should be indiscriminately sold. Objects sold to someone who does not care deeply about the work might as well not be sold at all. For an artist who has limited production, the dealer may be able to sell all of his work without making an effort. But the good dealer will be more concerned with where the work goes; whether it will be seen again and cared for; whether it is becoming part of a collection that means something.

A good dealer will be of great assistance in reaching galleries in other cities to handle your work. You have already gone through this exercise once, and the last thing you should be doing is trying to do it all over again in another city. Your dealer should write you letters of introduction to dealers he respects but might not know, or convince dealers in other cities that he knows of your worth as an artist. Now the tables turn, and it becomes the dealer's turn to be subtle. Getting your work into fine collections, museums, or other cities will most likely be done by word of mouth. It will be up to the dealer to build on a larger scale the type of enthusiasm for your work I recommended for you earlier.

Also, as your real talent as an artist begins to surface, the dealer's talent in his craft will emerge also.The dealer's talent will not be simply in selling, as he would probably be better off selling cars, but will appear more in his ability to assess the whims of his clients, the strange quirks in tastes of the people who frequent his gallery. It will be knowledge of the collections of the clients with whom he works that will enable him to bring your work up at the moment when it might actually do some good. It will be his ability to earn the respect of your artistic community in order to better convince them of your true quality as an artist.

These are the types of qualities in a dealer that will be hard to judge until you have worked together for a while. But they are the types of things to look for in a dealer, and the types of things you will want him to bring to the fine balance of your relationship. Your paintings, sculpture, or whatever media you work in must come first and be of a certain quality. If they do, then you are in the position to demand an equal level of quality in the representation of your work.

THE WASHINGTON, D.C., SCENE

As far as the actual marketplace goes, Washington has evolved from a sleepy southern city of ten years ago, to an active almost thriving art center. Beginning with the Kennedy Center, Washington has seen the arrival of the Hirshhorn, the East Wing of the National Gallery and the new Air and Space Museum change, enhance and pick up the pace of the cultural activity in the city. At the same time new commercial galleries have sprung up all over; hundreds of artists have moved here and collectors are now starting to come as well.

Even with this frenzy of new activity, Washington is a tenuous art market. The major collectors have always chosen to go to New York to buy, and rightfully so, as there were not major pictures for them here. Now there are, but it is difficult to break them of their old habits. But the new collectors and the increased interest in collecting by corporations have stimulated the art market here. This combined with the tremendous influx of foreign and American visitors has caused many galleries to thrive, and made Washington an exciting and visible place for any artist to exhibit.

Yet it is still true that the market for art is created in New York. It is possible for an artist to survive and thrive in D.C., but to expand his or her market, to gain a national following and reputation, and to achieve major prices, the artist must be represented and shown in New York.

19

Dealing from Chicago

by
Rhona Hoffman

◆ ◆ ◆ ◆

RHONA HOFFMAN is co-owner of the Young Hoffman Gallery in Chicago.

◆◆◆◆

THE CHICAGO SCENE

Chicago is a large and diverse city renowned for having a Second City complex. With respect to the art world, it is perhaps less an indication of an inferiority complex than an acknowledgment of fact to say New York City is *the* world art market place and, regardless of what is exhibited and/or purchased in other parts of the world, most museums and collectors also go to New York to see and buy art. New York is also, and very importantly, the home of the national art press, a press which writes primarily about what is being shown in New York. Almost everything outside of New York is designated as "Art news from..." and the interest is mostly, if not exclusively, in local or regional art and artists.

In the last five years the number and quality of galleries in Chicago have increased considerably, and today the scene is fairly sizeable and definitely very varied. Though several galleries specialize in only certain types of work such as photography and sculpture, most handle a wider range of material—painting, sculpture, installations, prints and drawings, ceramic and glass works, crafts.

Though Chicago may not have a very large national support system, it does have an exceptionally large private, museum and corporate patronage. For years, and most particularly in the last several years, it has been noted by the press (almost ad nauseum) that the per capita number of collectors from Chicago and the Midwest is enormous. However, it must here be noted again that these same people buy not only in Chicago, but in New York and in almost any city they visit during their fairly extensive travels, where they see art they wish to acquire.

It is possible for a Chicago artist, or one who moves to Chicago and stays here for some extended period, never to achieve a national reputation while, nevertheless, enjoying an important local one—

usually accompanied by a good teaching position and successful gallery representation. It is not totally unusual for artists to get their "starts" here and then go on to broader recognition. There is an impressive list of famous graduates from the School of the Art Institute of Chicago. The Chicago Imagists went from exhibitions at the School of the Art Institute to shows at the Hyde Park Art Center; from a private gallery in Chicago to one in New York as well; from museum exhibitions in Chicago, New York, and other parts of this country to Europe.

BEING AN ARTIST IN YOUR HOME TOWN

It is probably wise and expedient for artists to establish themselves first in their home town or the largest local city near there. In Chicago there is a decided prejudice *for* the local artist. Here one finds home town chauvinism at its best—the art and the artists are accessible, and there is a built-in private and corporate support system. Many corporations and private collections buy *only* Chicago art. Galleries are encouraged, by public enthusiasm and sales, to support their local artists. The Museum of Contemporary Art, through its curators and collector-board members, has been diligent in looking at the work of young unrepresented artists from Chicago and elsewhere. The Borg Warner Corporation in fact has recently endowed two galleries, one at the Museum of Contemporary Art and the other at the Art Institute, where *only* Chicago artists' work may be shown. The Museum of Contemporary Art has an "Options" program where contemporary and often controversial work by younger artists, regardless of domicile, is shown on a regular basis. The Young Hoffman Gallery represents many artists from outside of Chicago, and while our choices are based on consideration of work on a national and sometimes international basis, we represent more than a few Chicago-based artists.

There are thousands of artists looking for gallery representation each year and so it is very difficult for most artists to gain access to the private gallery system. Most galleries have about ten exhibitions per season. Since most artists wish to have shows every other year, the galleries can represent a maximum of about twenty artists on a permanent basis. Although some private galleries in Chicago have group and new talent exhibitions, alternative spaces and cooperative galleries tend to have more. Thus, the opportunity for exhibition in alternative spaces and cooperative galleries is vastly greater. Following is a partial list of spaces which regularly, if not exclusively, exhibit younger artists' work: A.R.C., Art in Public Places, Artemesia (women only), Chicago Artist Coalition, DePaul University, Facets Multi-Media, Hyde Park Art Center, Illinois Center, N.A.M.W. Gallery, Randolph Street Gallery, RAW Space (part of A.R.C.), West Hubbard Gallery.

ALTERNATIVE SPACES

Commercial galleries are not necessarily the wisest first stop for the younger unrepresented artist. Looking over the biographies of hundreds of known exhibiting artists, I have found that most have worked at least ten years before having significant one-person exhibitions at commercial galleries. It takes time to gain experience and maturity in the work necessary for representation in many galleries. Galleries who do take work by young artists as well as those galleries who wish to keep abreast of what work is being done, go to as many of the alternative spaces as possible. My partner and I go to such spaces not only in Chicago, but in every city we visit, as do many museum people and collectors. We are all searching and hoping to find new, long-lasting, valid, exciting work. Since no one person can possibly go blindly from studio to studio across the country, we must rely in part on some pre-selection method, be it the alternative or cooperative spaces, recommendations from collectors, museum curators and directors, or artists whose taste and intellect we respect. It is often the case that we see the work long before we ever meet the artist.

Our gallery and several others in Chicago like to look at younger work, and yet we will not usually give a show to someone until the work has reached some maturity. On the other hand, there is a significant number of galleries in Chicago who are primarily interested in the younger developing artists' work, and those galleries may be approached successfully early on in one's career. In Chicago there are also galleries who do not represent artists on an ongoing basis, and therefore are able to show many more artists.

Since there are so many different kinds of art, and different types and qualities of galleries, the talent and goals of the artists must be sorted out before anyone can recommend which gallery to approach. My impressions from the NEA-sponsored panel I attended a few years ago dealing with this question made me realize how heterogeneous the community is. It is truly difficult to answer questions except on a one-to-one basis. To judge from the questions I received while on the NEA panel, some artists simply want to make a living, some want to make good art, some *can* make good art. Some will be significant for many years. Others, like the author of the single great novel, live only for a short while. It is often the artist who must be honest and decide not only what he or she desires, but what is possible. Talent and goals and tenacity will determine to whom, when and where the artist should take his or her work.

LOOKING FOR A GALLERY

If you are not from the immediate Chicago area, do some advance research before entering the city limits. As I mentioned in the beginning of this essay, the number of galleries and other spaces has grown too big for anyone to "do" Chicago in a day or two. Try to get a list of the galleries in Chicago. The Chicago Art Dealers Association (312/944-2066) will mail you its member brochure, which has not only gallery names, addresses and telephone numbers but also brief descriptions of the kinds of work they normally handle. It also includes maps of the gallery areas in the city. The newly published "Art Now/Chicago Gallery Guide (Art Now, Inc., 144 N. 14th Street, Kenilworth, New Jersey 07033—201/272-5006) identical to the guide which has been available in New York for years, lists *all* the galleries here. *Chicago Magazine* also has a full listing of exhibition spaces in Chicago. If you can do none of the above, plan a few extra days in Chicago to visit all the galleries and to study the listings mentioned above. There are some galleries that would be totally unsuitable for certain work.

If you can, call for an appointment. Different galleries have different rules for viewing work. Some see artists only on certain days or at certain hours, or not at all. Mention that you are from out-of-town, because I would guess that they, like us, would make every effort to see you. Young Hoffman Gallery looks at all work that could possibly interest us, but without an appointment we cannot put aside a reasonable amount of time for you. I must honestly add here that, even with an appointment, we cannot guarantee that clients and/or telephone calls will not interrupt.

If you are from Chicago you probably know or think you know the gallery situation, but you might also have unwarranted prejudices for or against some of them regarding what work does or does not interest them. Make believe you are from out of town and reexamine the scene. It is, furthermore, doubly important for you to call for an appointment since, no matter how we try not to punish the local artist, there is, in fact, not the same urgency to drop everything to see you.

No matter how long the gallery spends with you it won't seem long enough. Remember, however, most of us have seen lots of work and know rather quickly, almost instinctively, when something is for us. Speaking only for the Young Hoffman Gallery, even if we like your slides we still have to visit your studio, see your work, and talk with you for a longer period of time than a gallery visit will allow. There are no quick, on-the-spot "yes" decisions. We represent a limited number of people and have to make sure that we believe in work enough to make a long-term commitment to an artist. There are, however, many galleries in Chicago that are willing and even anxious to take work on a more casual basis and that will make their decision based on living with the work and on the public's reaction to work taken on consignment. If a gallery says they find your work interesting but don't want to make any commitment at the moment, it is not necessarily a way to get rid of you. It is really true that most gallery owners like much more art than they can show in their own gallery. If someone tells you to "stay in touch," DO. It is probably an honest response. Time passes, work changes and matures, and gallery representation shifts. If a gallery likes your work but cannot deal with it, ask them to recommend another gallery that might. We do that as a matter of course. Remember, always, that galleries are delighted to find new artists. We need you.

Most of what I discussed in the preceding paragraphs deals with artists who feel their work is significant to the contemporary art world, but I know that all artists are not looking for a niche in the history books. There are many artists interested in making a living by using their artistic talents with no goal of making fine art. In the Chicago area there are a great number of purely commercial galleries, often located in fashionable high-rent boutique areas of the city and suburbs, which supply skillfully worked paintings, sculpture, prints, drawings, etc., for clients who are basically interested in decorating their homes and offices. I suggest that with the exception of the search for museums and similar institutional representation, you can follow the same suggestions for galleries— just different galleries.

No slide ever substituted for the real work. Some work looks better in slides than in reality, while other work simply cannot be seen well in slides. Nonetheless, slides are what artists have to show when they approach galleries. Bring a small magnifier with you in case the gallery cannot project them. If your work is sculpture, take slides of each work from several angles. Mark slides with title, media, and size. If you can afford to, have a few color transparencies to show. Don't show me black and white photographs of color work. If the work is small, bring it with you. If it is large and you want to bring it, ask the gallery in advance if they wish to see it. Don't just bring slides of new work. Although that is what I want to see first, I also like to see earlier work.

Biographies are not terribly important to us but they do give a quick idea of how much and what kind of exposure the work has had. As for reviews, I don't have time to read them at this preliminary meeting and I always assume that the artist would not show me a bad review anyway! A bibliography, if there is one, is good enough for the time being.

If you get the gallery you set out to get, and you get the show and if the show sells out, and you get great reviews and everything is wonderful, wonderful, still plan on another job. It simply is not true that all famous, widely exhibited, greatly heralded artists make a lot of money—or even enough money to "live off their art." The list of those who do not is considerably longer than the list of those who do.

There are many museum jobs that allow you to do your work and stay close to the art world, while at the same time making money to pay the rent—security guards, construction crew, museum store clerks. Shopping and framing art, assisting other artists with their work, and teaching art are other popular jobs in Chicago.

I hope you can gather from all that I have said that Chicago today has a very viable art community composed of artists and active collectors and galleries. Its reputation for being the Windy City is still true. Its capacity for welcoming newcomers is not as well known, but it is equally true.

20

Dealing from Houston

by

Janie C. Lee

◆—◆—◆—◆

JANIE C. LEE opened her first gallery in Texas 15 years ago. The gallery originally introduced to Texas many of the major artists of the 60's, such as Johns, Stella, and Frankenthaler. It primarily exhibits American art from the 50's and 60's to the present, and also has a great interest in drawings of every period.

Ms. Lee serves on the Board of Directors of the Art Dealers Association of America as well as being a member of the Houston Art Dealers' Association.

◆ ◆ ◆ ◆

The Houston art scene is a healthy and active one. It is an exciting art community to be part of, for it is still emerging, maturing, and changing. If an artist is talented and willing to work ridiculously hard, he or she can and will succeed in Houston. Artists who become immersed in the Houston art community will probably shortly find themselves contributing to its development.

One reason for the health and growth of Houston's art scene is its museums, university exhibition spaces, and commercial galleries. Each institution has a different goal, or set of tastes, which contributes to the variety in the community.

VARIETY OF HOUSTON'S ART SCENE

The Museum of Fine Arts exhibits a fine permanent collection which includes the John and Audrey Beck Collection of Impressionist pictures—in itself an excellent teaching tool. The director of the museum continues to acquire important masterpieces for the museum.

The Contemporary Art Museum gives the Houston Community a superb overview of what is happening in the art world today. The contributions of the Museum of Fine Arts and the Contemporary Arts Museum, which are directly across the street from one another, are a perfect complement to each other: one institution concentrates on exhibitions and acquisitions of the past or the proven present; the other creates superb large and small exhibitions of every description, informing the public about the best new work of living artists irrespective of age or geographic location.

In addition to the above, there is the Institute for the Arts at Rice University. The Institute creates some of the most unusual exhibitions in the United States, ranging from theme exhibitions of ancient times to European masters and American contemporary art.

The University of Houston and Rice University both have active
and important exhibition galleries—the Sarah Campbell Blaffer
Gallery and the Sewall Art Gallery, respectively. These spaces have
good educational exhibitions as well as student and faculty
exhibitions.

There is also the non-profit Lawndale Annex, which functions
as an exhibition space for artists who have shown extensively in
Texas, the Southwest and elsewhere, as well as those artists who
have had few or no prior exhibits. Under the auspices of the
University of Houston Art Department, the Lawndale Annex has
organized comprehensive group exhibitions, and has hosted traveling exhibitions and many groups of several simultaneous one-
person shows. The Annex also provides a forum for multimedia and
performance events.

COMMERCIAL GALLERIES

Houston has a variety of good, respected, commercial galleries
unequaled in this part of the country. Most of them have an area in
which they specialize, such as 19th or 20th century art, Texas art,
Southwest art, photography, and prints. Some address themselves
to even more specialization, such as minimal art or colorfield
painting. The large number of professional galleries and the variety
of their tastes are tremendous assets to the community and the
young artists.

At the time of this writing, the Janie C. Lee Gallery has been in
Texas for fifteen years. During this period there have been many
changes in the Texas art community, and in the gallery itself. My
basic premise, however, remains the same. The gallery is interested
in, and committed to, exhibiting the best quality mature work we
can find. The work we usually show is from established artists. It is
not our objective to show primarily New York artists any more than
we set out to show Houston artists, but the artists to whom we have
been committed for many years—Johns, Stella, Frankenthaler and
Motherwell, to name a few—happen to live in the Eastern part of
the United States. The gallery exhibits artists from Houston, Dallas,
and other areas of the United States because their work is also of
high quality. Our goal is to find the best quality art, and to exhibit
and sell it.

Our format is a little different from that of other galleries. We
have very few major exhibitions, often as few as five a year. When
possible we create a uniquely original exhibition such as the

retrospective exhibition of Robert Motherwell drawings (1980) which was accompanied by a catalogue and an essay by a distinguished art historian. Our only other exhibitions are small drawing or collage shows.

We try to have a large diversity of works in our showing room. For instance, there will be work from our "stable" of artists; individual well-known pictures consigned to the gallery for sale by collectors; work by artists with whom we would like to have more of a commitment; pictures by artists we want to observe more; work by artists we believe are talented, but with whom we have not made a gallery commitment to exhibit. We commit very slowly in taking on an artist; however, if we do take one on, we feel a great sense of responsibility toward him or her.

Our primary energies are spent caring for the art and artists we represent. This means working with the artists to obtain new work, curating and caring for their work, setting new exhibitions, selling the work, keeping the artists informed by regular reports on the activity of their work, and maintaining records for the artists in the gallery.

The second part of our activity, and our second priority, is looking for new art. First, we're looking for art by artists whose work we were previously familiar with, but who may have had a period of nonproductivity, or a change in their work. Second, we are looking for new and young artists. But I repeat, this is not the gallery's top priority as it is in other galleries in Houston.

The manner in which we approach new artists usually follows one of two patterns. First, and most interesting, information comes to us via an artist, curator, art historian, or dealer for whom we have great respect and whom we know personally. Our informer calls us or sends us information on an artist whom he considers talented, although still quite young. Or he may say that an artist, no longer young, still has extraordinary qualities that have not been recognized. Following the receipt of such information, we definitely want to see slides of the work. If we like the slides, and are interested, we then follow up by making an appointment to meet the artist to see his or her work. We also very much want to make a studio visit.

In the second pattern, we receive unsolicited slides or other photographic material on an artist's work. (We prefer to receive slides.) The director of the gallery and I review slides every two weeks, at which time we decide whether the material is of interest to us. All photographic material is inadequate to express the quality of the artwork itself—everyone in the business knows this. When we receive slides, we project them to see the work in the best possible light, review them, and, if we are interested, get in touch with the artist to find out how we can see more actual work. If we are not interested, we return the slides and tell the artist our reactions.

Artists who arrive at the gallery without an appointment will be asked to leave their slides, or send them to us. If they arrive with actual works of art, we will request them to submit slides instead. As are many galleries, we are understaffed and usually can't stop what we are doing to give unannounced artists the time and courtesy they and their work probably warrant. We regularly allocate time to study slides sent to us in order to be able to give them our full attention.

The community in Houston that collects and purchases art is still small. It has grown consistently each year, which is, I think, a productive, positive, working situation. Most galleries I have spoken to tell me that they are doing good business, as are we. Those who buy art are a diverse group, ranging from the young couple with very little money to spend, to large corporations with big art budgets, with all different sorts of purchasers in between. But in Houston there only a few whom I would call real collectors.

There can never be too many collectors. A collector does not say that he has no more space on his wall. A collector buys a work of art because he loves it, and feels it is of great quality—then he worries about wall space!

One major facet of a healthy art community that is lacking in Houston is in-depth press coverage of the art being exhibited—or, for that matter, of art that should be exhibited. The local newspapers attempt to cover the scene, but are given inadequate space to write on the subject in depth. It would be a tremendous asset if Houston had an arts magazine, staffed by people who understood the visual arts. Such a magazine could include articles from art historians, museum curators, newspaper writers, and artists living in Houston. The city, with its community of museums, galleries and artists, has proven itself worthy of such a publication.

I believe that artists need representation. If a gallery represents an artist, it has a tremendous obligation to assist the artist in every way it can. After all, the gallery is only as good as the artists it represents.

THE NEW YORK CITY EXPERIENCE

The emerging artists have a very real and difficult problem in bringing their art to the attention of those who can recognize its quality and want to acquire it. I think that the gallery should help such artists—it is to the gallery's advantage to do so. I must also mention, since my gallery is located in Houston, that I believe artists need to spend time in New York City. I do not mean that they must make a permanent residence in New York, but I am deeply committed to the results of the experience of a few years in New York: the art in the museums; the dialogue among one's colleagues; the advantage of seeing art that is being shown in the hundreds of galleries. All of the advantages New York City offers, in addition to the above, are an intrinsic part of an artist's development. I am not suggesting that it is easy to live in New York, but then it's not easy to be an artist either. But somehow, even though it is difficult, many people have done it. Most of those who are recognized as our greatest artists today have managed to live in New York City. Eventually, many of those artists do indeed live out of New York, but they spent some of their time in the city. I believe the New York experience is pivotal to the maturity of the artist and his or her work.

In reviewing the Houston art scene, I find the activity, the variety of galleries, museums, exhibition spaces, and cooperative galleries, are what make it an interesting artistic community. Were we to have one museum, or one or two good galleries, or one university art department, I believe it would be much less a viable opportunity for young artists. There are good artists who have had to leave Houston to become recognized, but they are not the majority.

All the people I've met connected with the art scene in Houston, genuinely want to make it better—myself included. We may differ as to how to make it better, but that too can be productive.

I can think of very few professions more difficult than that of an artist. It is so hard, one must be a little crazy to want it at all. It can also be very rewarding.

Houston is not a city suffering from feelings of self-sufficiency. It still respects nothing as much as it does the best talent. It welcomes it. It is not important where you came from; it's what you do and how you do it when you arrive. If you're good in medicine, finance, or any field—including art—Houston will give you a chance. Then it's up to you.

21

Dealing Wholesale

A Conversation with
Harry H. Lunn

◆ ◆ ◆ ◆

HARRY H. LUNN, JR., president of Lunn Gallery/Graphics International Ltd., is a Washington, D.C.-based art dealer specializing in rare and vintage photography throughout the United States and Europe. He is also active as a dealer of graphics, drawings, and paintings.

◆◆◆◆

The following are excerpts from an interview of Harry Lunn by editor Lee Caplin.

LEC: As a gallery owner, how important do you feel the commercial art gallery is in the total art marketplace?

HHL: It is vital, particularly in marketing contemporary work, since the ability of a promising artist to make his statement depends largely upon his entry into a commercial art gallery. Commercial gallery exhibits usually precede museum interest in a given artist. On the New York scene the young artist is eager to get into the Whitney Biennial, but his entry most often is through one of the galleries specializing in contemporary art.

There's a good deal of competition among the galleries: "I have three artists who were in the Whitney exhibition...," etc. A gallery's ability to attract the finest of the important younger artists depends on its track record in gaining museum recognition for them. Out of any hundred artists, I would say there may be three who can write their own ticket. The other 97 are begging to get in. Certain artists clearly stand out in the beginning. Johns and Rauschenberg were obvious talents to Leo Castelli when he first met them in the 1950's.

LEC: Do you think the situation is any different for photographers as opposed to painters or sculptors?

HHL: No. I think one of the major errors in viewing the world of photography in a commercial sense is thinking that photography has to be handled differently than other forms of art. There are some differences, but they relate more to the fact that in photography, as in prints, one deals with a multiple medium. In dealing in paintings, you're dealing with unique objects. And the way you market unique objects is obviously somewhat different from the way you market multiples. But beyond that, photography to me is simply another art form that has to be marketed like other art forms.

LEC: Do collectors perceive differently those artists who have gallery representation?

HHL: Most collectors, including relatively sophisticated collectors, have a remarkable lack of confidence in their own reaction to art. The context in which they are introduced to an art object is crucial. There are ranks of galleries, and clients are much more likely to be impressed by whether a photographer has shown with Castelli or whether he's shown at SoHo Photo than they are by their own response. In other words, if he walks into the Castelli Graphics gallery, which is where the photographs are housed, and sees the work of an artist, he's much more likely to be impressed by that artist and that photograph than he would be if he saw it in another context far less prestigious than Castelli. It could be the same artist, the same photograph, but he would be far more likely to buy at Castelli than he would at a cooperative gallery in SoHo.

LEC: But in terms of the high quality galleries such as Castelli and Light, you are making a difference without a distinction.

HHL: A number of photographers greatly prefer to be shown in the context of an art gallery as opposed to a purely photographic gallery. In other words, certain collectors would never consider Witkin, because it is entirely a photographic gallery. This is no critique of Witkin's operation, which is very serious, professional and successful—but an artist like Robert Mapplethorpe prefers to show at the Robert Miller Gallery because Miller maintains a full spectrum and an excellent track record in promoting artists in all media. His museum contacts are excellent, increasing the probability that Mapplethorpe's work will be acquired by museums or included in shows. The chances are much higher than they would be if he were represented by a purely photographic gallery less frequented by museum curators. Collectors are also looking to Miller's judgment, which has been very good. So the fact that Miller becomes interested in photography and particular photographers makes it important for the curators and collectors, because his track record for spotting young talent in all fields has been excellent in competition with his other colleagues in New York.

LEC: Have you made a conscious decision to have your gallery exhibit art in many different media?

HHL   Yes. I consider myself an art dealer, not a photography dealer, even though 95 percent of our turnover is photography. But I've always believed in a total art context, and I think this is one reason we've been successful. We've managed to interest many clients who were collecting prints and paintings in purchasing photographs as well, while continuing their other collecting interest.

LEC: How far would you, or, to your knowledge, other dealers go in taking on new or young artists? Do you just rely on your taste or do you have a sense of a particular artist's marketability?

HHL   Most dealers, especially at the outset, must be preoccupied with survival and with paying the bills. After a dealer becomes more successful, he can afford to take greater risks with exhibits he's not so sure are going to be fantastic commercial successes. He can then do things for the pleasure of doing them, and if they work, so much the better. And if they're not particularly commercially successful, it doesn't sink his operation, because he's doing enough other things. He cannot stage a number of risky shows in a row, though. Our approach in Washington is mostly oriented to painting, drawing, and fine prints, because the retail market in Washington is more interested in art of that character than in photographic art. Collectors in California, New York, and other parts of the country seem to be much more interested in collecting photographs than the local Washington crowd. What is exhibited on the walls here relates more to our local retail clientele, but this is only ten percent of turnover. What's really going on with us is wholesale sales worldwide at auction and through other dealers. At any given moment, I've got three or four exhibits in galleries elsewhere in this country or abroad, and these dealer sales account for 40 percent of our gross.

LEC: In other words, there is a Harry Lunn exhibit in someone else's gallery.

HHL: Yes. The Light Gallery recently had a major Robert Frank show and all the images belonged to us. Not long ago we mounted, in Paris, a very important Walker Evans show with 270 prints, which will circulate in Europe. I did a Steichen exhibit a few years ago with the same dealer in Paris. He sold the entire exhibit to a museum. You know, I never met the curator from the museum. The other dealer did it all.

LEC: What's the incentive for somebody else to take on your show?

HHL: The reputation of the artist and the ability to stage a major exhibition without significant financial commitment, but with the possibility of earning substantial commissions on the sale of the prints.

LEC: But doesn't it detract from another gallery's relationship with its community when it has a whole show of Lunn's come into town?

HHL: No. Most of them are very happy to have that relationship. A fundamental point about the art business is that most galleries are undercapitalized, and this is even more the case with galleries specializing in photography. Consequently they really have to take these shows on consignment from me.

LEC: Is that because of the high price of vintage photography on the market?

HHL: In part, but primarily it is a case of scale. We own an inventory that was acquired over the years for more than two million dollars. The total retail value is twelve million, but certainly we couldn't sell each and every object at full retail. This inventory permits us to consign material very broadly to other dealers around the country. It's really the basis of our business.

LEC: I get the impression that the bulk of your business is the so-called "blue chip" art.

HHL: It is.

LEC: What is the proportion of blue chip artists to lesser known contemporary artists in your business?

HHL: I doubt if contemporary photographs amount to more than five percent of our turnover, if that. When I talk about contemporary, I'm not talking about Robert Frank. Robert Frank has become a classic. I'm talking about the younger, up-and-coming photographers. Frankly, this is because most collectors prefer to acquire the so-called blue chip items because they are rare and they may not be long on the market. Collectors might respect an excellent contemporary—a John Gossage or Lewis Baltz—but they would think, "In three or four years I may have to pay twenty percent or even fifty percent more for the work if the guy gets hot, but in the meantime I know I can still acquire the picture. But a fine Man Ray, Paul Strand, or Robert Frank may not be available when I want it." People aren't standing in line outside my door, but really the easiest thing to sell in any field of art is the superb individual object. If you stand in a room of Miro paintings, there is always a stellar one which is also the most expensive and the easiest to sell. The same lesson is true with photography, because collectors exist who can afford to acquire what they want. Much of my time is devoted to locating very special objects for a very small group of buyers.

LEC: Going back to when you entered the whole realm of marketing photographs, what was your role in creating public acceptance of photography as an art form?

HHL: We began by organizing exhibits that treated rare photography with respect—the same respect we would show to an exhibition of Picasso prints. We framed the photographs elegantly, we prepared checklists, and then later catalogues. I began to introduce photographs in my annual print

catalogues along with the prints, and not in a special
section. We usually organized catalogues alphabetically.
The photographs would be in sequence with the prints: a
Braque etching and on a facing page a Brassai photograph.
It forced both collectors and dealers to look at this material
with a new interest. This came at a time when the print
market peaked and began to decline in late 1973. At this
point photographs began rising in price. Moreover, there
was a certain freshness to the photographic images. They
were new to people. It wasn't the same old recycled Picasso
that everyone had in his catalogue. We gambled on the
development of an acceptance of photography as a collect-
ible art field.

At that moment we decided to make a heavy financial
investment in photography. In effect, what I did was to sell
off my print inventory and buy photographs. The reversal
now has become complete; our non-photographic inventory
is nine percent of the total value of inventory. This investment began in 1972, and intensified in 1974 and 1975 when
we made a very major commitment to the work of Ansel
Adams.

LEC: And that was the first big step.

HHL: The Ansel Adams acquisition was the first, but soon after we
also acquired the Walker Evans archive and made arrangements with Marlborough to acquire the Berenice Abbott
archive.

LEC: Was there a single event that did it?

HHL   The Ansel Adams explosion. We began to have incredible
success selling Adams prints and realized there was a vast
market for his work.

LEC: You'd already bought the collection?

HHL: We were in the process of acquisition, and we could have
been wrong. But from my experience in the print field, I
realized that while it was fun to buy and introduce younger
artists, the major clients were really preoccupied with
acquiring the cream. By that time in the print field, sources
were very well known, and competition was keen, but I
looked at photography and the people like Adams who were

comparable to the Miros and Picassos of the print world, and they were untouched really. You could pick up the phone and call Ansel; he would be delighted to work out all the arrangements. I decided to start with the outstanding living artists and then as I learned about the history of photography, I went after the finest material available in Europe of the French and English photographers of the 19th century.

LEC: I'm not going to try to distinguish really between the contemporaries and the blue chip, but thinking about the contemporaries a little bit, how do you go about picking whose work you want to represent? What I'm looking for is a sense of those we were talking about earlier, the young up-and-coming, or people who are just starting in the field. Where do they fit in?

HHL: An enormous number of people regard themselves as "art" photographers not making their living in commercial work but attempting to survive economically as artists. There are tons of them. We are frequently requested to look at port-folios to give advice on artistic direction. Of all these photographers, only a relatively minor number will make it. This is true of every generation: Walker Evans in the 1930's and 1940's; Robert Frank in the 1940's and 1950's; William Eggleston and possibly Gary Winogrand and Lee Friedlander in the 1960's and 1970's. The photographers who are most important change our way of looking at things. It's true with any art field. Why is Johns important? Because he changed our perception of vision in painting and prints. He presaged a radical departure and was the most important figure in that period of departure. That's why Robert Frank is so important. *The Americans* as a book has had an incredible influence on all photography. Some-where out of all the activity now going on in the early 1980's, there will emerge one or two figures of importance. It's too soon to make an evaluation of superstars, and what makes photography different from other art forms is that one needs to look at a body of the work over a ten- to fifteen-year span. Some talents are very self-evident at the begin-ning. Frank had early recognition. When he came to this country, people realized there was something really exceptional going on in his work. Walker Evans was a protégé of Lincoln Kirsten, who commissioned a series of architectural photographs in New England, which in turn resulted in Evans' first exhibit at the Museum of Modern Art in 1936, and the influential book of the same title, *American Photographs*. It was clear that Evans was someone significant, even though many of his most important images had not yet been made. The Evans example is rare. Imagine all the other people who were taking photographs at the same time, some of whom we still recognize as very important and others who have gone into complete oblivion, maybe to be resurrected someday, who knows. But you're talking about a handful of names, which is what is very frustrating about contemporary photographers swarming all over the place. There are dozens and dozens of people all fighting for gallery space, museum space, Guggenheim fellowships, Endowment fellowships.

LEC: And you can't accommodate them all.

HHL: Much of it is very boring art.

LEC: Well then, how do you go about creating a market for an artist you believe in?

HHL: Contemporary?

LEC: Yes.

HHL: You exhibit it; you publish a portfolio; you write a catalogue. I'm more interested at the moment in some of the people who got lost, who are now in their 50s and 60s, who are very important but who for one reason or another went into an eclipse. A good example is Louis Faurer, an important artist rediscovered largely by Walter Hopps. A few years ago, Faurer was actually destitute, and Hopps introduced us to see if I could help. This led to our acquisition of his vintage prints.

LEC: What do you look for when you're evaluating contemporary work?

HHL: Whether I think it's an interesting picture. Some images grab you immediately and others take more time. In the case of Faurer, it was very clear to me that he was a bridging point between Evans and Frank.

LEC: When you represent a living artist, what types of things are you going to be doing for that artist?

HHL: An exhibit at the gallery here is less important than organizing exhibits in other parts of the country.

LEC: Do you write letters?

HHL: I live on the telephone and I travel constantly.

LEC: So you're really marketing.

HHL: Once you start to market one artist, the roughly parallel techniques can be used to market others. If I go to San Francisco and visit three or four galleries there, the dealers and I confer on the next year. Obviously, if you have four dealers you work with in the same town, one of them is going to exhibit Karsh, another Adams, Evans or Frank. You can't run two Karsh shows in the same town.

LEC: I infer from what you're saying that in the same way you would rely on a museum director to give you some insight, other dealers rely on you to give them similar insight on ...

HHL: On what sells.

LEC: Of course you're not relying on the museum guy to know what sells; why do you even listen to him?

HHL: I listen to him in terms of new talent—or old talent in the case of Faurer—that comes to my attention.

LEC: Regarding your living artists, how do you compare what you do to what you know other galleries do? It sounds to me as if you're a very conscientious marketer of the work.

HHL: We're in the wholesale market. Most galleries are in the retail business.

LEC: In other words you're selling large blocks of work.

HHL: Or organizing a traveling museum exhibition, or specific exhibitions for other art galleries which then attempt to sell the material. But we're primarily in the wholesale role, and we are not particularly dependent on what sells off the wall in any given week in Washington, although when something is bought locally we love it. There's nothing nicer than someone coming in and paying the full retail price.

LEC: Why do you have such an investment in beautiful light and space for exhibits when basically as a business it's happening for you elsewhere?

HHL: We need a certain amount of space in which to operate and it might as well be functional, elegant, and fun. I have six people working for me. There's a tremendous administrative burden when you get into wholesaling, because you have to keep track of inventory and have several private exhibition areas in which to present the art.

LEC: Say you found a living artist, which you have done in a couple of cases, who you feel is worth the trouble. Do you sit down with him and plan what's going to happen or does he just go back to the studio and make prints? Is there a whole set of steps that you follow? For example, holding back work, suggesting limited editions, suggesting that artists always sign their work?

HHL: Signature has become pro forma now, but you have to tailor advice on other issues individually to each artist. You must decide whether the artist's chief need is for museum shows from which spring commercial interest or if he should concentrate on just printing for the next two or three years to develop an inventory. Should there be a limited portfolio for someone like Eggleston? That often works out very well, because he does series of images which make sense as a unit. That's why a number of portfolios of his work have been published. Other artists need different formats. The portfolio is not necessarily the most appropriate way to advance work. It's a case-by-case situation and there are not many general rules.

LEC: Do you believe in limited editions? Or do you believe in cutting off a particular print at a given number?

HHL: It depends on the artist and the image. With Karsh I don't, because there are certain images like the portrait of Georgia

O'Keeffe that we can sell endlessly, and it doesn't seem to make any difference to people that there is not a limit. So for Karsh I don't limit. For some of the other people, yes.

LEC: You tell them?

HHL: I don't tell them what to do, but I make recommendations. Since it's considered that I know a bit about marketing, they generally listen. In my experience the more successful younger contemporary photographers are the people who have decided to limit their prints to a relatively low number of editions. Mark Cohen has done editions of three; Duane Michals who, of course, is rather a senior figure at this point, 25. And in my experience, if collectors are faced with two images they like relatively well, and if X is unlimited and Y is in an edition of five or 10 or 25, Y will get sold. Y will then be off the market, and it will make the remaining ones that much more valuable.

LEC: Do you tell artists to keep their negatives or destroy them so there can't be reprints?

HHL: No. I don't believe in destroying negatives, because you need them later on for books and other projects.

LEC: We're really talking about how much influence you have or how you and the artist working together reach agreements on what external activities make the work desirable or marketable.

HHL: You have to be careful that the work is not overly accessible. You don't arrange ten shows for an artist around the country in a period of six months, because the overexposure bores collectors. Also, if you own a large archive of material—the work of an individual photographer—you make only a certain amount available at any one time, because if 1,000 prints hang over in the marketplace, you cannot create the sense of rarity that induces collectors to acquire. All of these techniques are common to marketing any kind of art, or, for that matter, any commodity. The easiest way to make a sale is to tell the client the picture is not for sale!

LEC: Is the artist a passive producer in the marketing process?

HHL: It all depends on how the artists gets involved. Some are marvelous at public relations for themselves, and others are a disaster. There are some artists you pay to stay away from an opening, and there are others, like Ansel Adams, who are superstars. Ansel's kind of a cult hero. He packs 'em in. People love him. It's a great asset. Karsh is the same way. Some of the others are bitter and difficult and you want to keep them away from clients.

LEC: Do you sit down with them and talk about what you're going to do for them?

HHL: Of course.

LEC: Is there a set program?

HHL: As I said earlier, each artist is unique. You have to decide whether the person needs a lot of attention in terms of business activity, in terms of placing his work in important collections, and then develop a strategy by which you hope to get museums to purchase his work, or arrange donations of material to them. Then you schedule a series of shows here and about, consider a catalogue, attempt to negotiate a monograph.

LEC: Where do you see the market in photography, not only for the "blue chip" artists but the numerous people who are out there making photographs now? Do you have any sense of where it's going? Whether there's hope for young photographers?

HHL: I think photography will be a dominant art form for the next 20 years and probably beyond. Technology will play a role, especially in regard to color photography, which at the moment is relatively difficult to market because of the impermanence of most color printing processes. If, as I expect, color technology produces prints as permanent as black and white, a great increase in activity with color will occur overnight. Not only that, but you'll see color in large format and considerable technical experimentation. Color photographs will not necessarily look like paintings, but they'll have the kind of objective quality of a major painting.

The market currently is obsessed with superb individual images by the important photographers, and this will continue. There is not the collecting in depth in photography that exists in the fine print field. If you're really a serious collector of German expressionist prints, and you can afford it, you want to have more than just one Ludwig Kirchner print. You might want two or three different states of the same print, to study the way Kirchner worked. By contrast, it is rare to find people collecting a particular Robert Frank and then two or three variants that were a frame before or a frame after, or even two or three images from a particular period, even though to me that kind of development is every bit as interesting as looking at three state proofs of a Kirchner image. It is the same didactic experience. On the contrary, most collecting involves finding a famous or historic image. Clients demand Berenice Abbott's "New York at Night"; no other image will do. Many collections include only one photograph by each of the major artists: Karsh's portrait of O'Keeffe, Kertesz's "Modrian's Studio." This is the sort of collecting going on now, which is why after a while some of the auctions become very boring, since each year each auction house has at least 20 to 30 images that are appearing simultaneously in each of the other auction houses.

LEC: That's more like the resale of certain commodities.

HHL: That's what people want. More and more of these icons are being ground out, and it's come to a point where if you want to sell a "New York at Night" at Parke-Bernet, you probably will be scheduled for a sale years in the future because PB has ten others ahead of you in line with the same image.

LEC: All of which will sell?

HHL: All of which, in time, will sell. But you can sell only one per auction. You can't put up five copies of a print in the same sale.

LEC: What is the role of the photographer who is a photojournalist?

HHL: I like photojournalism; some of the most interesting work of the 1930's, 1940's and early 1950's was photojournalism. I think photojournalism now is less interesting in this country because it is limited to newspapers, *People Magazine* and *Life*. But it's not like the old days when Eugene Smith went out and created essays for *Life*. The political photojournalist essay is a dying art form, but in its time it produced great photographs.

LEC: So you, as a dealer, do have a role in keeping photography that was a product of photojournalism at the same level of desirability as art photographs?

HHL: Right. A good picture is a good picture whatever the circumstances in which it was made. Weegee was an incredible photographer whose work derived entirely from journalistic assignments. The prints that survive are usually in pretty rough shape physically, because that's the way Weegee printed and kept them. This gives them their own charm. It's different from looking an an Ansel Adams print, which is impeccably made, superbly printed, correctly mounted and signed ... a kind of deliberate museum object. A Weegee is likely to be slightly crumpled in one corner, and that's what makes it a Weegee.

LEC: Also signed?

HHL: Usually it has a stamp on the back saying, "Weegee the Famous." He obviously had an incredible sense of humor and irony about what he was doing, but also a sense of its value.

LEC: Is your eye still out for the diamond in the rough? Are you always seeking that fresh way of looking at things? What's the chance it'll come in the door?

HHL: Very little has come in the door—ever. Our Photo Secession catalogue brought together material from several important family collections, but everything in that catalogue resulted from our research and from leads given to me by scholars or collectors. Museum curators have been very helpful in the past, referring people to me who were interested in selling works that the museums did not have funds to acquire.

LEC: For contemporary photography, does the same hold true?

HHL: No, it's a completely different thing.

LEC: How much of that comes walking in the door?

HHL: Too much. Everyone is out hawking his wares, and I've found very little I like.

LEC: So what advice would you give the emerging artist?

HHL: Don't come here. There are many more photographic galleries around the country than there were five years ago, and they work on a retail basis. They need exhibitions and are forced to work, to an extent, with contemporary artists. In any city there's usually someone specializing in contemporary work. It's a totally different market: collectors who can't afford to spend $10,000 on a rare 19th century photograph will spend $200 or $300 on a contemporary photograph and buy an object they like, put in on their walls, and enjoy it. If the artist becomes famous ten years down the road, the picture will also have been a good investment.

LEC: Are there any centers for this?

HHL: The principal center is of course New York; also Chicago, Washington, San Francisco, Los Angeles, New Orleans, Dallas, Houston, and Boston. Those are the major commercial centers in the country.

LEC: So in the absence of the gallery system for the emerging photographer...

HHL: They would be in very bad shape. Publication in something like *Camera Magazine* or *American Photography* is also an avenue for exposure. Those publications are sources of ideas for dealers, collectors, and museums. I subscribe to all of them. I look through them, and if work interests me I get in touch with the artist.

Finding Alternatives

part five

22

Museums—
The Artist
and the Museum:
How to Crack
the Sight Barrier

by

Tom L. Freudenheim

◆–◆–◆–◆

TOM L. FREUDENHEIM is the Director of the Museum Program at the National Endowment for the Arts. Before he came to the Endowment, Mr. Freudenheim served for eight years as Director of the Baltimore Museum of Art.

◆ ◆ ◆ ◆

The artist-museum relationship seems eternally strained—a reflection of the outsider trying to get in, with those on the inside closing shades and shutters (or eyes?) to keep the outsider an outsider. The exception, of course, is in those instances when a living artist *is* shown in the museum. In this case, the ranks of outsiders have been diminished by a single unit, not assuaging the feelings of those left out. Moreover, the outsiders generally are convinced that some highly illicit relationship lies behind the fact of the exhibition and the choice of the artist.

Like all simple-minded explanations, this one probably contains a certain amount of truth, even as to the questionable relationship between exhibited artist and exhibiting museum. But it also explains nothing. If it contains some truth, it is nevertheless not actually true. The artist-museum issue is complicated, cannot be simply stated, and depends greatly on which artist and which museum one is discussing. But this is not to say one cannot attempt to clarify matters or even advise artists on how they might relate to museums.

MANY KINDS OF MUSEUMS

First of all the artist must realize (as he/she presumably already does), that there are many artists, and each one (or almost each of them), is trying to be seen somewhere—in studio, gallery, museum or collection. Knowing that one is not unique is probably small comfort, but it ought to provide some sense of perspective. On the so-called other side—that is, the museum—there are a number of factors which must be understood. All museums are not alike. Some range widely through the history of art, and may have little or no interest in the work of living artists (this extreme is relatively rare). Other museums specialize in modern and contemporary art. In between lie as many variations as there are museums. And in these museums there are people working (directors and curators, to name some that may be of interest to the artist), who may also vary in terms of personality, interest in living artists, time to spend seeing artists or slides or studios, and even ability to make judgments. The artist sees himself as a major figure, but may not be. Why should not the same be true for those people who work in museums and make decisions about what art is shown? It is a field of human relations and personal choices (we would hope informed choices, but nonetheless personal ones); it is not a field of litmus paper tests for quality or eventual impact on the history of art.

DIFFERENCES IN ATTITUDES

Adding to this mix of museum type and staff type is the matter of institutional policy. Even among those museums that do exhibit the work of living artists, there are many variations, based on opinion or official policies. Thus, one museum may be interested only in established contemporary art that has met the test of audience and critical viewing in commercial galleries or art publications. Another museum may take special interest in local or regional artists. The artist has a responsibility to understand these issues and factor them into any view of museums. It makes no sense for an artist to spend a great deal of time trying to be shown in a museum that has never shown any work similar to his—not so much in terms of style, but in terms of being local or relatively unknown. Many artists work in vain in such situations, and it is heartbreaking both for the artist and (believe it or not) for the people working in the museum who somehow share in the sense of the artist's frustration.

And it is from these kinds of tense beginnings that adversarial relationships begin, in spite of the fact that artists and museums ought to have at least one thing in common: art. After all, the direction of art has been changed on occasion because of the impact on artists of an exhibition. Historically, artists have enjoyed looking at the work of artists who came before them (or even those working at the same time), and have found this information a source of energy, inspiration or reaction. From the museum's point of view, the artist is in some ways the ideal visitor-viewer. The artist knows how to look, and can use visual information creatively; those are goals that many museums set for all viewers. Therefore, the notion that artist-museum relationships should be adversary relationships is somewhat absurd, and ought to be fought or rejected.

TIPS FOR APPROACHING MUSEUMS

As a general guide to artists, one can suggest a number of simple approaches to the museum.

1. Don't start out resenting the idea that the museum's prime interest is not in your work. The museum has numerous tasks and obligations; seeing new work may be only one of them.

2. Find out about the viewing policies of the museum. Some museums have viewing days for seeing artists' work. Others accept slides throughout the year. Some will see slides but not warm bodies. There are many policies, and a call to the museum should tell you that institution's approach. (Some don't want any new work brought to them; those are the breaks!)

3. Along with formal policies (where they exist), it is important to find out the interests of the staff. By looking at a year's exhibition cycle, you can sometimes get a sense of taste and directions and interest of directors and curators. Read their catalogues or other published writings to grasp how they might relate to viewing your work. (You may end up psyching it out incorrectly, but it's worth a try.)

4. Try for other visibility first. A museum is seldom the place for your first exhibition or group show. Museums are not the same things as galleries. Most contemporary art curators see other exhibitions in their area—at commercial galleries, schools, banks, or other such places. Sending an invitation with a personal note can't hurt, but may not help at all. Being noticed by your local paper's art critic might assist visibility in general, but not necessarily as far as the museum person is concerned. Museum people have their own strong convictions, and will frequently be unmoved by the comments of the critics (except when the critics are praising their own exhibitions).

5. Enter regional and local juried exhibitions when they come around in your area. Those exhibitions are frequently juried by notable museum people from around the country, and the best of those people take notes on what they have seen. You may end up being discovered through a juried exhibition, just as you may be asked to pick up your rejected work the next day. The artist has to be prepared for that, too, alas.

6. If you do find a museum willing to accept your slides for viewing, try to be sensible about the number of slides you submit. Try to get some distance from the material—perhaps have a friend help you make the most judicious selection of your work. The artist is seldom the best judge of his or her own work, and you want to make certain you have submitted the best.

7. If you are represented by a gallery, it never hurts to have the gallery try to show your work to the museum staff. Gallery people often have their own special relationships with curators, and thus can promote work more easily.

8. There is no evidence that socializing with museum people is of direct assistance in the system of showing contemporary art, but there is also no evidence that it has hurt too many artists. So whatever opportunities the so-called "art world" affords for developing personal relationships are probably worth pursuing. If the result is not useful for exhibitions, you still might develop some friendships, or at the least a better mutual understanding of the world of the artist and the world of the museum-worker.

9. Try to understand that the museum director or curator may have literally hundreds of artists like you wanting to be viewed and shown. Even the interested and willing museum person has other things to do (like directing or curating), and cannot spend all day seeing artists, visiting studios, and viewing slides. In a few instances, there are museums with curators assigned to do mostly or exclusively that, but such are exceptions, and even those curators eventually have to spend time writing the catalogues or installing the exhibitions of the work they selected from slides or studios.

The artist who *does* manage to arrange for museum exhibition, having conquered the so-called heights, then has a new set of concerns to deal with. There ought to be some kind of formal written agreement, stating the fact that the museum has agreed on the exhibition, with dates, if possible, and whatever other formal arrangements are involved. It is not unusual for an artist to believe that an agreement has been reached, while the museum may have only the most tentative of plans. Staffs change occasionally, and commitments are either not met or are not even seen as commitments. Formalities may seem intrusive, but they are appropriate and businesslike, and they protect both artist and museum because they clarify the relationship.

Having overcome the general problem of the exhibition's really taking place, there are many other details that ought to be worked out formally. Will there be a catalogue? Who will write the essay? What else will it contain (bibliography, list of exhibitions, biography)? Will it be sold? For how much? Will the artist get any free copies and how many? Who will pay the costs for production? (The museum ought to do this.) But is the artist expected to supply photographs and research materials, and at whose expense are the photographs taken? Such costs are generally the responsibility of the museum, but taking it for granted does not make it so, and the cost of photography alone can be quite expensive. There ought to be clear understandings on the size of the catalogue, number of photos reproduced, and number of color plates, if any. Design decisions can also be an issue. All of these matters should be mutually understood and agreed on, if the artist-museum relationship is to be sound.

Another issue that can and does arise involves the identification of gallery spaces in the museum. The artist may believe that the museum is using one space, while the museum is planning quite another space for the exhibition. Agreements about sales of works in the exhibition should be made, since the museum may want to take a commission for sales of works sold while on display, and the artist ought to know this in advance. Loan forms should be issued for all loans, with the museum providing wall-to-wall insurance. Packing, shipping, travel, conservation questions should all be answered in advance, lest the project be underway and the artist find that the responsibilities are not clearly assigned. Museums generally have conventional ways of dealing with these situations, and the artist has a right to be treated with the same respect as any other lender to an exhibition, just as the works ought to be handled carefully whether they are from another museum or "just" from a local artist.

It may be excessively cautious to suggest that the artist use legal advice to make certain that all such items are carefully covered. But in some instances it is the lack of such advice that creates situations for which the artist later needs legal assistance, so it might not be a bad idea to start out with the best advice.

There is no easy route, but that doesn't mean there is no way at all. In any given year, hundreds of new artists are shown in our museums—not just the same old names, but artists totally new to the museums where they are being seen. The museum must be understood as only one part of the complex world with which the artist deals. And while it may superficially appear to be the most important, the museum as a factor in the artist's career goals should be kept in perspective.

23

Commissions

by
Helen and Newton Harrison

◆ ◆ ◆ ◆

THE HARRISONS are a collaborative team, working across media. Essentially they are conceptualists and story-tellers. Their subject matter often deals with reclamation and environmental and social issues. They work variously with performance, large-scale murals and massive proposals, which often take humorous and ironic turns. They live in Del Mar, California.

◆ ◆ ◆

Editor's note: Conceptual artists Newton and Helen Harrison individually discuss their early experiences with commissions, and then reflect on their experiences together.

Newton: There is great romance surrounding commissions as well as many peculiar expectations. My early experience with commissions began in 1946 when I was an apprentice to a sculptor in the National Sculpture Society. I was 14 years old at the time and got the job simply by going to the studio and knocking on his door. He hired me, because I modeled horses better than he had when he was 14. I worked for him for three years—casting, chasing bronze, making models, pointing up small figures and the like. He did commissions and earned his living by making medallions and reliefs with industrial and war memorial themes. He had himself apprenticed to master sculptor Lee Laurie, who had designed the Atlas figure in Rockefeller Center. As did my teacher and his before him, I experimented with the neo-classical themes of giant horses being restrained by giant men with oversized forearms and thighs, until I eventually found myself in an aesthetic wasteland.

However, the apprenticeship experience was illuminating, in part because of the skills I gained, and in part because of the image I formed of studio as shop, sculpture as profession, production as craft, and commission as business. The business of it followed a rather standard format. An architect would send plans of a wall needing a relief, or an open space needing a fountain or figure. Often the subject matter was predetermined. My boss would then make a model, scaled at one inch to the foot, submit it, and receive a modest fee. If the model was accepted, an agreement was reached on materials and price. Then the sculptor would make a quarter-sized model in plaster, which, if approved, was followed by the full-sized piece in plaster. The model was then either cast in metal or concrete, or transferred to stone, usually by someone else. After it was installed, there was an unveiling ceremony, and the sculptor received his final payment. The experience, in retelling, sounds quaint. Most art isn't like that anymore and, since the passing of the Academy in the nineteenth century, many artists find the restrictions of meeting requirements for professional commissions appalling.

Helen: My first experience with a commission was for a university gallery for an exhibition called "In a Bottle." The exhibition director requested—commissioned—all participants to do works in bottles. No contracts were given, no scale models were viewed for approval, no quarter-sized models were made, and no full-sized models were made in plaster and transferred to another material. There were no preliminary, intermediate, or final payments. In fact, the piece cost me $75 and several weeks' work once I had decided on the concept. The work was well liked, well received, and was shown several other times. My gain was the work itself.

THE VARIETY OF COMMISSIONS

Newton and Helen: These two examples of our personal experiences with commissions we perceive as opposite in poles, two ends of the spectrum of commissioning. After all, what is a commission in art but a request by somebody to a somebody else for a something to be done? The variations of agreements, outcomes, gains, losses, and possible misunderstandings are endless and amazing.

To us there is an inherent contradiction in an artist becoming a "professional." According to our definition of art, the value often appears in a work's spontaneity and risk. Risk means an artist cannot always deliver the goods. A professional, on the other hand, is expected to deliver the goods on time and in a prescribed manner. A corporation wants the risk eliminated and the outcome predictable, and to the extent that the outcome is predictable, any spontaneity, improvisation and pursuit of a vision, wherever it may lead, is lost. But someone who commissions a major artist—because of that artist's unique vision—may run into quite a problem. It can be quite a problem for the artist as well.

We were once commissioned to do a water piece for the backyard of an elegant Spanish-style house in North Hollywood. The cost was to be about $8,000, the design fee, about $3,000, and we were to be the overseers. The work was to be subcontracted. We agreed that if the cost overran $12,000 we would give up the design fee. The work was inspected by the building inspector half-way into completion. The inspector insisted that we add a complex concrete support system dug into the adjacent hillside in order to secure the work. As a result of this decision, the piece had to be done over again. Its cost went up by a factor of three. We ourselves lost not only the design fee, but about $5,000 in expenses as well.

However, the money problem alone was minor when compared with the human misunderstandings that grew from conflicting expectations and desires that both we and the man who commissioned the work encountered along the way.

Our water piece was in effect a crab farm. We were doing cannibalism experiments in it as part of an ongoing work on art, ecology, and habitat reclamation. One of our incentives and conditions for agreeing to proceed at so low a fee was the information we would gain in the process. However, we believe the client saw the piece more as an investment which, if successful, would give him the opportunity of patenting a crab-mating process and ultimately cornering the crab market. Thus, when we asked for our information, he perceived it as his possession to use as he saw fit, and refused to give it. We then refused to offer more information on habitat control. His net product was a few crabs in an elegantly conceived pond, along with a business loss. Our net product was a lot of experience in making outdoor ponds, but no additional ecological information, and a business loss to boot. After that, we made the decision to be as specific as possible in our requirements before accepting any future commissions; specific not only as to costs, but also as to expectations, desires, and intentions of everyone concerned. In the case of commissions, human interaction is more important than any contract. But the bottom line may be the letter of the contract, even though with trust and good faith, contracts can be easily changed or adjusted.

The stories of artists' experiences with commissions abound. For instance, during the 1930's depression, artists were commissioned by the WPA to do murals in public buildings. The pay was minimal and varied from job to job. Artists responded in their own way, depending on the deal. If the pay appeared too low, an artist might choose to paint people only in profile, or as figures whose hands were in their pockets in order to complete the work quickly.

Another type of commission can emerge from a circle of friends. Matthew Rothenberg is the 14-year-old son of Dianne Rothenberg, an anthropologist, and Jerome Rothenberg, a poet. Walter Munk, an oceanographer, and Judy Munk, who is involved in community planning, are friends of the Rothenbergs. The Munks heard that Matthew and a small group of his friends had done some murals and went to see the 8x10 version of the Mona Lisa that Matthew had done in his room. They commissioned Matthew to do a 14-foot mural in a large room in their house. They agreed upon a Rousseau-style image for the mural, to be done on various walls with special treatment for doorways. An agreement was reached: the Munks would pay for the materials and a fee on top. (This arrangement is one that industry calls "cost plus.")

Matthew assembled his team of two friends. They had worked together before and were confident of their abilities. The trio worked for about five months, averaging three days' work per week, which totaled 180 work days. The work was completed to everyone's satisfaction. The team received its fee of $500, or about $2.79 per day per person. If Matthew and team had worked out an arrangement with the Munks on the basis of materials, wages and overhead (i.e. cost of travel, the bus or parents driving them), and as beginners charged $3.00 per hour, their 180 days of work would have cost about $4,320. Had this been the case we doubt the Munks would have wanted to invest about $5,000 in three ambitious but untested 14-year-olds. They, in turn, would not have gained their first and very valuable experience in taking on such a major project.

CORPORATE COMMISSIONS

As we all know, the great commissions in the Renaissance came from the Church, the Kings and the city states, which, with the newly emerging banker/merchant class, began the great collections of art. Along with the emerging middle class, these remained the chief sources of commissions or patronage for several hundred years. However, the forms of these sources changed. Public and private museums were founded and often commissioned works. In recent years corporations have also become involved in commissioning art: sometimes to build an image; sometimes for investment, tax or other benefits. We argue with the treatment of art as a commodity, with prices that can be inflated or manipulated. This is ultimately to the disadvantage of both the artist and the art community. However, when strings are not attached, a corporate commission can be as viable as any grant that is relatively economically and politically neutral.

Four years ago Metromedia commissioned us to complete a large work in which we were already deeply involved. We had expected the work to take another ten years to finish at our own pace. The work is called the Lagoon Cycle. It has about 50 panels, each eight feet high, and altogether it will cover about 350 running feet of wall space.

The few stipulations made by the company actually turned out to be very useful. The contract, however, was astonishing in its scope and detail. It was ten pages long and treated our work as a physical property. Their lawyers proposed, for example, that we do no other Lagoon Cycles. We agreed. Further, they proposed that we do the best possible Lagoon Cycle we were capable of doing. Naturally, we agreed enthusiastically. The idea that anyone might assume we would work below our best capacity had never occurred to us. However, they also stipulated that any material used in the Lagoon Cycle was not to be used in any other work or referred to in any way. That is to say, they assumed we would turn over to them not only the images, but the ideas that generated the images. At this point all other negotiation stopped. We explained that all artists—authors, moviemakers, whatever—often cite prior themes in new work. If a work were completely new, communication would come to a standstill. Moreover, the Lagoon Cycle itself was derived from prior art and experience and contained understandings which even cited earlier works. Finally we arrived at a satisfactory agreement, and the contract was signed in sextuplicate. Actually, the contract as a model is a unique and valuable document, and at some point it might be useful to publish it.

Now, for our problem: Metromedia did not bargain or haggle with us. They asked for our price and our justification for it, and they paid us exactly what we asked. Our price, however, was based on the costs of materials and labor—both our own and our assistants'—in 1977. We calculated our overhead to be 20 percent, and added another ten percent as a hedge against inflation. As a result of not accurately factoring inflation into our calculations, each year we work on this piece we lose about 15 percent more. Yet, if we hurry in any way, we risk debasing a project which has taken up a good part of the last ten years. So our profit is rapidly evaporating, and our empathy for all people on fixed incomes is growing.

How to summarize....We think commissions fall into a number of categories. There are corporate commissions, architectural commissions, museum commissions, government or public commissions, private and individual commissions (which, if they are not done for professional collectors, often evolve from friendships).

CHARACTERISTICS COMMON TO ALL COMMISSIONS

We have found all commissions have two common properties: (1) request and (2) expectation of gain by all parties involved. Museum commissions rarely entail financial profit, but they do advance careers. Generally, if a museum asks us to do something substantial—an installation, for instance—they will pay for the cost of production, shipping, installation, travel, per diem, and occasionally a modest honorarium. This is not unfair since we keep the installation. However, we feel that a wiser choice for the future might be for museums to pay artists either fees or wages and keep the installation, since these are often created for a specific site and are therefore unsalable.

With museums, and with other types of commissions as well, we regard the essential precondition to be that the artist's work has evoked critical discourse among other artists, dealers, collectors, and museum directors. Thereafter, personal preference, friendship, or the "buddy system" may speed things up. Conversely, clashing personalities, hostility, and antisocial behavior may slow things down. In all events the likelihood of obtaining commissions is not great even under the best of circumstances.

We regard any invitation to do a work we would not normally do, or any request for a proposal that is not self-generated, as a commission. We tend to treat these as opportunities to experiment. Generally, the lower the fee, the greater the freedom to be playful.

Art Park in Lewiston, N.Y., regularly commissions artists to do temporary work—mostly on a 40-acre flat area, which is a former quarry refilled with rock from the Niagara Power Project. The area is called a "spoils pile." An honorarium, per diem, and a materials budget are offered. Artists are expected to do their work in the open, and part of the bargain is direct intereaction with the public.

Having been invited to do a work there, we proposed to transform the whole 40-acre spoils pile into a meadow surrounded by trees. Our plan was to persuade the various towns in the area, who by law had to rebuild their sewer systems, to dump all excess dirt and all compostable material on the spoils pile site. Art Park agreed; the clients agreed. The contractors would save money using close-by Art Park as a dump site instead of others farther away. The work proceeded. We saw the piece as particularly simple and direct. It was congruent with ideas of joining art and reclamation, and art and utility, which have been our chief preoccupations since the early 1970's.

However, again there was an unexpected conflict: this time between Art Park's vision of our proposal and our own. By the time 3,000 truck loads had been dumped, the scale of the work infringed on the Art Park's notion about how much space a work, even one such as our own, should take up. The Director called off the dumping, and finally we settled for a 20-acre meadow instead of the 40 acres originally planned.

Other stories we've told exemplify the various forms of

commissions and the pitfalls awaiting the unwary. Contrary to expectations, we find that the benefits of being unwary have outweighed the disadvantages, since overcontrol limits freedom of invention. In this game every commission has its original problem. Each piece is one of a kind and is finally valued for its uniqueness and quality of expression.

In conclusion, we wish to mention a type of commission that has no name—where the outcome is a surprise to all parties. This type of commission involves utility, play, social change and community—both within and outside of art. Often this kind of commission does not have the expected object-like outcome. After all, one may be commissioned to do anything, and one thing leads to another.

In the spring of 1977, we were approached by the president of a small San Diego based company that does Environmental Impact Reports (EIR). He had read an article about us, describing us as environmental artists with social and political concerns. His company was competing to do the EIR for a particular project in the center of the downtown area of the city of San Diego. We reviewed the qualifications of his people, and he reviewed ours. Finally we agreed to do the aesthetic section of the report. Since we had no idea how to do an EIR, we began by looking at similar sections of earlier reports. Mostly the EIRs were done by architects. Mostly they seemed underconsidered, with the definition of aesthetics narrowed down to simply whether the project looked good or not. Generally the EIRs said "yes" to the plans, if this or that small change were made. Requesting a small change was called "remediation." The project called for a scaled-down version of a suburban shopping center, two stories high, with a five-block solid wall offering one entrance and one exit. Elderly people would be displaced, and the views of the ocean would be blocked. The space above the city streets was not considered, nor were the city streets themselves—nor any intereaction between them. A historic small park was to be made the entry to a bank. In short, the entire seven-square-block area was to be walled and devoured. We wrote a 20-page argument, which essentially pointed out the anomalies, and we called the plan irremedial. Our question was whether the people of San Diego wanted a single-purpose, fortress-like, suburban shopping center to be the metaphor for the "Center of the City." This question was picked up by the newspapers and made a cause célèbre. The redevelopment agency was furious and attempted to call the EIR illegal. The developer threatened to pull out. There were many meetings and much fuss. Finally the original plan was abandoned and a new architect was hired. The elderly people were included in the project's housing plans, and a more open design was adapted. Needless to say, since that time we have not been asked to do any more "Aesthetic EIRs" in the San Diego area! We were paid $1,600 for what was to be four days' work for the two of us. We estimate our actual pay at about $60 per week. We consider it a bargain.

Fortunately, information travels in odd ways, and life is enhanced as much by serendipity as by design. Our plaza critique came to the attention of an East Coast arts administrator, whom we met by accident at a sculpture exhibit. He commented on our critique and asked if we would like to criticize the Baltimore City plan, with an eye to possibly proposing an alternative. We said we would, and the plan was sent. We visited Baltimore and found ourselves in conceptual agreement with the city planners. We proposed a work called Baltimore Promenade, based on the concept that the promenade is a universal urban form, central to the well-being of urban ecology. Our ideas were accepted in general; a plan for action and a design fee were agreed upon, and the actual work began.

This most recent of our commissions will, from one point of view, have no "object outcome" at all. From another perspective, the object and transactional results, if our design is put into practice over the next decade, will be rather complex. We are actually proposing to set up a promenade network that will make Baltimore a place where walking is a central means of experiencing the city. Our art, if successful, will simply be a background to everyday life.

We feel that anyone who hopes to live entirely off the proceeds of commissions while maintaining his integrity as an artist is likely to have a hard time of it. But from our own experience, our recommendation to those who want to engage in public art is to regard their work as a form of public service, and then to simply put one foot in front of the other.

24

Corporate Art Collections

by

Mary Lanier

◆ ◆ ◆ ◆

MARY LANIER is president of Mary Lanier, Inc., and founder and president of the Association of Professional Art Advisors in New York City. She is an independent advisor to Philip Morris, Inc., Metropolitan Life Insurance Co., Becton Dickinson and Co., among others. Formerly she was curator of the art program for Chase Manhattan Bank.

◆ ◆ ◆ ◆

THE ART OF ART IN BUSINESS

Corporate support of the arts is a burgeoning activity in American business. Recent figures show that corporations have poured millions of dollars into one form or another of arts support. Exactly how this breaks down into art acquisitions is unknown, given the fact that a significant amount of art adorning the walls of American corporations is not recorded as Fine Art or Capital Asset, but rather as decoration, and therefore is lost statistically in renovation and decorating costs. Nevertheless, one need only set foot inside any modern corporate headquarters to see the evidence of a new kind of consciousness about art in the work place. Even throughout the local branch facilities of corporate giants and indeed in most small firms there is some evidence of what employees have come to call "the artwork," or the obligatory finishing touch in the office.

Realizing that it is difficult to determine precisely which corporations are buying what, it will be useful for the artist to understand as much as possible about the realities of corporate art collecting in order to have a clear picture of how to approach this market. Indeed, a knowledge of these realities may serve to discourage artists working in certain styles from exposing themselves and their work to audiences and settings that are impractical or inhospitable. The most important thing to understand is that corporate art collections are only as sophisticated as the people who select the art, and where one corporation may have a reputation for volume buying, another may be quietly acquiring a small number of superb examples from a carefully defined scholarly area.

While the best collections have a point of view and experienced advisors, others use art to perform the artless function of Muzak—to blend in, to soothe, or to continue the tradition of the wall calendar.

It is important to be able to distinguish between serious corporate collecting and that which is not.

WHAT MOTIVATES CORPORATIONS TO COLLECT ART?

It should be understood that business is business and that fundamentally corporate interest in the arts is self-interest. Corporations need to know there is something in it for them, because, after all, art is a luxury, not a necessity of life in the work place. Keeping in mind that all of life's endeavors contain self-interest, it should be determined just how enlightened corporate self-interest is in order to evaluate the possibilities for the artist in the corporate marketplace.

For the corporation, the challenge is to pick up, in many cases, where private collectors and museums are slowing down. This must be done in a bureaucratic context where art is often expected to fill many needs beyond the pure enjoyment of it. Some of the needs that corporations must satisfy with Fine Art are listed below:

- improve corporate image and visibility;
- decorate the walls and public spaces;
- support design schemes and correct design deficiencies;
- provide good investment;
- please people, boost morale, and improve productivity.

While most corporations do not set out to fill this tall order, it is important to remember that the constituency is broad based and that corporate management is usually intent upon improving the work environment. In addition, management often has to answer to stockholders who question the appreciability of such expenditures and employees who feel the art budget should be applied to salary increases and additional benefits.

Even given all this, it is possible, with the courage of conviction, good advice and a decent budget, for the corporation to become an important catalyst between the artist and the public.

WHICH CORPORATIONS COLLECT ART?

There are major companies such as Chase Manhattan Bank, Prudential, McCrory Corporation, Security Pacific Bank, First National Bank of Chicago, Atlantic Richfield, Owens-Corning, ATT, and IBM who have collected art for several years and who have established reputations for fine collections. Each has done this in the context of using art in the working environment, and each reports satisfying results from within. Certainly the art world recognizes the importance of such collections and enthusiastically supports the continuation of these programs. The companies listed above are household words in corporate collecting. Yet there are many more throughout the country that have begun collections, and it is the job of the artist to find out which and where these are. Learning this requires keeping eyes and ears open to news of corporate art buying. One good method is to obtain the biographies from the galleries of well-known artists whose work can be found in major museum and corporate collections. These biographies usually list the collections and often new corporate collections come to light. Another good place to start is at the switchboard of the company, large or small. Asking for the name of the Art Director, Public Relations Director, Corporate Communications Director or even the construction and property management people and inquiring in any of these areas will often reveal whether there is an art-buying program. After determining who is in charge of the art buying and whether that person is "in-house" or independent, the next step is to contact that person with a cover letter, slides, resumé, and a self-addressed stamped return envelope.

The suggestions above apply to companies that have established or are beginning art programs. There is also the possibility that a company will need to obtain works of art to fill very specific spaces and that will be the end of it. Getting in touch with interior designers and architects may be a method of approaching a one-shot situation like this. In any case, a brief, polite letter with accompanying slides is the best way to approach architects, corporations, art advisors, and even galleries. Being able to address the key people by name is, of course, helpful. Obviously, a personal recommendation from someone is preferable to any of this, and should be used when possible.

"CORPORATE ART" AND THE "ART CONSULTANT"

The phenomenon of corporate collecting has created two distinct yet unfortunate concepts that threaten to separate corporate collecting from the traditional, serious kind. One of these concepts is "Corporate Art," an unhappy term that implies that which is facile, easy-to-live-with, uninspired, and not-of-museum-quality. "Corporate Art" is the decorative stuff made for offices and touted by its manufacturer as "looking great in a bank lobby or airline terminal" (visual Muzak). One sees it everywhere. It is meant not to be noticed and, while those in the art world do not recognize it as art, the innocent, untrained eye thinks it is, and is often willing to pay dearly for it. Much "Corporate Art" is finding its way into corporate settings as a result of "art consultants" who peddle it to unsuspecting corporate buyers who want to be certain it matches the rug and chair. The challenge for the qualified art advisor is to help corporate collectors discern between art and corporate art.

The untrained art consultant is the second *negative* aspect of the new industry and can be held responsible for perpetuating mediocrity. When corporations began to spend large sums of money on art, the "art consultant" appeared on the scene to help them spend it. Many art consultants were unqualified and their corporate customers did not know what to require of them. Being an art consultant often meant simply that one carried a card with that title. Recently, however, a group of professionals has emerged by virtue of their extensive training and experience. These professionals have determined that the term art advisor should replace the term art consultant with its negative connotations from the past. The job of the art advisor/consultant should be to counsel the client on the acquisition and/or programmatic use of fine art without reference to any particular inventory or artist and to assist in the client's understanding and appreciation of such object(s). The Association of Professional Art Advisors was incorporated in 1980 to devise standards of conduct and procedure so that artists, dealers, and corporations can work more effectively toward good collecting. The Association has determined that an art advisor should be a full-time professional and should be paid by his client or employer and not by the artist or seller. The art advisor does not sell art, but rather sells time and knowledge. If an art advisor keeps an inventory, takes commissions, or sells art to a corporate client, he is considered a dealer and not an art advisor *per se*. The Association recognizes the integrity of dealers, but wishes to keep the two activities—dealing and advising—professionally separate. When an art advisor arranges a sale to a corporate client, he will often negotiate a standard discount, and ask that it be passed on directly to his client. This assures the client and the artist or dealer that the advice is free of conflict of interest.

Art advisors are considered go-betweens, bringing the art and the corporate client together. Other types of go-betweens include commercial galleries and private dealers who buy directly from the artist and resell at a mark-up to the client. In addition, there are consultants who sell objects to the corporation and take a commission from the artist or dealer.*

An artist should evaluate a consultant/advisor, not necessarily by the way he is compensated, but rather by his knowledge and reputation. Art prices are higher than necessary because of the various "discounts" built into the costs in order to cover consultants' commissions. The Association hopes the the terms *wholesale* and *retail* can some day be eliminated from the art market and that added-on costs will be reduced because consultant/advisors will be paid strictly by their clients. In any case the key person in the selection process is the advisor/consultant, whether he is in-house or independent. The advisor/consultant will either make the selection himself, or will advise someone within the company to do so. Sometimes there is a committee that deliberates on the advisor's recommendations. It is difficult and usually unnecessary to know how decisions are made internally.

WHAT DO CORPORATIONS BUY?

The answer varies as much as do the eyes, sophistication, and budget of those who make the selection. Earlier, in discussing why corporations buy art, we determined that the main concern is usually the visual quality of the environment. That being so, then it is reasonable that most corporations will want art that has a visual presence. This basic need limits the acquisition of conceptual and minimal objects (although there are collections such as that owned by Gilman Paper Company, which have concentrated specifically in these areas). There are important collections specializing in constructivist art, landscapes, abstraction, photographs, and sculpture.

---

*One should be particularly wary of the consultant who "takes it from both sides"—i.e., client fees plus commission without disclosure. In general, art "advisors" or consultants can be located by asking gallery owners who deal in contemporary art as well as the appropriate official in corporations known to buy art.

One would do well to determine which corporations are focusing on particular points of view. Yet, for the most part, corporations are collecting "eclectically," experimenting with all media, periods, and styles. It makes sense that unless a corporation begins with a particular focus, the quickest way to introduce a wide audience to the broad possibilities is to present a sampling of everything. (Still, looking at corporate collections, one is aware of not seeing much religious art, political art, or art with the nude figure.) The fact that many corporations are hoping to improve their working environment by having a variety of work to which a variety of people relate, opens doors for emerging and lesser known artists.

Beginning collectors do not want to spend vast sums on art that is untested in the market, and at the same time they do not want to invest in blue chip items. Therefore, their budgets are modest and they are willing to consider things that interest them in their own right. This thinking does not require "big names," and represents a market opportunity for lesser knowns.

The kind of corporate thinking described here presents advantages for the artist who needs a sale and the company who wants art. This kind of symbiosis should provide a way to keep the art community alive and enrich the lives of the millions who work and do business within the corporate setting.

The challenge, of course, is to do it well. Artistic energies should be applied to the work itself. Marketing of this work presents a different problem; yet we are now seeing a tradition developing— the corporate art collection. There are indications that a structure of communication is emerging that will enable the artist to reach that market.

25

Craft Fairs

by
Carol Sedestrom

◆ ◆ ◆ ◆

CAROL SEDESTROM is President of American Craft Enterprises, Inc., the marketing subsidiary of the American Craft Council, an educational organization with a national membership of 35,000. The Council publishes *American Craft* Magazine bi-monthly and maintains the American Craft Museum in New York City, as well as sponsoring marketing events for craftspeople.

◆ ◆ ◆ ◆

During the past fifteen years, the sales volume of handmade objects has increased by quantum leaps annually. While there are no reliable statistics about the growth of the "industry" in general, reported sales figures from the nation's largest craft marketing event, the Northeast Craft Fair—held annually in Rhinebeck, New York—relate the consistently developing interest in contemporary crafts. The first event, held in 1965 in northern Vermont, reported 60 exhibitors and sales of $18,000, with "several thousand" guests in attendance. That same event in 1980 (having moved to four different sites because of its growth), reported 2,000 applicants for its 500 available spaces. Four thousand shops, department stores, galleries, and museums registered to buy on wholesale trade days, and approximately 60,000 people attended on the three-day weekend. Four and one half million dollars in sales were reported by the participating craftspeople.

Events through which a craftsperson may sell his work range from Sunday afternoon "bazaars" to major events like those sponsored by American Craft Enterprises, the marketing arm of the American Crafts Council. Sylvia Porter, author of a syndicated column on financial management, reported in June 1980 that sales of crafts would top two billion dollars that year. The majority of these sales were made at "events," rather than through normal marketing channels.

ADVANTAGES OF CRAFT FAIRS

From the customer's point of view, craft shows offer several interesting advantages. Only at a show does one have the opportunity to meet and get to know the artist who made the unique piece of work that is about to become part of one's daily life. At shows, visitors have the chance to see artists working, and learn about the skills and expertise that are required to create a piece of pottery or an enameled brooch. Shows offer an enormous variety of choices not to be found in any other shopping opportunity. Furthermore, many craft shows feature interesting food booths and occasional music and casual entertainment, thereby offering a cultural experience for the whole family. Craft shows have become an important addition to the leisure activity alternatives of the American public.

From the craftsman's point of view, participating in a craft show provides an excellent means of selling handmade objects. Being in one of the largest wholesale-retail shows is the fastest way to gain exposure and begin setting up one's business. Shows provide an excellent opportunity for feedback from potential customers, and are an outstanding way to develop custom work or commissions for unique pieces. Educational opportunities abound in shows, either for material in the form of seminars on pricing, promotion, packing and shipping, etc., or even more importantly, in the form of "hand-me-down" information from contemporaries operating in the field. In addition, most craftspeople, who generally live very isolated lives, enjoy the social aspects of fairs: seeing old friends, making new ones, and being part of the warm camaraderie.

HOW TO SELECT A CRAFT SHOW

Shows vary in size, quality, and standards, and it behooves the newcomer to do some "homework" before signing up to exhibit.

The best way to assess a show and its potential as a means of selling your work is to visit the show personally. This will help you understand what kind of work is featured, what kind of clientele visits the show, and how the show itself is managed. If you feel you want to be part of the event, ask exhibitors how they became involved, or ask for the manager's office or information booth.

Obviously, one can't visit craft shows all over the country. The next most reliable source for information about shows is other craftspeople who have been in them. They may not be able to assess whether your type of work would sell—particularly if they are involved in jewelry and you are in pottery—but they should have facts on the management policies, clientele, and general attendance of shows in which you may be interested.

Another source of information is your local craft shop. Most shop managers and owners attend numerous fairs every year, and are generally pleased to advise a newcomer on which ones they consider to be good resources.

If none of these avenues is available to you, it is possible to assess a show without recommendation. There are several publications that list shows—some even evaluate them. Three such publications are *Sunshine Artists U.S.A.* (501-503 North Virginia Avenue, Winter Park, FL 32789); *The Crafts Report* (700 Orange Street, Wilmington, DE 19801); and *American Craft* (published by the American Crafts Council, 22 W. 55th Street, New York, NY 10022).

Write to numerous shows for applications, and then compare the applications themselves. Scrutinize the requirements and standards set up by the show management in its material. It is generally considered that juried events produce a higher standard of quality than nonjuried events. A further tip to the wise: be certain the management publishes the names of the jurors in the preliminary material. Some shows charge a percentage of sales and are juried by the management—not on the aesthetic quality of the objects, but on the basis of what sells the best, thereby ensuring a profitable event for the management, rather than one that upholds the standards of the craft movement. Most craft shows with integrity require that the artist accompany his or her work to the show. They do not permit sales representatives or importers. This requirement generally ensures a legitimate craft event.

Events are sponsored by craft organizations and by promoters. It is generally felt in the craft community that events sponsored by organizations are more likely to produce results that are beneficial to the individual. Some promoters' primary interest is in their profit, not in their exhibitors. Craftspeople have been badly taken advantage of by this kind of promoter.

If you are satisfied with the general integrity of the show, its size, location, and philosophy, the next step is preparing an application.

The application material should inform you whether the show focuses on retail sales, wholesale or trade sales, or a combination of both. "Selling to the public" shows are generally shorter, are not as expensive, and do not require as much preparation as wholesale or combination shows. To do a retail show, you need a certain body of work to sell and a booth or display from which to sell it. Wholesale shows where you would be dealing with buyers who are writing orders for future delivery require a commitment on your part to produce work for delivery in the future—as well as more extensive displays, price lists, brochures, order books, and packaging materials for immediate deliveries. There are very few "wholesale only" shows; most wholesale events open first to the trade and then to the public for two or three days. The combination shows are generally longer than public shows, are more expensive to participate in, and require more professionalism from exhibitors. If, however, you are interested in developing your work as a business, they are definitely the best vehicle.

WHAT SHOWS COST

Fees range from as low as $10 at local bazaars to as high as several hundred dollars charged at the larger, more successful shows. The fees should be commensurate with the services offered. In other words, if you have to put your booth up every morning and take it down every night, if there is no security, and if there may be little or no publicity or advertising, you shouldn't have to pay much for the show. On the other hand, a show that guarantees services is generally worth the extra money.

HOW TO APPLY

Almost all craft events—whether they are sales expositions or museum exhibitions—select their participants on the basis of slides of your work. Your slide will become a surrogate for your work, and the preparation of your slides should be approached with the same degree of professionalism with which you approach the making of your craft.

The purpose of the slide is to focus the viewer's attention on the object. You should avoid the common problems of using a background that is too "busy" or too textured or too distracting, thereby diminishing the viewer's attention to the object. Your object should be framed in the center of the slide—not too small or too overpowering. Photographic problems like focus, distortion, over- and under-exposure, hot spots, and incorrect use of film should be avoided. Choose a background color that will enhance your subject, use appropriate lighting, and frame your object well. Slides should be simple, accurate records—not cute or clever.

If you don't want to invest the time and money in learning how to take your own slides, then contract for the services of a professional photographer. Remember, though, that you must offer editorial guidance. Most professionals are used to "jazzing up" product shots and, while appropriate for consumer magazines or catalogues, that type of shot is inappropriate for a craft exhibitor. Writing to American Craft Enterprises for an application is worth the time if for no other reason than to receive their full-color brochure on how slides should look.

If your work is rejected from a show, remember, it is not the end of the world and does not necessarily mean that your work is inferior. It may be that your work is inappropriate for the show, or that the competition that year was very strong. Don't be discouraged. Continue to apply, because most shows have a new jury each year. Perhaps the next year's group will be more favorable toward your work.

After you have been accepted for a show, the next consideration is what kind of display you plan to use. Most fairs that operate in an indoor or tent facility (an event where you can leave your booth intact at night) encourage their exhibitors to spend time and create energy on their displays. Your booth is your most important marketing tool at a craft event. It is a showcase for your work and a vital factor influencing traffic and sales. It should provide an attractive and advantageous environment in which potential customers can view your work. One publication credited the Northeast Craft Fair as being "like a series of 500 individual boutiques, one more exciting than the next."

The temporary nature and diverse physical circumstances of fairs present a number of special display problems.

From an aesthetic point of view ...

—Begin by thinking of your space as a total environment for your work. Keep it simple, uncluttered, so that objects are presented as dramatically as possible. Your most important objective is to enhance your work.
—The setting should be complementary to the work displayed. Think about color and texture that are in character with your work so that you create a harmonious whole.
—Be aware of scale. Consider the proportion of the displays (cases, pedestals, shelves, racks) in relation to your work. Don't let them overpower your objects.
—Pay attention to details of execution and finishing; your work deserves careful as well as creative presentation.

—Consider your neighbors and the appearance of the event as a whole; finish the back and sides of your booth. If possible, consult with your neighbors; often, people working together can arrive at extremely effective display solutions.

From a practical point of view ...

—Display your work at an eye-level that is comfortable for visitors. Displays that are too low cause backaches; those that are too high lose their audience.

—Build a secure structure that will stand the strain of crowds, curious young visitors, baby strollers, and other hazards of busy, eventful days. Avoid protruding shelves or dangerous support wires.

—Protect your work. Shoplifting is always a problem; display your objects so they are enclosed, attached or anchored, or so they can be watched. Don't leave your booth unattended.

—When planning your booth, consider who will be setting it up at the fair. If one person will be setting up, design units that can be managed by one individual working alone.

—Secure your work. If it is breakable, anchor it in place as unobtrusively as possible. Visitors should feel comfortable in your booth; objects should seem accessible, yet not be precariously displayed.

—You are there to do business—provide an area where orders can be written and other business transacted.

—Make certain your booth is properly lighted. Some objects benefit from spot-lighting; other crafts look best bathed in a clear, even light.

—Bring a hand-truck, dolly, wagon, or other wheeled conveyance to move and carry your work and display materials.

—Be flexible when planning your display. Not all space assignments are exact, and sometimes the loss of six inches can be a catastrophe if your display is rigid. Adjustable units that can be used for various size spaces work best.

And don't forget to ...

—Construct a display that fits easily in your car or van, and that is comparatively quick to set up and break down. (Some craftspeople find that modular units that can be used together or separately in more than one situation pay for themselves many times over.)

—Provide space to display your name and/or logo, and room for business cards and display literature—and to store back-up stock and packing materials.

—Keep your booth and the area around it neat and tidy. Boxes, papers, and packing materials can distract greatly from your display. A broom, dustpan and garbage bag or wastebasket are very helpful. Build or set aside an area where these materials can be hidden from view.

—Consider weather protection gear if you are planning your booth for an outside event.

You might consider ...

—Using part of your booth to educate the visitor in the processes involved in your craft. Or you may want to display your work in different stages of creation.

—Showing slides of a wider range of your work, or of the processes involved in creating it.

Some craftspeople prefer to use commercial sources, such as Abstrata, for their displays, and others prefer to rent drape and tables from decorators affiliated with commercial exhibit halls. Your most important objective is to present your work in the most favorable fashion.

BEFORE GOING TO THE FAIR

Once you are amidst the hubbub and confusion of a big fair, it is difficult to determine policies and approaches to selling. So before you go, be sure to cover the following points:

1. Determine your policy concerning consignment: do you consign, or only sell outright? If you consign, what are your terms? Ask about insurance of work while in the shop's possession. Establish the length of time the work is to be consigned. All arrangements should be clearly understood and be stated *in writing* and signed by both you and the shop owner.

2. State your minimum order, if you have one, either in the number of pieces or dollar amount. Many shops have expressed concern about what they feel are unrealistic minimum orders set by craftspeople. Sometimes a "number of pieces" minimum works better for everyone. Offer any guidance you can in helping a shop make a selection of your work, and try to guide the buyers in the most salable pieces for their kind of shop.

3. Please be sure your name and address are on your order pads, packing slips, and billing invoices. Be *certain* that any order you

take is signed by the buyer; without signature, the order could be refused later. Some craftspeople reconfirm all orders taken at a marketing event, just to avoid unfortunate confusion.

4. State your business terms and payment terms. (Some fairs provide you a card on which to do this and which you can post in your booth during trade days.) If you make a service charge for late payment, this should be stated on your order forms and billing invoice. If you charge for packing and shipping, alert the buyer and state this on your order form. If your prices are subject to change, that should also be noted.

5. Business cards and/or printed information about you and your work are invaluable. These need not be expensive, and are extremely good for your business as a way of advertising. Craft events have a very high rate of "call back" business, and many exhibitors find themselves receiving new business for months after a show.

6. Establish a delivery date, and if you can't keep it, *notify* the shop that you will deliver late. If you cannot deliver at all, give the shop ample notice so they can fill their stock another way. Do not attempt to deliver orders that are very late; the shop has the right to refuse delivery.

There are other ways to sell one's work beyond craft fairs, but they are usually more time-consuming, more costly, and generally less productive. Most people who plan to make their living from the sale of their work begin their careers at a craft fair.

26

Prints and Collecting

by

Clinton Adams

◆◆◆◆

CLINTON ADAMS is Director of Tamarind Institute at the University of New Mexico at Albuquerque. Long known as an artist, he is also author of two books and numerous articles, principally on the history, art, and techniques of lithography.

◆ ◆ ◆ ◆

THE CHANGING SCENE IN AMERICAN
PRINTMAKING

American printmaking has so greatly changed during the past fifty years that it has become all but a different art. Today, every artist who makes prints faces the consequences of these changes—changes that have combined to create a new range of opportunities, as well as to create an obstacle course of problems which we must understand if we are to overcome them.

As an illustration of the changes, I ask you to imagine two hypothetical exhibitions: one, a complete and well-chosen survey of the best and most important prints created in the United States during the past five years; the other, an equally representative survey of the finest prints created during the 1920's and '30s.

We find the large and colorful prints included in the contemporary exhibition prominently displayed in fine, well-lighted galleries, perhaps in the East Wing of the National Gallery or at the Museum of Modern Art. They are accompanied by a big, handsome catalogue, resplendent with color plates ($14.95 in paperback). Among the artists represented are the biggest names in American painting and sculpture, from Motherwell and Johns on down, one right after another. Some of the prints are immense in scale, perhaps 60 or 70 inches in their longer dimension. Almost all are technically complex, often mixing photographic processes with traditional printmaking techniques. Many use blended inking. A majority of the lithographs, the most popular medium, were printed collaboratively in one of the well-known workshops—Universal Limited Art Editions (U.L.A.E.), Gemini G.E.L., or Tamarind—and it is these lithographs which in their color, size and power tend to dominate the exhibition.

When we step back in time to view the exhibition of prints from the 1920's and '30s, we can hardly avoid being depressed by the contrast. Even to see the show we have to make a special effort, for it is at a second-rank museum, off the beaten track. Clearly not a main event, it is installed in a series of dingy, low-ceilinged galleries in the museum's basement. Its catalogue is little more than a check-list, with only a few illustrations (although by way of consolation its price is twenty-five cents). The prints themselves are small in size and most are in black and white. The etchings outnumber the prints in other media; the technical methods are simple and direct. While a few of the prints on exhibition are the work of prominent painters of the period, most are by artists who are known primarily as printmakers.

The striking contrast between these two very different exhibitions (and their different surroundings) tells us a lot about the recent history of printmaking in the United States. In nineteenth century France there was a strong tradition of the *peintre-graveur*—the painter who also made prints—and with few exceptions the greatest prints of the century were made by the greatest painters, from Delacroix and Goya to Bonnard and Toulouse-Lautrec. In the United States no such tradition existed. There were in this country no counterparts of the printmaking workshops that existed in France, and the two most important American artist-printmakers of that period, James McNeill Whistler and Mary Cassatt, lived and worked abroad.

Beginning in the mid-nineteenth century, a market for popular prints began to develop throughout the United States, and to satisfy this demand, prints were produced in great quantity. But just as the routine work of commercial publishers had given lithography a bad name earlier, now a flood of repetitious etchings—"original" only in the sense that they were hand-drawn, handpainted and signed—caused serious artists to question the value of making prints. One writer observed in 1891 that "it is obvious the public will have to be educated. Collectors will soon learn the difference between manufacture and art."

In this circumstance, I find it easy to understand why young artists studying in American art schools and academies were in no way encouraged to explore printmaking. Lithography was still seen as a purely commercial process, and while etching enjoyed a slightly higher status, its reputation was hurt by the cheap, popular prints sold in every gallery and department store.

Early in the twentieth century things began to change. Among the young realist artists of the so-called "ash can" school were several—John Sloan and George Bellows in particular—who found the original print an ideal vehicle for their images. Other American artists returned from Europe with a new enthusiasm for printmaking. Some had worked collaboratively with European master-printers and now sought to find comparable opportunities in the United States. Although such opportunities were few, it was sometimes possible to find commercial printers who were willing to undertake work for artists, usually while moonlighting after hours. In 1918 one of these printers, George C. Miller, established a lithographic workshop in New York and began to work exclusively with artists. At this time there was only a single school in the entire United States, the Mechanics Ohio Institute in Cincinnati, where lithography was taught. Even etching was taught in very few places. It was not until 1921, when Joseph Pennell took over the classes at the Art Students League in New York, that printmaking received serious attention there.

The dichotomy that then began between two very different modes of printmaking continues to the present day. In one of these modes artists work collaboratively with professional printers; in the other they learn to print for themselves. To some degree the distinction is one of medium. Both Whistler and Pennell printed their own etchings but took their lithographs to professional printers, and other artists would continue to follow this practice later on. But in the 1920's first a few and then an increasing number of art schools began to offer instruction in lithography as well as etching; young artists learned how to print and began to think of themselves as "printmakers," a category set apart.

Meanwhile, something akin to the European tradition developed as during the 1920's a number of the more prominent American painters of the period made lithographs (and occasionally etchings) in collaboration with printers either here or in Europe. Frequent trips to Paris became all but obligatory for American artists. Not only was there the great magnet of modernist art, but travel was cheap in those days. Life was pleasant in Paris, and it cost very little to live there. If, at the same time, you wanted to make a few lithographs, the price (in those uninflated dollars) was very low indeed. The studio most frequented was that of Desjobert, who printed for Stuart Davis, Yasuo Kuniyoshi, Adolf Dehn, and other Americans.

The motivation for making prints varied as did the mode. For some artists, printmaking was little more than a brief encounter. They made a few etchings or lithographs but with no deep commitment to the process. During the depression years of the 1930's, some were interested in making prints as a source of much-needed income. Although the artist received only a few hundred dollars when commissioned to make a print for Associated American Artists or for one of the print clubs, that was good money then.

Other artists made prints at least in part for social reasons. They strongly believed in prints as an art for the masses and thought that prints could (and should) be made available in large numbers at low prices. They condemned what they conceived to be the artificial elitism of etchers who deliberately limited their editions. Many of these artists were attracted by the political thought and artistic styles of the Mexican artists, Diego Rivera and José Clemente Orozco, who strongly influenced an entire generation of American printmakers. A parallel impetus came from establishment of the Federal Art Project of the Works Progress Administration, which during the 1930's operated print workshops throughout the United States.

Still a third group, composed primarily of artists who printed their own work, was fascinated by the printmaking process itself. For them the complexity and even the sheer laboriousness of printmaking was its own reward. This attitude was particularly at home in America, where the work-ethic had long favored styles and forms of art in which the virtuosity of the artist was made evident. The intaglio print was thus favored over lithography, for lithography permitted access by painters and sculptors who might all too easily draw on the stone without having paid their dues as printmakers.

This point of view gained all but total ascendancy after World War II, during the late 1940's and into the 1950's, when there was an explosive growth in intaglio printmaking, first under the influence of Stanley William Hayter at his Atelier 17 in New York, then of Mauricio Lasansky at the University of Iowa. Before the war, although instruction in printmaking was provided in most of the independent art schools, it was not common in university art departments. Now, with enrollments rapidly rising as a result of the G.I. boom, faculties expanded and funds became available to establish printmaking workshops at one school after another. Many of these new workshops were staffed by printmakers who had studied with either Hayter or Lasansky. Intaglio printmaking, and to a lesser extent the woodblock, became a standard part of the fine arts curriculum.

Museums responded by establishing annual juried exhibitions which provided the printmakers trained in the postwar art departments with an outlet for their work. And it was easy to participate. Entry fees were either low or nonexistent; most of the prints were still small enough to ship through the mails, and the postal service was then both cheap and reliable. Despite a great increase in printmaking activity, the number of aspiring artists remained far smaller than it has become today, so that it was possible for them to look forward realistically to success, as measured by regular acceptance in the exhibitions and receipt of occasional prizes and purchase awards. Further, as their work developed and their list of exhibitions lengthened, young printmakers could with reasonable assurance count on a faculty appointment as a printmaking teacher.

THE REVIVAL OF LITHOGRAPHY

Lithography was in disrepute not only among intalgio printmakers but also among modernist artists who associated it closely with the rejected style of the social realist painters. Although the firm of George C. Miller & Son (now under the direction of Burr Miller) continued to print for artists, few among the new generation of American painters were attracted to lithography. Printers elsewhere in the country—Kistler in Los Angeles, Barrett in Colorado Springs—were no longer active. It was not until after the founding of U.L.A.E. in New York (1957) and Tamarind Lithography Workshop in Los Angeles (1960) that a rebirth of lithography could begin.

By fortunate coincidence, the revival of lithography, like the earlier revival of intaglio printmaking, came at a time when university enrollments were rapidly expanding. New campuses were being established within state university systems and new art buildings were being constructed on both new and old campuses. In the twenty years between 1960 and 1980 more than 200 art schools, colleges and universities equipped new lithography workshops;

others expanded existing facilities. Many intaglio programs were likewise begun or expanded, screenprinting was developed, and a new relationship between printmaking and photography was explored. In short, it was a period of unequalled growth in instruction during which the concept of "a major in printmaking" became firmly established, and also a period in which a very large number of young intaglio printmakers and lithographers were appointed to university faculties.

Simultaneously, it was a period in which the original print once again became a major medium as many of the nation's most significant artists discovered the immense range and vitality of a medium too long neglected. By 1969, when a major exhibition of Tamarind lithographs was shown at the Museum of Modern Art in New York, it was possible to say that "while few American artists made lithographs in the 1950's, there are few in the 1960's who have not done so, either at Tamarind or at the workshops established as a consequence of the Tamarind programs."

One effect of this new interest in the print was to intensify the dichotomy between the printmakers who printed for themselves—most of whom either taught printmaking at art schools or universities or who had received their training there—and the painter-printmakers who worked collaboratively with the professional printers now available to them. A second effect was to lift the original print into an entirely new level of visibility; one in which that hypothetical exhibition I spoke of earlier might be presented as a major event at an important museum. A new market was created, and for the first time American art dealers began to take the fine contemporary print seriously as a potential source of income. Not far behind came the inevitable side effect, as another group of less scrupulous dealers, more interested in profit than quality, saw a chance to exploit the situation. Which is where we are today.

THE SCENE TODAY

Whatever conclusions we reach about the general health of printmaking depend upon our point of view. From the vantage point of a Robert Motherwell, Jasper Johns or Robert Rauschenberg, it could hardly be better. They are among a very small number of artists who have access at any time to the finest printers; their editions are sold out almost before the ink is dry and at very good prices. Their prints deservedly enter the most prestigious museum collections and occupy an important position in the history of the modern art.

From the other end of the scale, that of the commercial print dealer or publisher, the view is equally rosy. We may think of the prints they produce as kitsch or schlock, but we cannot escape the fact that such prints have found a very substantial market. Their sales give proof once more to a cynical comment: "No one ever went broke underestimating the taste of the American public." The rip-off artists could not care less.

But if you are caught somewhere between these extremes, as most artist-printmakers are, your response may be quite different. From this perspective, printmaking is in a state not of good health but of crisis: a crisis which, like so many problems today, arises from several causes, each of which adds to the others, making the situation worse.

First among these causes is the evolution of what I will call the high-technology print. It is taken for granted today that "important" prints are large in size and complex in execution. They must compete with the prints produced at the professional printmaking workshops. Even worse, it is expected at least unconsciously that they must compete with paintings in color, size and power. The essentially *graphic* character of the print has been lost, and the high-tech print now often resembles a painting. Part of this change stems from the fact that many prints are made by artists who seek to multiply their already discovered "trademark" images rather than to explore the new vocabulary of the print. Part of it stems from a characteristically American fascination with technology for its own sake. During the past twenty years young printmakers have received their training in studios which, in their size, complexity and wealth of equipment, could not even have been imagined by an earlier generation. The best modern presses are at hand, along with large-diameter rollers for blended inking, lights and cameras for the making of photo-plates, and all kinds of fine papers, inks and chemicals. To replicate the studio space and equipment of a typical print shop in any large state university would easily cost in excess of a half-million dollars. Typically, the faculty members who are in charge of print instruction are themselves artist-printmakers who are deeply involved in the making of high-tech prints, and it is natural that they will wish to compete with their peers in leading students further and further along the path of technological complexity. Nor are students led unwillingly. The photographic image, the rainbow roll and the multicolor print are immensely fascinating, and rare are the young artists who resist their lure. But then comes the day when all requirements have been met, when final exhibitions have been held, when degrees have been awarded. What now? Where do they go from here?

The dilemma faced by American printmakers is a genuine one. The cost of making prints has been pushed high by inflation, which has drastically increased the price of plates, inks, paper, and other materials. Most younger printmakers cannot afford to work in the professional workshops on a contract basis, so in order to continue to make prints they must gain access to necessary equipment. In the past, the usual way to do this has been through appointment to the printmaking faculty of a well-equipped art school or university. But now the catch is that in order to get such an appointment it is necessary *first* to have produced and exhibited a substantial body of recent prints. It will not do to rely upon prints made while in graduate school, not after a couple of years have gone by. The question is sure to be asked: What have you done lately?

SEEKING ALTERNATIVES TO THE PROFESSIONAL
WORKSHOP AND UNIVERSITY

To say that prospective teachers of printmakers are encountering a tight job-market is to understate the problem. Nor will the problem diminish. A long period of declining university enrollments, caused by low birthrates twenty years before, will persist during most of the 1980's and, as a consequence, there will be no growth in the size of faculties. Because the printmaking instructors hired during the great expansion of the 1960's are still young, the number of vacancies in this field may be smaller than in others. Add to this the effect of a new law which forbids mandatory retirement at age 65 and it is apparent that the number of new faculty appointments is likely to be small indeed.

But if it is possible to make prints neither in a professional workshop nor in a university, what are the alternatives?

One might be to make prints in a cooperative workshop. In some countries, notably Canada and Scotland, the national arts councils (the counterparts to our National Endowment for the Arts) maintain well-equipped, government-supported workshops to which all artists may have access. Unfortunately, no such program has been developed in the United States, nor is it likely in the economic climate of the 1980's that one will soon come about. In the past we did not perceive a need to develop this alternative because young printmakers found ample opportunities for employment as teachers and, through employment, access to equipment. Only recently has this situation changed.

A second alternative might be to move away from the oversize, high-tech print toward an image that can be printed with minimal equipment. Gauguin, after all, printed masterpieces in Tahiti, and Picasso revolutionized our perception of the linoleum cut. Artistic quality has little to do with complexity or size: this we know. But unfortunately, we also know from experience that artists who submit small black and white prints to exhibition juries or faculty search committees do so at their own risk. Far too often juries and committees are attracted either consciously or unconsciously to works that reflect a command of advanced printing techniques, those that have scale, those that cry out their own importance. A similar preference for large and colorful prints exists in the marketplace. Dealers who sell contemporary prints are well aware of the difficulty they encounter in sale of smaller prints, particularly in black and white. Few buyers of prints are traditional print collectors; most want prints to frame and hang on the wall as surrogates for the paintings they want but cannot afford.

The problem we face is real. There are no easy answers. We confront simultaneously the consequences of technological and financial inflation, both of which have escalated the cost of making prints. Of the two, the technological inflation is the lesser problem. It is essentially a reflection of attitudes, perceptions, and expectations that evolved between 1950 and 1980, all of which can be changed. It is not a fact of life. If artists find themselves in a situation where they cannot produce high-tech prints, they will turn to simpler means, and I am enough an optimist to believe that if they make fine prints—and simple prints *can* be fine—they will find an audience: perhaps not a mass audience, but a sufficient one.

I am far more concerned about financial inflation. It would take an optimist with rosier glasses than mine to predict that it will soon subside. Yet while the inflation persists the problems of the printmaker grow ever more difficult. Not only does inflation add to the direct cost of making prints by causing the price of paper, plates and

workshop supplies to head for the moon; it also attacks the
marketplace and multiplies indirect costs. Very probably, as the
government seeks to attack the causes of inflation, there will also be
a reduction in outside support, particularly support in the form of
grants to individuals and institutions. In any adverse economic
climate, the arts are sure to feel the pain.

In such a climate it will pay you as a printmaker to examine all
expenses with care. If you seek a teaching position, you will have no
choice but to submit to the search committee procedure, cumber-
some and frustrating though it may be. But juried exhibitions are
another matter entirely. Their value should be questioned, or at
least examined, in terms of what an economist would call their cost-
benefit ratio. On the benefit side are the ego-massage of acceptance,
the added entry on an exhibition record, the possible sale, the
occasional prize. Counterbalancing these are the numerous costs:
excessive entry fees, through which the participating artists often
find themselves not only paying for the exhibition but also providing the funds for the purchase awards; skyrocketing shipping
charges; frequently damaged prints; and, not to be discounted, the
time spent in submitting work. Balancing these all out, it is clear
that discriminations should be made. Perhaps it is worthwhile to
send prints to an exhibition if it is in a good museum, if the entry
fees are moderate, and if the jurors command respect. But is there
really any good reason to send work to every trivial but expensive
exhibition that clutters the calendar? I think not. Only when
printmakers stop subsidizing such activities will a new and more
favorable exhibition structure emerge.

EXPLORING EXHIBITION ALTERNATIVES

In the meantime, in the exhibition as well as in the production
of your work, you should look for alternatives. There are commercial
galleries in most sections of the country, and each year they are
successful in marketing a high volume of original prints. Cooperative galleries and alternative spaces also provide access to the
marketplace. But the marketing of prints is a business, and like all
businesses it requires skill, effort, and careful organization if it is to
be successful. As a printmaker you must learn to maintain careful
records: not only the full documentation of your editions, required
by law in some states, but also a log in which you record the

whereabouts of each impression, particularly those you place on consignment with dealers. To enter loose arrangements with respect to consignments is to invite trouble. You must learn to protect your own interests; no one will do it for you.

The price structure of your work should be clear and simple. One simple system is a schedule of prices based on size, perhaps with one range for color prints and a second for black and white. You should know what it costs you to produce your work, and you should take this into account in establishing these prices. In art, however, the competitive forces of the marketplace have far more to do with pricing policies than do the costs of production. You should therefore inform yourself about the marketplace. You should price the work of other artists whose work is comparable to yours and get the opinions of dealers. What you seek to do is establish a price that will provide you with a reasonable reward for your work while still permitting it to move freely in the marketplace. Remember that it is very easy to raise the price of a print after a portion of the edition has been sold, but very poor policy to lower it. It may thus pay to sell the first few impressions from a new edition at a modest publication price. If they move quickly at that price, thus justifying an increase, dealers and collectors will soon come to think of you as an artist whose work is in demand, which is precisely the image you wish to create.

You must learn to keep track of collectors who purchase your work so you can let them know of new publications. In order to do this, you should insist that dealers provide you with the full names and addresses of those who purchase your work through their galleries. This list may become the most important marketing tool you have. The size and complexity of the national art market can be a severe barrier to emerging artists trying to "break in." But your personal mailing list can be a key element in developing a local following—local in terms of where you live, sell, and show work. By developing and expanding the local interest in your work, the ripple effect can produce good consequences for your reputation and, ultimately, for the sale of your work. Your mailing list, like all of your business records, should be maintained regularly and professionally. You need such records not only for obvious legal reasons (depending upon the state and city of your residence you may be subject to a variety of licensing and tax requirements), but also because the business of the artist *is* a business and must be run like one. It is unfortunate that more art schools and universities do not offer art students basic courses in business practices and law; in the absence of such courses, you must dig out the necessary information by yourself. Although this is not difficult to do, too many artists fail to do it. Forget the romantic myths! It is very expensive to learn the hard way.

THE OUTLOOK FOR THE FUTURE

With all the problems you face as a printmaker, there is, at end, some consolation in the knowledge that others have faced and survived them. Inflation and its consequences are dangerous enemies. A scarcity of teaching positions is an unfortunate fact. But in other ways the present situation is far from bleak: excellent technical information is now at hand in all parts of the country; fine papers, supplies and equipment (though expensive) are readily available; the original print has gained prestige, and at least some American artists have established an active market for their work at very substantial prices; a new generation of American master-printers is unrivaled in the world; and these printers are employed in a diversity of workshops, serving a multitude of artists. Change is both inevitable and healthy in the arts. The hypothetical exhibitions we contemplated at the beginning of this chapter will be replaced by some very different kinds of exhibitions fifty years from now. We cannot even imagine the specific character of the prints that will be shown but, barring the holocaust, there is every reason to expect that the print will continue to attract artists of high creative energy, as it has for hundreds of years.

27

Alternative Spaces

by
Nancy Drew

◆-◆-◆-◆

NANCY DREW is a New York arts consultant who served as the Coordinator for Artists Programs at the National Endowment for the Arts from 1979 until 1981. Previously she was the curator of the Long Beach Museum and the owner of Some Serious Business, and Artist Space in Los Angeles.

◆ ◆ ◆ ◆

Throughout history artists have taken the initiative in establishing organizations to increase both support for and exposure of their work. Such organizations provide assistance and materials to artists as well as exhibition opportunities. From the Renaissance Guilds through the Paris Salons to the new Alternative Spaces, artist-initiated groups have encouraged dialogue among artists and provided community resource centers.

"In the '70s the single most important development in art was the inception of Alternative Spaces," observed Director of the NEA Media Arts Program, Brian O'Doherty. Today, a constellation of over 500 spaces, located throughout the U.S. and Europe, furnish artists opportunities for exhibition and education. Although they may differ in structure, staff and ambition, the goal of each alternative space is the same: to provide artists with services, and to give artists direct input and involvement at all levels.

THE LARGER MEANING OF "SPACES"

In talking about alternative spaces the word "space," denoting a gallery or exhibition area, can be misleading. Often an alternative space is a conceptual vision, using the city as a resource or the downtown as installation site. For example, during the '70s and into the '80s "spaces" offered the following facilities to the artists:

- Implementing the commission of new works of art—assisting in acquisition of materials, labor, money and site.
- Providing a support structure—including publicity and documentation—that calls attention to the art. Channeling direct financial assistance in the form of honoraria and residencies, as well as emergency grants and material stipends.

Although alternative spaces sometimes sell works of art, this is not their primary role. They are not concerned with "get-rich-quick" schemes. Rather they are more useful for other provided services.

The administration policies of individual alternative spaces are determined by the needs of the artists involved. A.I.R. in New York, a feminist cooperative gallery, and N.A.M.E. in Chicago, an artist-run co-op, are collectively run: their primary objective is to exhibit the work of collective members and to import significant shows from the outside. Both New York's institute of Art and Urban Resources (which runs The Clocktower and P.S. 1), and the Los Angeles Institute of Contemporary Art (LAICA) have a director who coordinates the various activities. At The Clocktower and LAICA, the director and curators seek out important work that would not be shown in official metropolitan spaces because of the avant-garde, controversial, or unusual nature of the work.

Some alternative spaces are interdisciplinary art centers. They explore the entire spectrum of art forms, from theater to music to film to the visual arts; they offer audio and video postproduction facilities to artists; they coordinate multimedia events. Examples of interdisciplinary centers include The Kitchen in New York and "and/or" in Seattle. Others are totally service-oriented, providing seminars, lectures, workshops, job referrals, and equipment and skill exchanges. NOVA in Cleveland and the Boston Visual Artists Union (BVAU), Boston, fall into this category.

"ANTI-SPACES"

As there are alternative spaces, there are alternatives to the alternatives. New "anti-spaces" have cropped up coast to coast—as Jet Wave in San Francisco and Collaborative Projects (Colab) in New York, for example. These loosely knit groups sponsor guerrilla exhibitions and hit-and-run art. A recent example was the Times Square Show, for which Colab converted a condemned massage parlor in the Times Square tenderloin into a Salon des Refusées—or, as some have observed, a Salon de Refuse—democratically exhibiting work by many artists.

TWO EXAMPLES OF CREATING "SPACES"

Because alternative spaces exist as options to the familiar and traditional types of art outlets, it is impossible to describe them in general terms. Each space evolves organically and is unique. Just Above Midtown in Manhattan and "and/or" in Seattle are two thriving "spaces" which illustrate what can be created.

"and/or"

"and/or," in Seattle, defines itself as "a Center for New Art." Early in 1974 five artists, working in painting, video, and music got together, pooled their resources from part-time jobs, art sales, and studio rentals and were able to rent 3,000 square feet on the first floor of an Odd-Fellows Temple. The building was designed as a public gathering hall and was well suited to the presentation of artwork. The rent was cheap, the location ideal—right near the hub of the downtown area. The five artists immediately declared themselves the Board of Directors and began the needed renovations, which included installation of walls and electrical wiring. Exhibitions, performance, and programs grew out of the interests of the Board, and eventually "and/or" came to have a twofold purpose. Its first aim was the presentation of new work—painting, video, and music. Its second aim, the development of a range of services to the local arts community—a library, a collection of video tapes, a video-editing facility, an electronic music studio, a resource center for composers, a xerox room, a monthly publication (by subscription), and frequent workshops by accountants, Volunteer Lawyers for the Arts and the like.

The staff, initially the founders volunteering in their free time, now has expanded to include two full-time administrators, a business manager, and nine part-time workers. The original Board still exists, and under it "and/or" has become an umbrella for several groups that function autonomously in their creative directions, but collaboratively as businesses.

It was never the intention of the Board to institutionalize the character of "and/or." Indeed, when it began they weren't quite sure what the "space" was going to turn out to be. Therefore, they felt they couldn't seek outside funding at the outset, until they had a known commodity with precisely defined activities. For the first nine or ten months, money was contributed out of the founders' pockets or raised by admissions to exhibits and musical performances. No salaries were paid. As the character of the organization began to reveal itself, the Board then sought corporate government (local, state and federal) and foundation support to augment revenues from membership. (Membership requires yearly dues of $20 with higher patronage categories available. Membership was made available to the public nine months after "and/or" opened its doors.)

Anne Focke, cofounder and present director of "and/or," strongly believes that the integrity and value of the artwork should come first, regardless of public impression. She also maintains that it is completely wrong (a) to assume that granting agencies will ever be a primary funding source; and (b) to mold programs to suit funding guidelines for those agencies. The "and/or" Board reserves one meeting a year for articulating its present identity and future direction. It can then seek funds from appropriate sources and plan for the next year's activities in reasoned but flexible manner.

"and/or" is in its seventh year and has expanded in program, scope, and physical size. According to Ann Focke, "We are a group of groups, all artists, and 'and/or' could only exist in Seattle. If we were in New York, we'd be something different."

"Just Above Midtown"

Simultaneously, in New York, Just Above Midtown was developing. This organization too represents the vision and commitment of a small group of people dedicated to the support and exposure of contemporary art. Linda Goode Bryant recounts Just Above Midtown's downtown beginning days:

"The idea for Just Above Midtown grew out of a dining room conversation I had with two friends at my apartment on Riverside Drive. This was in July of 1974. They are artists and I considered myself an artist, although I was working as an administrator at the Studio Museum and had worked in the Education Department at the Met. We talked about the fact that there just didn't seem to be the right structures for emerging artists—certainly not the right platform for Afro-American Art. So I said, 'Let's start a gallery,' and they said, 'Yeah.' And I said 'No. Let's really start a gallery,' and they said, 'Yeah.' This went on for a couple of weeks and finally I got one friend out of everyone I knew to take the idea seriously. Anyway, I started to call realtors and finally I found one. We blew his mind: 'We need a space and don't have any money.' He nearly choked: 'But you're talking about 57th Street between 5th and 6th!' We told him all the reasons why it was a good idea, and I guess he liked our energy and we settled on $300 a month! I borrowed $1,000 from a friend and my parents, and all their friends chipped in money. A group of us did all the renovations ourselves. It had been a hair salon before and needed a lot of work. I took the money my parents gave us and we laid a new floor.

"Oh, we were so naive. We decided to have the opening on November 18th, 1974. We all just saw membership money pouring in after that. So the opening came and more than a thousand people showed up, and by the end of the night we had one $15 membership. I called my parents. Then a friend came down from Boston. She lived with a family and took care of their kids at night and worked with us during the day. We were starving. We didn't have any money, so we wouldn't eat all day until 1:00 p.m. when one of us would go out for buttered rolls. Then we'd all have dinner at my house—a pot of something cheap, like chili. Then my friend Pat from Boston went home to see her family in Virginia. She called one day to say she'd been really sick and had had to have her stomach pumped. You know what it was? The buttered rolls! We can all laugh now, but it was really unbelievable.

"Anyway—we opened on not even a shoestring, and as I say we had no members after that. But in December Stevie Wonder came in and bought some art and that got us through another month. Then Robert Flack introduced us to some artists. At one point I was so confused and demoralized, I sublet the gallery and went out to Los Angeles. A few friends took me out to dinner and explained about funding, and started to teach me about how to survive. Then one day Patrick McGuiness, who was the Commissioner of Cultural Affairs, came in and said, 'You ought to go nonprofit.' He hooked us up with a lawyer who represented a number of artists and he [the lawyer] volunteered to help us. So I started to learn. Our first grant came from the Rockefeller Foundation. Then in 1976 we applied for and got our first government grant. So things started to roll. But the beginning was something else! I was a single mother at the time. My kids were little and we just lived at the gallery. We sure weren't your typical 57th Street gallery, but I guess people liked our energy, even though they didn't know *what* to think."

Just Above Midtown has been relocated in downtown Manhattan. It continues to hold group and solo exhibitions, to sponsor appearances on artist seminars and such programs as The Artists/ The Public, and to encourage exposure through publication and performance. It is an organization that responds primarily, although not exclusively, to the needs of Afro-American non-white artists.

For every alternative space there is a personal story on "How and Why It Began." There has been no set of rules for anyone to follow. This factor has contributed to the diversity and richness of the field. Vision, commitment, and courage were seen as necessary initial ingredients.

As many of the spaces become larger and develop more sophisticated and complex structures, traditional business skills and services are incorporated. Operating budgets now range from $2,500 to 1.5 million dollars. Funds are derived from the private sector, State-Federal sources, as well as generated and earned income. These organizations approach fund raising as creatively as they have their programming.

Each alternative space has different policies regarding new members and sponsored artists, but all are established with the unaffiliated artists in mind. Consequently they are much more receptive to new ideas than are official institutions like museums. They are dedicated to maintaining flexibility, and because their trade is new art, their benefit is vitality.

Alternative spaces are the artworld's equivalent of scientific laboratories. By providing an exchange between the individual artist and the community at large, they provide a rich environment for the production of art, beneficial to both parties.

Index